THE PIPES OF WAR

GLASGOW

PRINTED AT THE UNIVERSITY PRESS BY
ROBERT MACLEHOSE & COMPANY LTD. FOR
MACLEHOSE, JACKSON AND CO., PUBLISHERS
TO THE UNIVERSITY OF GLASGOW

MACMILLAN AND CO. LTD.	LONDON
THE MACMILLAN CO.	NEW YORK
MACMILLAN CO. OF CANADA	TORONTO
SIMPKIN, HAMILTON AND CO.	LONDON
BOWES AND BOWES	CAMBRIDGE
DOUGLAS AND FOULIS	EDINBURGH

MCMXX

PIPER JAMES RICHARDSON, V.C., 16TH CANADIAN SCOTTISH
AT REGINA TRENCH, VIMY RIDGE
From the Painting by J. Prinsep Beadle

THE PIPES OF WAR

A Record of the Achievements of Pipers of Scottish and Overseas Regiments during the War 1914-18

BY

BREVET-COL. SIR BRUCE SETON, Bart., of Abercorn, C.B.

AND

PIPE-MAJOR JOHN GRANT

WITH CONTRIBUTIONS BY

NEIL MUNRO, BOYD CABLE, PHILIP GIBBS, AND OTHERS

GLASGOW

MACLEHOSE, JACKSON & CO.

PUBLISHERS TO THE UNIVERSITY

1920

WHEREVER Scottish troops have fought the sound of the pipes has been heard, speaking to us of our beloved native land, bringing back to our memories the proud traditions of our race, and stimulating our spirits to fresh efforts in the cause of freedom. The cry of "The Lament" over our fallen heroes has reminded us of the undying spirit of the Scottish race, and of the sacredness of our cause.

The Pipers of Scotland may well be proud of the part they have played in this war. In the heat of battle, by the lonely grave, and during the long hours of waiting, they have called to us to show ourselves worthy of the land to which we belong. Many have fallen in the fight for liberty, but their memories remain. Their fame will inspire others to learn the pipes, and keep alive their music in the Land of the Gael.

D. Haig. F.M.

6 Decr. 1918.

PREFACE

This record of the achievements of pipers during the war of 1914-18 is not intended to be an appeal to emotionalism. It aims at showing that, in spite of the efforts of a very efficient enemy to prevent individual gallantry, in spite of the physical conditions of the modern battlefield, the pipes of war, the oldest instrument in the world, have played an even greater part in the orchestra of battle in this than they have in past campaigns.

The piper, be he Highlander, or Lowlander, or Scot from Overseas, has accomplished the impossible—not rarely and under favourable conditions, but almost as a matter of routine; and to him not Scotland only but the British Empire owes more than they have yet appreciated.

In doing so he has sacrificed himself; and Scotland—and the world—must face the fact that a large proportion of the men who played the instrument and kept alive the old traditions have completed their self-imposed task. With 500 pipers killed and 600 wounded something must be done to raise a new generation of players; it is a matter of national importance that this should be taken in hand at once, and that the sons of those who have gone should follow in the footsteps of their fathers.

This is the best tribute that can be offered to them.

The Piobaireachd Society intend to institute a Memorial School of piping for this purpose, and all profits from the sale of this book will be handed over to their fund.

The compilation of the statistical portions of the work has involved correspondence with commanding officers, pipe presidents and pipe majors of many units in the Imperial armies; to them, for their enthusiastic assistance in obtaining information, is due the credit for the mass of detail that has been made available.

To the other contributors—authors, artists and poets—is due in large measure such success as may follow the publication of this work. They have helped a cause worthy of their efforts.

It is earnestly to be hoped that Scotland will rise to the occasion. To the compilers it has been a privilege to record the achievements of men—many of them personal friends—who contributed so largely to the success of their gallant regiments.

B. S.
J. G.

CONTENTS

PAGE

Foreword by Field-Marshal Earl Haig of Bemersyde, K.T. - - v

Preface - - - - - - - - - - - - - - - - vii

THE PIPES OF WAR. By Brevet Col. Sir Bruce Seton, Bart., of Abercorn, C.B.

Introduction - - - - - - - - - - - - - - 3

A History of the Pipes - - - - - - - - - - - 9

The Pipes in the War, 1914-1918

The Western Front - - - - - - - - - - - - - 18
Gallipoli - - - - - - - - - - - - - - - 31
Salonika - - - - - - - - - - - - - - - 33
Mesopotamia - - - - - - - - - - - - - - 33
The Last Stage - - - - - - - - - - - - - 34
Pipers in the Ranks - - - - - - - - - - - - 35
Pipers on the March - - - - - - - - - - - - 37
Pipe Tunes - - - - - - - - - - - - - - 42
Individual Achievements - - - - - - - - - - - 46
Foreigners and the Pipes - - - - - - - - - - 63
The Pipes in Captivity - - - - - - - - - - - 64

Military Pipe Bands and Reform - - - - - - - - - 66

Regimental Records

The Scots Guards - - - - - - - - - - - - - 71
The Royal Scots - - - - - - - - - - - - - 73
The Royal Scots Fusiliers - - - - - - - - - - 82
The King's Own Scottish Borderers - - - - - - - - 86
The Cameronians (The Scottish Rifles) - - - - - - - - 91
The Royal Highlanders (The Black Watch) - - - - - - - 96
The Highland Light Infantry - - - - - - - - - - 105
The Seaforth Highlanders - - - - - - - - - - 114
The Gordon Highlanders - - - - - - - - - - - 124
The Cameron Highlanders - - - - - - - - - - 130
The Argyll and Sutherland Highlanders - - - - - - - - 135
The London Scottish - - - - - - - - - - - - 143
The Tyneside Scottish - - - - - - - - - - - 145

CONTENTS

REGIMENTAL RECORDS PAGE

The Middlesex Regiment - 146
The Liverpool Scottish - 147
The Royal Fusiliers - 147
The Argyllshire Mountain Battery - 148
The Ross and Cromarty Battery - 148
Miscellaneous - 148
The Pipe Band of the 52nd (Lowland) Division - 149
Prisoners of War Band - 150
Princess Patricia's Canadian Light Infantry - 150
The Royal Highlanders of Canada - 151
The 48th Highlanders of Canada - 152
The Canadian Scottish - 153
The Cameron Highlanders of Canada - 154
The 21st Canadians - 155
The 25th Canadians - 155
The 29th Canadians - 156
The 236th Canadians - 157
The Canadian Pioneers - 158
The 2nd Auckland Regiment - 158
The 42nd Australians - 159
The South African Scottish - 159

ROLL OF HONOUR, 1914-1918 - 161

CANNTAIREACHD. By MAJOR J. P. GRANT, M.C., Yr. of Rothiemurchus - 179

THE IRISH PIPES: THEIR HISTORY, DEVELOPMENT AND DIVERGENCE FROM THE SIMPLE HIGHLAND TYPE. By W. H. GRATTAN FLOOD, Mus.D., K.S.G. - 191

THE TUITION OF YOUNG REGIMENTAL PIPERS. By JOHN GRANT, Pipe Major 195

THE SPIRIT OF THE MACCRIMMONS. By FRED. T. MACLEOD, F.S.A.(Scot.) - 201

A GOSSIP ABOUT THE GORDON HIGHLANDERS. By J. M. BULLOCH - 219

TO THE LION RAMPANT. By ALICE C. MACDONELL OF KEPPOCH - 228

THE MUSIC OF BATTLE. By PHILIP GIBBS - 232

THE PIPES IN THE EVERYDAY LIFE OF THE WAR. By ARTHUR FETTERLESS - 239

THE OLDEST AIR IN THE WORLD. By NEIL MUNRO - 246

THE PIPES: ONSET. By JOSEPH LEE, Lieut. - 255

FLESH TO THE EAGLES. By BOYD CABLE - 258

THE BLACK CHANTER. By CHARLES LAING WARR - 267

THE PIPES. By EDMUND CANDLER - 286

ILLUSTRATIONS

PIPER JAMES RICHARDSON, V.C., 16TH CANADIAN SCOTTISH, AT REGINA TRENCH, VIMY RIDGE
From the Painting by J. PRINSEP BEADLE.

PIPER DANIEL LAIDLAW, V.C., 7TH KING'S OWN SCOTTISH BORDERERS, AT LOOS
From the Drawing by LOUIS WEIRTER, R.B.A.

" THE COMRADES WE LEFT IN GALLIPOLI "
From the Pipe Tune composed by COLONEL H. A. C. MACLEAN of Pennycross, C.M.G. Set by MRS. A. C. MACDIARMID.

PIPER KENNETH MACKAY, CAMERON HIGHLANDERS, AT QUATRE-BRAS
From the Painting by LOCKHART BOGLE, by kind permission of the Officers of the 1st Cameron Highlanders.

PIPE-MAJOR HOWARTH, D.C.M., 6TH GORDON HIGHLANDERS, AT NEUVE CHAPELLE
From the Painting by J. PRINSEP BEADLE.

BEN BUIDHE, ARGYLLSHIRE
From the Water-colour Drawing by GEORGE HOUSTON, A.R.S.A.

BORDER OF CELTIC DESIGN BY ALEXANDER RITCHIE, IONA

THE PIBROCH
From the Painting by LOCKHART BOGLE.

DUNIQUAICH, LOCH FYNE
From the Water-colour Drawing by GEORGE HOUSTON, A.R.S.A.

THE PIPES OF WAR

BY

BREVET-COL. SIR BRUCE SETON, BART.
OF ABERCORN, C.B.

INTRODUCTION

THE history of the bagpipes as a military institution is a long and honourable one, inseparable from that of Scottish troops, Highland and Lowland, wherever they have fought, for centuries past. The strains of *piob mhor* have been heard all over those bloody European battlefields on which Scottish soldiers of fortune died—too often for lost causes—from the time when Buchan's force joined the Lilies of France in 1422, throughout the Hundred Years' War, in the Low Countries, in Germany, in Austria; and they have handed on a tradition which has been lived up to in the later days of the regular Scottish units of the British Army.

But memories are short; and, in the army as elsewhere, the passion for reform before the greatest war of all was threatening many old-established institutions whose utility was not immediately apparent.

And so it came about that to many observers, indeed to a considerable section of military opinion, it appeared likely that along with the kilt, the use of tartan, bonnet, doublet and other special features of the dress of Scottish regiments, the bagpipe must be regarded as a picturesque anachronism destined to disappear as the conditions of war changed and as the yearning of high military authorities for a deadly khaki uniformity of clothing and equipment became more insistent.

"Why," it has often been said, "should Scottish units find it necessary, either in peace or on active service to retain an obsolete musical instrument of their own? In days past, before the rifle had revolutionised tactics, when shooting was erratic at 100 yards' range, there might have been something to say for an instrument which experience showed to be capable of stimulating men at the psychological moment when effort was failing; but is it reasonable to expect that the educated twentieth century soldier will prove to be responsive to any such stimulus—even if it were possible, under modern conditions of rifle and shell fire, to provide it ? "

The reply to such a line of argument is clear enough ; and its truth has been demonstrated in every action in which Scottish troops have taken part during the war.

The strength of an army depends, to an incalculable degree, on the strength not only of individual regimental *esprit de corps*, but of the national sentiment of its units. The retention of time-honoured territorial titles in the New Armies, instead of a soulless numbering of units, was itself due to a recognition by the authorities of the principle that the individual soldier is a better fighting man when he feels that he has to live up to an ancient and brilliant regimental record. The Rifleman, even in peace, would never voluntarily be transferred to a " red " regiment, nor does a 10th Hussar yearn for the cuirass of the Life Guardsman. When a man joins a regiment, voluntarily or compulsorily, he adopts for the whole period of his military service the customs, the prejudices, and the traditions of his unit, and is himself moulded by them in a manner which is as inexplicable as it is marked.

And if regimental *esprit de corps* and tradition are strong, national and territorial sentiment are stronger. In the old army, as a result of the system of recruitment, this factor was of less importance than in the, comparatively speaking, unmixed units of the new army of to-day. All our military history shows that the appeal to such national sentiment is as certain in its effects as the appeal to regimental tradition ; and this war has enormously accentuated its importance.

All observers agree—and military despatches confirm the view—that the rivalry of national sentiment has proved invaluable ; units, whether battalions or divisions, have literally competed for distinction for their own nationality, and have succeeded in associating particular exploits with themselves for ever. It may truly be said that behind the achievements of the 9th, 15th, 51st and 52nd and Canadian Divisions the motive impulse was national rather than merely regimental.

In the keeping alive of this national sentiment in Scottish units, their distinctive dress and, still more, the retention of the national instrument, have played an important part ; and this applies with equal force to units composed of Scotsmen who have left their native land permanently or temporarily.

Throughout the war these units have more than maintained the great traditions of their past history, carrying on the records of Scottish gallantry which have been excelled by no troops in the world and equalled by few.

And so with the pipers.

How important a contributory cause they have been to the success of their battalions is recognised by all alike, men and officers—and not least by the Field Marshal Commanding in Chief. In spite of modern conditions they have, in cases too numerous to record, played the part which was normally theirs in the olden days of set battles.

To many of the men in the ranks the music of the pipes in peace time may have had no special association other than with dances and gatherings ; but whenever the piper assumed his historic *rôle*—so long dormant—of fighting man, the inherited peculiarities of the Scottish soldier were aroused and the music made an overpowering appeal to his national sentiment.

Inherited sympathy of this kind is no doubt inexplicable—but it exists. It certainly cannot be ascribed to the Celtic strain in invididuals, for we know that the bagpipe was in general use for centuries all over the Lowlands —perhaps even before it displaced the bard and the harper and became the war instrument of the Highlands. We cannot analyse what Neil Munro describes as " the tune with the river in it, the fast river and the courageous, that kens not stop nor tarry, that runs round rock and over fall with a good humour, yet no mood for anything but the way before it " ; we only know that it works on some individuals and some races as no other instrument does, and we need not try to satisfy ourselves whether this is due to the flat seventh in the scale, or the ever-sounding drones, or the inherited memory it arouses.

The idea that the piper would be too conspicuous an object to be employed in his proper capacity has proved to be partly true, as indicated by the casualties among them when playing; but the same argument might be applied to any other soldier in the ranks. Shells show no discrimination in their objective.

To a certain extent this objection is a sound one; but it is all a matter of relative values. Many commanding officers have expressed the opinion that at times when, on account of the all-pervading noise of the battlefield, not a note of his music could be heard by the men nearest to him, it was the actual presence of the piper that supplied the stimulus to the men; in fact, it was the piper, not his instrument, that was followed.

For obvious reasons pipers are harder to replace than the ordinary soldier, and, in trench warfare especially, most regiments have tried to keep them in relative security; but in the records of units which follow it will be seen that, when the trouble comes, the piper has always been to the fore, and " the tune with the tartan of the clan in it " has been heard again as it has for centuries past.

From the military point of view the bagpipe has the merit of accentuating national sentiment at just those moments when the stimulus is most necessary, of rousing the " *mir cath,*" the frenzy of battle, and of rallying men when the ideal is liable to be lost sight of in the presence of the nerve shattering realities of action.

In all these ways the company pipers have justified their existence. In the discharge of a duty which may be regarded as sentimental in the highest sense of the term, they have, literally by hundreds, made the supreme sacrifice; wherever Scottish units have fought these men have exposed themselves, unhesitatingly, recklessly, playing their companies to the attack in conditions which, as regards intensity of personal risk, have never previously been experienced. Many battalions have lost all their pipers more than once, but, as long as reinforcements were available, there has never been any difficulty in getting fresh men out of the ranks or from home to take their place; and the new men have followed the old, just as heedless, as they played their comrades forward, knowing quite well that for many of them the urlar of " *Baile Inneraora* " or " *The March of the Cameron men*" might suddenly change to the taorluath of "*Ch till mi tuille.*"

The Germans at least, though they may not recognise the tune when they hear it in the streets of Cologne, appreciated the grim significance of *piob mhor* when "*I hear the pibroch sounding, sounding*" followed the lifting of the barrage.

The war also has afforded many instances of another function of the pipes in action. Charging the enemy at a foot pace through deep mud is after all but a "crowded hour of glorious life," which may or may not be completely or even partially successful, and men may have to be rallied when their nerves have given out under intolerable strain. Of this there have been several instances.

It must not, of course, be imagined that regimental pipers, during this or any other war, have been normally employed in playing their units to the attack; the whole condition of modern fighting makes this impossible in the same way and for the same reason that it has made impossible spectacular charges by battalions in line.

It would be a more accurate presentment of the case to say that the military piper, *qua* piper, normally exercises his functions behind the front line, in billets and on the line of march; and in this respect he resembles other army musicians whose duty—according to old Army Regulations of 300 years ago—is "to excite cheerfulness and alacrity in the souldier."

But, recognising all this, the peculiarity of the piper is that, in open fighting, when his unit has been committed to the attack, he often assumes the *rôle* which distinguishes him from all other musicians, and takes his place at the head of his company.

Instances of this during the war are innumerable, and those which are detailed below are but typical of what has occurred in every field of operations, and in most units which possessed pipers.

And if it is impossible to say too much of the regimental pipers of the British Army, it is equally so in the case of those of Overseas units, notably of the Canadians. From the point of view of the historian who wishes to demonstrate what pipers have done during this war, no more remarkable case could be selected than that of the 16th Canadian Scottish. The pipers of this distinguished battalion won one V.C., one D.C.M., one Military Medal and Bar, and eight plain Military Medals—a record which is unique. No man was put up for a decoration unless he had played his company over the top at least twice, and no piper was ever ordered to play in action—it was left to volunteers, who, it was found, had to resort to the drawing of lots to obtain the coveted privilege of playing.

The colonel of the regiment—himself a V.C.—commenting on the casualties says: "I believe the purpose of war is to win victories, and if one can do this better by encouraging certain sentiments and traditions why shouldn't it be done? The heroic and dramatic effect of a piper stoically playing his way across the ghastly modern battlefield, altogether oblivious to danger, has an extraordinary effect on the spirit and enterprise of his comrades. His example inspires all those about him."

And so it comes to this: the method of employment of the regimental piper during this war has depended largely on opportunity—and still more on the individuality of commanding officers. Men vary within very wide limits in the price they are prepared to pay for attaining their object; and where one man will deliberately sacrifice a certain number of men to get a position, another will as deliberately avoid the sacrifice, even if it costs him his objective.

As far as pipers are concerned, the decision arrived at by commanding officers of the two schools is equally indicative of the esteem in which they hold them.

A HISTORY OF THE PIPES

AT what stages of his development primitive man discovered he could obtain musical sounds by blowing on a hollow reed we cannot now ascertain; if we could do so we could at once determine when the pipe came into existence. It is unprofitable to speculate on this point.

What we do know, however, is that men playing the pipe are portrayed in sculptures the date of which is fixed by the best authorities as about 4000 B.C., and we conclude that in Chaldaea, Egypt, Assyria and Persia at least, the pipe—but not necessarily the bagpipe—had become a recognised musical instrument.

Actual specimens of the Egyptian pipe dating back to at least 1500 B.C. are in existence, and we know that they had a reed giving a scale almost identical with the chromatic scale; they also had a drone. Such a pipe had, clearly, advanced some way on the upward development to "*piob mhor.*"

Every stage in its evolution still persists in some country in the world, and by comparing these it is possible to trace the actual process. Thus, besides the single pipe, which is world-wide in its distribution, we have the Egyptian "arghool," which consists of a pipe "chanter" and drone lying side by side; and the later development, the "zummarah," has a bag. In India the twentieth century snake charmer has an instrument in which chanter and single drone lie side by side fixed into a small gourd with a lump of wax. The chanter has a small reed very similar to our own chanter reeds, and, although the scale differs, the sound produced is remarkably

Note.—The author takes this opportunity of acknowledging his indebtedness for much of the early history of the instrument to Manson's *The Highland Bagpipe* and Dr. Grattan Flood's *The Story of the Bagpipe*, both monuments of research.

similar. This instrument is essentially a single drone bagpipe, and is to be found all over India, in Yunnan and other parts of China.

It would have been more than surprising if the pipe, in some form or other, had not been used in ancient Greece and Rome. There are, in fact, very many references to it in classical literature, and by 100 A.D. we know that the " askaulos " had evolved into the bagpipe proper, and Chrysostomos speaks of a man who could " play the pipe with his mouth on the bag placed under his armpit."

Martial, Suetonius, Seneca, and other Latin writers refer to the " tibia utricularis," and there is practically no doubt that it was used as a marching instrument in the armies of Julius Caesar. A bronze showing a Roman soldier in marching order playing the utriculus has been discovered in England, and the writer Procopius refers to Roman pipe bands in this country.

But when we come to the question of the introduction of the bagpipe into the British Isles, and especially into Scotland, we are at once on highly controversial ground.

It is obvious enough that the instrument is not peculiar to the Celtic races ; that it has maintained its hold on them long after its disappearance in other European nations is equally so. But who introduced it into these favoured isles, whether the Cruithne or Prydani or Picts or the later " C " Gaidheal branch of the Celtic stem—who shall say ?

Some authorities—students of the subject would be a safer term—are prepared to assert that the bagpipe was introduced first into England, thence to Lowland Scotland, and only long afterwards into the Highlands ; and one recent writer in the *Celtic Magazine* says the evidence of its association with the Scottish Gaels does not go back beyond the middle of the sixteenth century !

The matter is one of academic interest, no doubt, but there is no likelihood of its ever being settled.

Records did not exist in the ancient Highlands, and we have to turn to early Irish literature for reference to the bagpipe. In the Brehon Laws of the fifth century it is spoken of as the " cuisle " ; and, although Tara's halls are usually associated with the harp, it is recorded that at the assemblies which took place there in pre-Christian days it was the custom for the pipes to play at the banquets.[1]

It is possible the bagpipe was brought over from the north of Ireland, " Scotia " as it then was, on the invasion of the Highlands by Cairbre Riada, who founded the kingdom of Dalriada in Argyle in A.D. 120; or in the later great colonisation, about A.D. 506, under Lorne and Angus, the sons of Erc.

It certainly does not appear likely that the bagpipe came over from " Scotia " in the first place, unless we are to accept the view that the Scottish Celt came over by the same route; unfortunately we have very little accurate knowledge of the early history of the Highlands, and there are no local written records extant to prove—as they do in the case of Ireland—that the instrument existed in those early days. We do know that the harper and the bard were national institutions of immense antiquity in the Highlands, and that, as the bagpipe became an increasingly important feature of everyday life, they were bitterly opposed to it.

Even Latin authors, who were familiar with the bagpipe as a marching instrument in their own army, omit to refer to the existence of *piob mhor* in the Highlands. The Greek writer Procopius, in 530 A.D., dismisses the Highlands with the statement that " in the west the air is infectious and mortal, the ground covered with serpents, and this dreary solitude is the region of departed spirits." And so we are thrown back on tradition.

In the absence of records of the employment of the bagpipe in war in the Highlands it is to Ireland, the so-called Lowlands of Scotland and to England that we have to turn for information; at the same time we must bear in mind that evolution of the instrument itself had begun to operate, and the English and Lowland pipes were different from the variety now known as the " Highland," which has supplanted all others.

As regards Ireland it is known that the Irish troops who fought in Gascony in 1286 had pipers with them, and a drawing of their instrument appears in a manuscript of 1300 A.D. in the British Museum. There were

[1] *The Bagpipe.* Grattan Flood.

also Irish pipers at the battle of Falkirk in 1298, and they are again referred to in contemporary accounts of the battle of Creçy.

The military piper therefore goes far back into history. But it was as a social instrument that one finds most frequent reference to bagpipes of some pattern or other in the Middle Ages. There was a pipe band at the English Court in 1327, and an old inventory of 1419 shows that at the Palace of St. James' were " foure baggpypes with pypes of ivorie . . . the bagge covered with purple vellat."

But, whereas the English pipes went the same way as the Continental varieties, it was otherwise in Scotland. Two institutions existed there which fostered the tradition and saved *piob mhor* from the fate of disappearance—the Burgh piper and the Clan piper; and by 1450 A.D. these had certainly become part of the national life.

In Edinburgh in 1487 A.D. there were three town pipers, who were paid three pence daily; one of their duties was " to accompany the toun's drummer throw toun morning and evening." In 1505 A.D. the town records of Dumbarton, Biggar, Wigton, Dumfries and Linlithgow refer to burgh pipers.

In Aberdeen in 1630 A.D. exception appears to have been taken to the custom of playing through the streets, as it is placed on record that this was to be stopped, " it being an uncivill forme to be usit uithin sic a famous burghe, and being oftene found fault uith als weill be sundrie niehbouris as by strangeris." That the citizens of this " famous burghe " are peculiarly susceptible to the criticisms of " strangeris " might never have been suspected by superficial observers, and it is well that there is official testimony to the fact.

The effect of their daily music on the inhabitants of Perth was different,—or perhaps Perth was less amenable to the criticisms of " strangeris." In any case it is recorded of a burgh piper, who used to rouse the citizens at 5 a.m., that his music was " inexpressibly soothing and delightful."

At Dundee the piper played through the town " every day in the morning at four hours and every nicht at aucht hours," and was paid twelve pennies yearly by each householder.

The pipes, at least in the pre-Reformation days—were sometimes played in church ; in course of time, however, piping on Sunday scandalised the authorities, religious and civil, and, in the burgh records, we find repeated instances of pipers being punished for this misdemeanour.

The burgh piper was a man of peace ; the clan piper was a man of war. For many centuries he had to compete with the "clarsair," or harper, and the bard, and aroused feelings of acute hostility from the latter. In 1411 A.D. one bard, MacMhurich of Clan Ranald, wrote a poem of a most uncomplimentary nature about the bagpipes.

The recitation of the bard before battle was probably last heard at Harlaw in 1411, and the clan bards disappeared finally in 1726 ; the last clan harper died in 1739, and the "croistara"—the fiery cross—was sent round the clans for the last time in the '45. The last Scottish piper will pass when the Scottish race itself passes—which will certainly be the last of all.

The clan pipers were highly esteemed as musicians—from the musical point of view they, no doubt, left us far behind. The courses of training, lasting over years, at the old piping schools such as existed at Boreraig, turned a man into a piper. As Neil Munro has it : "To the make of a piper go seven years of his own learning and seven generations before ; at the end of his seven years one born to it will stand at the start of knowledge, and, leaning a fond ear to the drone, he may have parley with old folks of old affairs."

One of the results of the Heritable Jurisdiction Act of 1747, which so completely altered the conditions of life in the Highlands, was the disappearance of the office of hereditary clan piper.

The tunes these men played were the old tunes we know so well ; and so it has happened that in this war we find companies marching into and through machine-gun and artillery barrage and into broken French villages and through German trenches while the company piper plays the same melodies that inspired their forebears to fight their neighbours lang syne—melodies which have been heard, too, in the same part of the world in the days when Scottish troops fought for the Lilies of France against all comers.

The association of the bagpipe with military operations is probably very ancient in Scotland. Perhaps the tradition that the Menzies pipers played at Bannockburn rests on an insecure foundation, but if the Bruce had no pipers, his son David most certainly had, as witness the Exchequer Rolls. In 1549 a French writer states that " the wild Scots encouraged themselves to arms by the sound of their bagpipes" ; and in 1598 Alexander Hume of Logie wrote :

> " Caus michtilie the warlic nottes brake
> On Heiland pipes, Scottes and Hyberniche."

Incidentally, this reference to three different kinds of pipes is interesting.

The first authentic reference to pipers in the Forces of the Crown appears to have been in 1627, when Alex. Macnaughton of Loch Fyne-side was commissioned by King Charles I. to " levie and transport twa hundredthe bowmen " for service in the French war. Writing in January 1628 to the Earl of Morton, Macnaughton says :

" As for newis from our selfis, our baggpyperis and marlit plaidis serwitt us in guid wise in the pursuit of ane man of war that hetlie followed us."

The records show that this company had a harper, " Harie M'Gra frae Larg," and a piper, "Allester Caddell," who, in accordance with the custom of the time, had his gillie to carry his pipes for him.

Regimental pipers undoubtedly existed in the numerous bodies of Scottish troops which served at various times on the Continent. Thus, in 1586, in the " State of War " of Captain Balfour's company in the Scots Brigade in Holland, there were two drummers and a piper ; and in " the worthy Scots regiment called Mackeye's " raised by Sir Donald Mackay in 1626 there was an establishment of thirty-six pipers.

Pipers are also found on the rolls of the " regiment d'Hebron "—now the Royal Scots—and to that very distinguished regiment we may safely accord the further distinction of being the first " Regular " regiment of the British Army to have pipes. The " North British Fusiliers," now one of the battalions of the Royal Scots Fusiliers, also had pipes as far back as 1678, and probably as early as 1642.

Writing in 1641, Lord Lothian said:

"I cannot out of our armie furnish you with a sober fiddler.... We are sadder and graver than ordinarie soldiers, only we are well provided with pypers. I have one for every company in my regiment, and I think they are as good as drummers."

The great Montrose had pipers in his armies, and tradition has it that, in the action of Philiphaugh in 1645, a piper stood on a small eminence and played the old Cavalier tune, "Whurry, Whigs, awa' man," until he was shot by one of Leslie's men, and fell into the "Piper's Pule" in Ettrick river.

An exactly similar incident occurred in the case of one of the pipers of Bonnie Dundee at Bothwell Brig in 1679.

At the Haughs o' Cromdale in 1690 a wounded piper climbed on to a big rock and went on playing till he died, thus setting an example which has been followed by his successors in many actions in this war. The stone on which this unknown hero stood is known to this day locally as "Clach a phiobair."

There are many such in France and elsewhere to-day.

In Wodrow's letters in 1716 there is a reference to the company pipers of the "Argyle's Highlanders": "They entered in three companies, and every company had their distinct pipers, playing three distinct springs. The first played "The Campbells are coming" . . . and when they entered Dundee the people thought they had been some of Mar's men, till some of the prisoners in the Tolbooth, understanding the first spring, swung the words of it out of the windows, which mortified the Jacobites."

Again, in 1715, when Argyle's troops marched to Leith, it was stated by Cockburn (Historical MSS. Commission): "While our generals were asleep the rebels marched to Seton House, leaving the piper in the citadel to amuse."

The piper, by this time, had clearly become a recognised military institution.

In the '45 the unfortunate Sir John Cope was undoubtedly aroused by the music of *piob mhor* at Prestonpans, though it is doubtful whether "Hey Johnnie Cope" was composed for the occasion.

Prince Charlie had thirty-two pipers of his own, besides those belonging to the clans with him. One of these men, James Reid, was taken prisoner in the operations of 1746. He pleaded that he had not carried arms, but the Court decided that " no Highland regiment ever marched without a piper : therefore his bag pipe, in the eye of the law, was an instrument of war "—and they dealt with him accordingly.

This view was confirmed by the Disarming Act of 1747, which nearly succeeded in attaining its object of abolishing the bagpipe, the kilt, the tartan and national sentiment generally—only Regular regiments being exempted from its operation.

Penal legislation against the bagpipe was no new thing. Cromwell had tried it in Ireland, and, under William II., 600 Irish pipers and harpers were persecuted with relentless rigour. And in Ireland it succeeded.

Saxon governments have always done the piper the honour of regarding him as an exponent and supporter of national sentiment.

Even in Scotland the years between 1747 and 1782, when the iniquitous Disarming Act was repealed, were very nearly fatal to the continued existence of the bagpipe as a national institution ; and it was the Regular Army which saved it—though no one could ever accuse the military authorities of unduly favouring the instrument. Even General Officers have publicly sneered at them—as when Wolfe at Quebec contemptuously refused to allow the pipes of the Fraser Highlanders to play, or when Sir Eyre Coote in 1778 described them as a " useless relic of the barbarous ages."

Both generals had to withdraw what they had said.

The opinion of the Court Martial which tried poor James Reid, that his bagpipe " was, in the eye of the law, an instrument of war," was after all as shrewd an expression of the truth as their sentence was harsh.

In later times the pipes in the army have received little official recognition. In 1858, when the King's Own Scottish Borderers applied for their pipers to be placed on the establishment, the Commander in Chief grudgingly consented " as the permission for these men is lost in time," but on condition that they were not to cost the public anything as regards their clothing.

Nor has the modern War Office shown more sympathy to an institution whose value, even on theoretical grounds, should have been recognised. The ancient and honourable title of Pipe Major has been abolished and that of "sergeant piper" has been substituted. Pipers themselves, on mobilisation, are returned to the ranks with the exception of six men. In Lowland regiments, indeed, the piper, though tolerated, is not officially recognised at all.

A bandsman may in due course become a first-class warrant officer—in one or two units, indeed, he has attained commissioned rank; but the "sergeant piper" remains a sergeant, and can hope for nothing more. This, surely, is an injustice which is remediable at small cost to the nation.

The apathy of the War Office in regard to the training of pipers as pipers is another matter which is in urgent need of reform. Commanding officers and pipe presidents are sometimes pipers themselves—though not always; it is absurd to leave to them the responsibility of training men in the art. The time has come for a thorough reform of the whole system and method of training of military pipe bands.

THE PIPES IN THE WAR, 1914-1918

THE WESTERN FRONT

DURING the autumn [1] and winter of 1914-15 pipers, for obvious reasons, had few opportunities of attracting much attention, still less of performing their highest duty, viz. playing their companies into action. They were necessarily, on account of the extreme shortage of men, for the most part employed in the ranks; and in many of the old Regular battalions pipe bands disappeared altogether.

For a time it seemed that the critics were right, and that in warfare in the twentieth century there was no longer a place for a class of man which was destined to disappear, as the bard and the harper had done in days lang syne.

This view was widely held, and in some regiments was never modified.

But gradually, as attacks became more frequent and movements set in, and as the British Army grew stronger in numbers, the position changed, and the piper became more than an invaluable marching instrumentalist or performer at *ceilidhs* in billets.

The first occasion on which pipers played, or tried to play, their companies into action was at Cuinchy on 25th January 1915, when the 1st Black Watch suffered such heavy casualties in advancing through deep mud up to their knees.

It was at Neuve Chapelle in March 1915 that the company piper really had his first chance of showing what he could do, as a piper, in action. On

[1] Probably the first pipers to play on French soil were those of the 2nd Argyll and Sutherland Highlanders on their landing at Boulogne.

this occasion the 20th Brigade had to carry the stronghold of Moulin du Piétre, and lost very heavily; the 2nd Gordons were in the main attack and the 6th Gordons, a Territorial unit, in reserve. The 6th Gordons were called upon to support their comrades of the old Regular Army, and advanced, headed by their pipes and drums, with a rush which carried many of them beyond their objective.

From that time onwards, right up to the end of the war, pipers have repeatedly played their units into action, in spite of the unfavourably conditions resulting from modern rifle and artillery fire and gas, and have established the standard of gallantry in this respect which has been at once the admiration of all observers and an incentive to their successors to emulate them.

During the first weeks' heavy fighting, in April-May 1915, on the left of the attenuated British line of the Ypres salient, the pipers of Canadian battalions took a prominent part. In their advance on the St. Julien wood the 16th Canadians were led by their company pipers, two of whom were killed and two wounded while playing; their places were at once taken by others, who played the battalion through the German trenches at the heels of the retiring enemy to the tune "We'll tak' the guid auld way." In many subsequent actions these men distinguished themselves in the same way.

After the failure of the first attack on the German line at Rue des Bois on 9th May 1915, in the action of Richebourg-Festubert, the 1st Black Watch were played to a fresh attack by their company pipers. "With their characteristic fury they had vanished into the smoke, and the only evidence that remained was the sound of the pipes." When they reached the German trenches a piper, Andrew Wishart, stood on the parados playing until he was wounded. Another piper, W. Stewart, was awarded the D.C.M. on this occasion.

The same thing happened in the case of the 2nd Black Watch at Festubert, the companies being led by their pipers. Of these men two, Pipers Gordon and Crichton, were specially mentioned for their gallantry. The Seaforth pipers, too, suffered heavily in this as in many later actions—"Caber Feidh" has often been heard along that line which looked so weak, but was too strong for the Germans.

In the action at Festubert on the 17th May the 4th Camerons got further than any other battalion, and were played in by their pipe major, J. Ross, and four pipers. These men got through untouched, though their pipes were all injured.

Later again, on 16th June 1915, when the Hooge salient was straightened by the 3rd Division, the attack was led by the 8th Brigade, and the enemy front and support lines were taken. On this occasion Pipe Major Daniel Campbell, although wounded, played his battalion, the 1st Royal Scots Fusiliers, over the top.

Dawn was just breaking when the Pipe Major scrambled out on the parapet and started playing. The men raced forward after him until stopped by uncut wire. In the hand-to-hand fighting which ensued the Pipe Major threw aside his pipes and, catching up a bayonet, joined in the attack.

It was during the Ypres fighting, where gas was first used against us, that an incident occurred of which the facts are as stated, but unfortunately it has been found impossible to get the names of the men concerned.

"The men, looking into the storm of shells that swept their course and at the awful cloud of death now almost on them, wavered, hung back —only for a moment. And who will dare to blame them?

"Two of the battalion pipers who were acting as stretcher bearers saw the situation in a moment. Dropping their stretcher they made for their dug-out and emerged a second later with their pipes. They sprang on the parapet, tore off their respirators and charged forward. Fierce and terrible the wild notes cleft the air . . . after fifteen yards the pibroch ceased; the two pipers, choked and suffocated with the gas fumes, staggered and fell." [1]

Although in these earlier actions pipers had done much to maintain the traditions of the past they had never had the opportunities of distinguishing themselves that came to them during the great operations about

[1] *Echoes of Flanders.* C. L. Warr.

Loos in September 1915. The attack of two army corps, in which were thirty Scottish battalions, along a seven-mile front, was a chance for these men, and one of which they were not slow to avail themselves. Three pipers at least earned the title of "The piper of Loos," and one of these, Daniel Laidlaw, of the 7th King's Own Scottish Borderers, was awarded the Victoria Cross; but, in the general orgie of gallantry which characterised those operations, individual pipers in very many cases won the highest praise in their own units but escaped the official recognition they had earned.

The attack by the 28th Brigade on the Hohenzollern Redoubt was accompanied by fearful casualties; with uncut wire in front, in an atmosphere heavily laden with gas, exposed to machine-gun fire in front and flank, the 6th K.O.S.B., 10th and 11th H.L.I. and 9th Seaforths were decimated. The K.O.S.B. were played over the top by their veteran Pipe Major, Robert Mackenzie, an old soldier of forty-two years' service. He was severely wounded and died the following day.

On the right of this Brigade the 26th had better luck, as the wire was found to be more thoroughly cut. The 5th Camerons and 7th Seaforths led the way followed by the 8th Gordons and 8th Black Watch, and reached Fosse 8, where they hung on, though reduced to the strength of a single battalion.

"The heroism of the pipers was splendid. In spite of murderous fire they continued playing. At one moment, when the fire of the machine guns was so terrific that it looked as if the attack must break down, a Seaforth piper dashed forward in front of the line and started 'Caber Feidh.' The effect was instantaneous—the sorely pressed men braced themselves together and charged forward. The Germans soon got to realise the value of the pipes and tried to pick off the pipers."

In this one attack the 5th Camerons had three pipers killed and eight wounded. Further south the pipers of the 2nd and 6th Gordons led their companies in the costly attack on Hulluch and the Quarries. An officer of the Devons, on their flank, writes:

"I shall never forget those pipes. . . . During the charge a Gordon piper continued playing after he was down."

On the other side of the Hulluch road the 15th Division received its baptism of fire, and lost 6000 men in the two days' fighting. One of the battalions of the 46th Brigade, the 7th King's Own Scottish Borderers, afforded an admirable example of the value of the pipes in rallying men when the position is critical. The piper concerned, Daniel Laidlaw, was awarded the Victoria Cross and the Croix de Guerre. The *London Gazette* Notification, which does not err on the side of uncontrolled emotionalism, describes the award as follows :

" For most conspicuous bravery. . . . During the worst of the bombardment, when the attack was about to commence, Piper Laidlaw, seeing that his company was somewhat shaken from the effects of gas, with absolute coolness and disregard of danger, mounted the parapet, marched up and down and played his company out of the trench. The effect of his splendid example was immediate, and the company dashed out to the assault. Piper Laidlaw continued playing his pipes until he was wounded."

The evidence of eye-witnesses shows that, at the time, a cloud of gas was settling down on the trench and there was heavy machine-gun fire. Laidlaw played " Blue Bonnets over the Border," and the effect on the men was indescribable ; as they followed him over the top he changed to " The Standard on the Braes of Mar." The old tune was surely never played to better purpose ; and if Laidlaw's action stood alone, if he were the only piper during the war who stimulated a company at the moment when things were at their worst, surely that achievement amply supports the view that, even in the warfare of to-day, *piob mhor* is an instrument of war which can justify all claims made for it. As it is, Piper Laidlaw, " the Piper of Loos," stands as type of a class of men who, throughout the war, have lived up to the traditions of a great past.

Another piper of the same battalion, Douglas Taylor, being wounded and unable to play, spent thirty-six hours bringing in gassed men without relief, until he himself was dangerously wounded. Further on, the 44th Brigade—the 8th Seaforths, 7th Camerons, 9th Black Watch and 10th Gordons—made the historic charge which captured Loos and then went on, until, for want of support, they could get no further and were compelled to retire. They rallied on Hill 70 round a tattered flag made out of a Cameron kilt. The battalions of this brigade were played into and beyond Loos; and, when they were widely scattered and mixed up, pipers played to rally the men of their own battalions. Among many others, Piper Charles Cameron of the 11th Argylls stood out in the open playing unconcernedly, and was thereafter known in his battalion as "the Piper of Loos."

The shattered remnants of the 15th Division were withdrawn in the evening from the blood-stained slopes of Hill 70, but the battalions were played in by their own pipers. The 9th Black Watch numbered only 100 of all ranks and one piper; the 7th Cameron pipers were practically annihilated, the 8th Seaforths lost ten, and others suffered in similar degree

It is a far cry from Hill 70 to Scaur Donald, and they were only regimental pipers, but to these brave men the words of the old song are surely applicable.

> "There let him rest in the lap of Scaur Donald,
> The wind for his watcher, the mist for his shroud,
> Where the green and the grey moss shall weave their wild tartan,
> A covering meet for a chieftain so proud."

In the fighting subsidiary to the main action of Loos, at Mauquissart and in the neighbourhood of Neuve Chapelle, the 2nd Black Watch pipers distinguished themselves greatly. They played their companies into and beyond the first line of German trenches. One of them, A. Macdonald, stood playing on the German parapet while the position was being cleared, and then on, through a hurricane of fire, over three lines of trenches, until dangerously wounded. For this he was given the D.C.M.

Three others, J. Galloway, R. Johnstone and David Armit, did precisely the same; and yet another, David Simpson, behaved with such gallantry that he also came to be known as "the Piper of Loos," the third of the brave trio to earn that honourable title. He had already played over three lines of German trenches, and was leading towards the fourth when he was killed. Johnstone, on this occasion, played till he fell gassed.

Throughout the long succession of actions which punctuated the Somme operations in 1916, the pipes continued to be much in evidence, and references to them and to their effect upon the men during that bloody fighting are frequent in the contemporary reports of observers, and in private letters subsequently published. French reports also have placed on record their admiration for the company pipers of Scottish regiments. "Some of the finest work," writes one well-known French military writer, "was accomplished at the very outset by the Highlanders, who carried the trenches in lightning fashion, urged on by the inspiriting music of their pipes."

The fighting at Loos had shown, on a comparatively small scale, that the pipes, when freed from the restrictions placed upon their employment by the exigencies of trench warfare, were still capable of fulfilling their historic *rôle* in open fighting The gallantry of the pipers at Hulluch and Hill 70 was worthy of the units they led, and established a record which was hard to beat; but for months on end their great achievements were emulated by those of their successors in the new armies which had poured into the field.

The opening attack on the 1st July affords numerous examples of pipers playing their companies into action, and a few may be taken as representative of the whole.

In the attack by the 32nd Division the 17th H.L.I. succeeded, with a loss of over 500 men, in capturing and holding part of the Leipzig redoubt, though unsupported for a considerable time. The Commanding Officer writes:

"I told the Pipe Major to play; he at once responded, getting into a small hollow, and playing and greatly heartening the men as they lay there hanging on to the captured position. Pipe Major Gilbert showed a total disregard of danger and played as if he were on a route march. For this action he obtained the Military Medal."

In the advance on Mametz on the same day the 2nd Gordons were led by their company pipers. An officer of an English battalion in the 20th Brigade describes how "we heard their pipes play these fellows over. It sounded grand against the noise of shells, machine guns and rifle fire. I shall never forget them."

The same thing occurred later when the battalion attacked the orchards of Ginchy: On both occasions the casualties were very heavy.

PIPER DANIEL LAIDLAW, V.C., 7TH KING'S OWN SCOTTISH BORDERERS
AT LOOS
From the Drawing by Louis Weirter, R.B.A.

At Fricourt Pipe Major David Anderson of the 15th Royal Scots stood out in front of the battalion until he was wounded, and played across shell-beaten ground under heavy fire. He was awarded the Croix de Guerre.

The two battalions of Tyneside Scottish were similarly played to their attack on La Boiselle and the ridge in front of it on the opening day of the battle of the Somme. A correspondent who was present says:

"The Tynesiders were on our right, and, as they got the signal to advance, I saw a piper—I think he was the Pipe Major—jump out of the trench and march straight towards the German lines. The tremendous rattle of machine-gun and rifle fire completely drowned the sound of his pipes, but he was obviously playing as though he would burst the bag, and, faintly through the roar of battle, we heard the mighty cheer his comrades gave as they swarmed after him. How he escaped I can't understand, for the ground was literally ploughed up by the hail of bullets; but he bore a charmed life, and the last glimpse I had of him as we, too, dashed out showed him still marching erect, playing on regardless of the flying bullets and of the men dropping all round him."

Of the two battalions 10 pipers were killed and 5 wounded, and Pipe Major Wilson and Piper G. Taylor both got the Military Medal. Many of these pipers, having played their companies up to the German trenches, took an active part in the fighting as bombers.

Again, at Longueval on 14th July, regimental pipers were conspicuous. As the 26th Brigade—8th Black Watch, 10th Argylls, 9th Seaforths, and 5th Camerons—commenced their advance, they were exposed to frontal and enfilading machine-gun fire, and shrapnel mowed them down; but their pipers led the way, and the men followed cheering and shouting.

"Where we were the brunt of the action fell on two New Army battalions of historic Highland regiments. Their advance was one of the most magnificent sights I have ever seen. They left their trenches at dawn, and a torrent of bullets met them. They answered immediately—with the shrill music of the pipes, and, indifferent apparently to the chaos around them, pushed steadily on towards their objective."

Describing the attack by the 10th Argylls, another observer writes:

" We came under a blistering hot fire, but the men never hesitated. In the middle of it all the pipes struck up " The Campbells are coming," and that made victory a certainty for us. We felt that whatever obstacles there barred our path they had to be overcome. . . . The last fight was the worst of all. It was at the extreme end of the village, where the enemy had possession of some ruined houses. They had a clear line of fire in all directions, and we were met with a murderous hail of fire. For a moment the men wavered. I doubted if they were equal to it. Then a piper sprang forward, and the strains broke out once more. The attacking line steadied and dashed at the last stronghold of the Huns. Their line snapped under our onslaught."

On this occasion the Pipe Major, Aitken, a man of sixty, was awarded the Distinguished Conduct Medal. One of the pipers referred to in the above incident was James Dall, and his Commanding Officer considers his action in playing the regimental march at this juncture was the means of his company gaining their objective; the other was D. Wilson, who was also mentioned in despatches with Dall.

Of the attack by the 9th Seaforths a wounded officer writes:

" We swept on until we finally carried the German trench with a rousing cheer to the strain of the pipes. The heroism of the pipers was splendid. In spite of murderous fire they kept playing on. At one moment, when the fire was so terrific it looked as if the attack must break down, one of the pipers dashed forward and started playing. The change could be felt at once, the sorely pressed men gave a mighty cheer and dashed forward with new zeal."

North of Longueval the 1st Gordons made a furious attack, on the 18th July, and on this occasion they were led by their pipers.

" They were out of sight over the parapet, but we could hear at intervals their shouts of ' Scotland for ever! ' and the faint strains of the pipes. Then we saw them reappear, and then came prisoners."

Similar accounts were given of the 6th and 7th Gordons. In the 6th Gordons Piper Charles Thomson had his arm blown off while playing. " The gallantry of these men who wear the tartans of the old Scottish clans would seem wonderful if it were not habitual with them. Their first dash for Longueval was one of the finest exploits of the war. They were led forward by the pipers, who went with them, not only towards the German lines, but across them and into the thick of the battle. . . . In that September fighting the pipe major of a Gordon battalion played his men forward and then was struck below the knee ; but he would not be touched by a doctor until the others had been tended. He was a giant of a man and so heavy that no stretcher could hold him, so they put him in a tarpaulin and carried him back. Then he had his leg amputated and died." [1]

On the 3rd September the 4th Black Watch were played into action and had to capture a village. According to an eye-witness :

" It was magnificent to see these men charge up the narrow street leading to the second barricade. Amid the ruined houses on each side the enemy were posted. At the moment when it was hottest the strains of the pipes were heard. The men answered with a cheer and swept steadily on over the barricade and through the ruins ; and the village was ours."

Of a Seaforth battalion a similar story is told :

" The men simply raced into the storm of bullets . . . at last it became too terrible for any human being to stand against it. The attacking lines melted away, the men seeking what cover could be found. . . . It was here that the pipers of the Seaforths had their chance. They took it. As the men advanced again to the attack they were cheered on by the strains of the pipes, which could just be heard. The men dashed through, clearing out the enemy as they went."

During the attack on Beaumont Hamel in October, as in the earlier fighting at Thiepval, the pipers of the 15th H.L.I. lost very heavily when leading their companies.

Such instances of the bravery of pipers and of the stimulus afforded by the pipes to men in action became matters of almost every-day occurrence, and, though everyone recognised the tremendous losses that were the result of their exposure, there were occasions when those losses were more

[1] Philip Gibbs.

than compensated for at the time by the results obtained. Everywhere, at Contalmaison, Martinpuich, Pozières, Delville Wood, wherever Scottish troops were employed, their pipers played their historic *rôle*, and, to quote Philip Gibbs, " over the open battlefields came the music of the Scottish pipes, shrill above the noise of gunfire."

Nor were the pipers of purely Scottish regiments left to establish these records of bravery unchallenged. They had keen rivals in battalions of overseas Scots, notably the South African Scottish and the Canadians.

During the fighting for Delville Wood in July the South Africans were torn to pieces by shell fire. The remains of the battalion hung on for days, losing all their officers but the colonel. When relief came their pipers headed the blackened and weary warriors out of the wood of death.

Similarly, the 16th Canadian Scottish pipers maintained the fine reputation they had earned on the Ypres salient. When the battalion moved up to the attack on the Regina trench on 8th October, there was keen competition among the pipers as to who should be allowed to play them over. " Four pipers, Richardson, Park, M'Kellar and Paul marched ahead of the battalion with the Commanding Officer for a distance of half a mile under intense machine-gun fire and escaped scatheless. They could be heard clearly as they played ' We'll take the good old way,' and, as they passed, wounded men lying in shell holes raised themselves on their elbows and cheered them. When they got near the German line the battalion encountered uncut wire which, being unusually heavy, took some time to cut. While this was going on Piper Richardson played up and down outside the wire for twenty minutes in the face of almost certain death. . . . Shortly afterwards a company sergeant major was wounded, and Richardson volunteered to take him out. After he had gone he remembered he had left his pipes behind. He left the sergeant major in safety in a shell hole and returned. He was never heard of again."

This brave man was awarded a posthumous V.C., the second piper to obtain this coveted distinction. Piper Paul was subsequently given the Military Medal.

At the capture of the Vimy Ridge on 9th April, 1917, by the Canadians, the pipers of some of their battalions took a prominent part. On this occasion the 16th Canadian Scottish repeated what they had done in previous engagements, their companies being led by pipers. The pipers concerned were Pipe Major Groat and Pipers M'Gillivray, M'Nab, M'Allister, M'Kellar and Paul, and they advanced a distance of over a mile under heavy fire without any casualties. The Pipe Major was awarded the Military Medal.

Similarly the 25th Canadians had their pipers out in this action, and Piper Walter Telfer, who went on playing after being severely wounded, was given the Military Medal; Piper Brand got the same decoration.

Later on, in the fighting round Arras, a battalion of the Camerons was played to the attack:

"When the order came our men went over with right good will. It was a thrilling moment, especially when the pipes struck up the Camerons' march. I believe it was that music, at that particular moment, which made it possible for us to go through the ordeal that followed."

Once again "The March of the Cameron Men" was the undoing of an enemy which had to stand up against the Camerons; and in one part of the line, when the attack was most furiously resisted, the company piper changed his tune to the old "Piobaireachd Dhomnuil Duibh"—

> "Fast they came, fast they come,
> See how they gather!
> Wide waves the eagle's plume
> Blended with heather."

An account of the few minutes before "zero" by a piper of this battalion appeared in the *Scottish Field* ("Pipes of the Misty Moorland," John M'Gibbon), and affords a good example of the steadying effect of the pipes in a period of great strain on morale:

"I looked down at the company and I could see they were shaken . . . I slung my rifle over my back and took up the pipes; that cheered them. I played through two or three tunes and then birled up 'Tullochgorum.' They fairly hooched it and stamped time with their feet. It was close on 'zero' . . . when I changed to 'The March of The Cameron Men.' Our guns burst out with drum fire behind us . . . and the men jumped the parapet like deer and raced over the broken ground at the double. I kept up 'The Cameron Men.' . . . I reached the parapet of the first enemy trench, when I 'stopped one' with my leg, and down I went in a heap."

The pipes were again to the front in the fighting for Hill 70 on the Lens-Loos line in August, 1917. It was surely appropriate enough that, in the advance over the very country in which so many Scottish regiments had fought, with only temporary success, two years before, the pipes should again be at the head of the units which recaptured those blood-soaked positions.

An officer, describing the advance of the 13th Royal Highlanders of Canada, says:

"Our advance was resumed and we swarmed over the top at three different points. Away to the left, which was the objective of our advance, the strains of the pipes could be heard, and across the hills, where so many Scottish lads had fallen two years ago, there burst a loud triumphant cheer as the Canadian Highlanders pressed on to complete their work."

And so it happened that the gallant lads of the 15th Division were avenged.

Opportunities for pipers continued during the later fighting in 1917-18. Records of individual companies and platoons show that on several occasions the pipes encouraged the men to further effort. In one case near Albert, a company of the Black Watch was temporarily cut off from its supports after getting into a German trench and suffered heavily; the men were crushed by superior numbers, and the prospect was black until the piper, who was present as a stretcher bearer, started playing. This had a great effect on the company, which held on to the position until reinforcements arrived.

In the fighting about Albert in August, 1918, several instances occurred of pipers playing their companies to the attack.

On the whole, however, at this stage in the war, it was being found increasingly difficult to renew the depleted ranks of the pipe bands, and most regiments were simply driven to keeping their pipers out of action as far as possible, except on special occasions. But there were still enough left of them to lead their units ever further eastward as the tide of war rolled back.

Incidents frequently occurred showing that their experience of four years' fighting had not damped the ardour of pipers in action.

On one occasion a 16th Canadian piper went into action playing on top of a tank, and was killed. At Amiens, the pipers of the 16th and 48th Highlanders of Canada played the battalions to the attack in August, 1918.

As the German defeat became increasingly apparent and the British forces drove the enemy before them, pipers again got an opportunity of leading their companies to the attack. During the fighting about Albert-Arras in August, 1918, Scottish troops were heavily engaged. Lieut. Edouard Ross, of the French interpreter staff, describes an attack by a battalion of the Black Watch in which a detachment with a piper got into the German trenches; they were all wounded, and their position was dangerous, but the piper started playing, and the sound rapidly brought reinforcements, who captured the position.

GALLIPOLI

In Gallipoli, as on the Western front, pipers added lustre to their reputation; and incidents which occurred to some of them showed that they were stout fighting men even after their pipes were put out of action.

The nature of the terrain generally precluded the more spectacular duty of playing their units to the attack, and the heavy casualties in the force and the constant demand for men resulted in their being frequently employed in the ranks; nevertheless, several cases did occur of company pipers acting as such.

On 12th July, 1916, when the 6th H.L.I. captured three lines of Turkish trenches, Pipers W. Mackenzie and M'Niven played at the head of their companies; M'Niven was killed, and Mackenzie, putting down his pipes, took part in the fighting with a Turkish shovel and did great execution.

On the same day the pipers of the 7th H.L.I. led their battalion into action, and only one of them was wounded. Of these men one, Piper Kenneth MacLennan, was subsequently awarded the Distinguished Conduct

Medal "for playing his pipes during the attack and advancing with the line after his pipes had been shattered by shrapnel, and heartening the wounded under fire." Another, Piper Cameron, played his company over three lines of trenches, with a revolver hanging on his wrist, and earned a mention in despatches; and Piper Macfarlane played through two bayonet charges until two of his drones were blown off by shell fragments.

Writing of the fighting on 12th July, a wounded officer writes:

"The sound of the pipes undoubtedly stirred them on, a piper belonging to each of the two battalions, 5th Argylls and 7th H.L.I., having mounted the parapets of their own trenches, and there in full danger played their comrades on to victory."

In the attack on Achi Baba there was no opportunity for pipers as such, though Pipe Major Andrew Buchan played the 4th Royal Scots "over the top," and, as an officer writes: "fearless of all danger went along the line and did much to hearten the men." Buchan was killed.

Of the pipers of the 5th Royal Scots none survived the early days of the fighting on the Peninsula. An officer of the regiment wrote that they "gloriously upheld the traditions established long ago." In the Achi Baba fighting four were killed and four wounded.

Casualties in action and by disease took heavy toll of the pipers of all these battalions, and after a few months on the Peninsula the pipe bands temporarily ceased to exist.

Even before the withdrawal of the force from Gallipoli it was found that so many casualties had occurred among the pipers of the battalions engaged that the bands were well on the way to extinction. Consequently, under the able management of Colonel Maclean of Pennycross a divisional band numbering twelve pipers and six drummers—all that remained—was organised out of the wreck of the pipe bands of the 52nd Division. That band, though never sent into action, individually or collectively played frequently under shell fire; and "Hey Johnnie Cope" could be heard quite distinctly every morning in the firing line up to within a few days of the evacuation.

The divisional band served on the Desert front in Egypt, and then

THE COMRADES WE LEFT IN GALLIPOLI.

Set by Mrs. A.C. MACDIARMID.

From the Pipe Tune Composed by
Col. H.A.C. MACLEAN C.M.G. of Pennycoss.

accompanied the Division right into Palestine, playing the leading battalion, the 4th K.O.S.B.'s, over the frontier to " Blue Bonnets over the Border."

Later on, more pipers and more Scottish units appeared; and so we find the 2nd London Scottish being played into Jerusalem, and "Dumbarton's Drums" sounding at the head of the Royal Scots as they took over the guard on the Holy Sepulchre—as is the right of "Pontius Pilate's Bodyguard."

SALONIKA

Opportunities for the employment of pipers as such were comparatively rare in the course of the Salonika operations, for obvious reasons. At Karadzakot Zir, however, the 1st Royal Scots pipers played their companies to the attack on the village, and the C.O. reported that, in his opinion,

" It was largely due to the presence of the pipers with the leading wave that the enemy evacuated their trenches and retired in disorder."

MESOPOTAMIA

Playing the pipes in the Golden East is a far greater effort than it is at home, and every piper who has soldiered there knows how the heat and the dryness of the atmosphere affect his bag and reeds. But the cult of *piob mhor* thrives east of Suez, and at least as much enthusiasm is shown by regiments stationed in India as in a home station.

And when Scottish troops were called upon to take their part in the Mesopotamia operations, we find the pipes as prominent a feature in the fighting as they were on the Western front. At Sheikh Saad on 7th January, 1916, the 1st Seaforths—the " Reismeid Caber Feidh "—were played to the attack across absolutely open ground by their Pipe Major Neil M'Kechnie and other pipers. An officer who was present describes the incident as follows:

" As we advanced over the dead flat open desert the Turks suddenly opened a very heavy fire from well concealed trenches at a range of from 600 to 800 yards. The battalion immediately advanced by rushes towards the enemy's position in spite of very heavy initial losses. Foremost among the men was our acting Pipe Major, M'Kechnie, who immediately struck up the regimental charge or 'onset,' 'Cabar Feidh.'

"His fine example as well as his music had a remarkable effect on the men at such a critical moment. He was shortly afterwards wounded, and had to drop behind as the lines went on."

In the same action the 2nd Black Watch were played in by their pipers just as they had been on many previous occasions in France. In the act of playing Corpl. Piper MacNee was mortally wounded. This brave man had been wounded before at Mauquissart and awarded the Distinguished Conduct Medal. The Pipe Major, John Keith, was awarded the D.C.M. for "gallant and distinguished service throughout the operations."

THE LAST STAGE

For four years and a half the pipes of war played their part in the greatest war in history; in the front, under conditions in which they could never have been expected to exist at all, they have led men to victory, have rallied them when victory eluded their grasp, and have marched them back undismayed by the tortures of battle; behind the lines they have headed the long columns of Scottish troops on their way up to the furnace in which the fate of nations was cast.

But, everywhere, they expressed the ideal of the race and led men to follow causes, even causes which appeared lost ones, through to the end.

When silence fell on the 11th November, 1918, along the blasted line where rival civilisations had so long struggled for mastery, the *rôle* of the pipes changed, and it was no longer the "onset" that the piper was impelled to play. The consummation of long effort had been attained—and what instrument more entitled to bear witness to the fact than the one which had sounded over the blood-stained slag-heaps of Loos, the shell-swept heights of Vimy?

As the British First Army entered Valenciennes, the pipers of a historic Scottish division played through the "place" opposite the Hotel de Ville, and must have awakened in the old gabled houses memories of the centuries old alliance between the Lilies of France and the Thistle.

Further east, along the roads that led to Cologne, the pipes played unceasingly, as befitted the occasion, impressing on the population that this was indeed the coming of " Scotland the Brave."

And so, over the great Rhine bridge, the pipes of the 9th and Canadian Divisions led the way, and Germany learnt at last that when *piob mhor* sounds " Gabhaidh sin an rathad mor " [1] it generally attains its objective.

PIPERS IN THE RANKS

The piper is, first and last, a fighting man ; and when a regiment is mobilised it at once loses most of its pipers. Whatever the strength of the band may have been in peace time, only the " sergeant piper "—a hideous official term for the pipe major—and five " full " pipers are normally retained as such. The remainder, while acting as pipers when opportunity offers—and designated accordingly—serve in the ranks.

During this war, and notably during the early years of it, it was often found necessary to make use of full and acting pipers in some purely military capacity, *i.e.* either in the ranks, or as Lewis gunners, bombers, orderlies, runners or stretcher bearers. This fact accounts for many of the honours awarded to pipers, and, at the same time, for the heavy casualties among them.

It is quite impossible to do justice to individuals or units in regard to the part they played in performing such duties ; for those who obtained official recognition, in some form or other, hundreds have merely had the satisfaction of playing the game, in accordance with the rules laid down by all ranks of the British army. The few examples given in this place are typical of the whole.

At Festubert in June, 1915, the pipers of the 6th Seaforths worked continuously day and night, and brought 170 casualties from the front line to the dressing station ; at Loos the 9th Black Watch lost nearly all

[1] " We will take the high road."

their pipers when similarly engaged, and at the two actions of Loos and Neuve Chapelle the 6th Gordons had two killed and ten wounded.

Again, the 2nd Royal Scots pipers lost heavily on the Somme, and were on one occasion highly commended for bringing water up to some newly captured trenches under heavy fire.

The comments of General Sir William Birdwood in a despatch to the Australian Government, though intended to apply to Australian stretcher bearers, are very applicable to pipers acting in this capacity, whether individually or collectively :

" Where all have done so well it is very hard to differentiate, but as a class the stretcher bearers have been beyond praise. Never for a second have they flinched from going forward time after time, absolutely regardless of the fire brought against them ; and I so deeply regret that they should have suffered in consequence."

Another and most hazardous class of duty, which was largely performed by pipers in some battalions, was that of " runners " or despatch carriers ; this often involved crossing heavily shelled country, and has resulted in many casualties. Notable cases have occurred of men carrying despatches through intense barrages, and some have received rewards ; the majority of such cases, however, have necessarily been unnoticed.

Some men appear to have specialised in this duty, *e.g.* Pipe Major Matheson, 1st Seaforths, who got the D.C.M. " for gallant conduct on many occasions in conveying messages under heavy fire," and Lance-Corpl. Piper Dyce, 13th Royal Highlanders of Canada, who on one occasion carried a most urgent despatch through artillery barrage when badly wounded.

In other cases pipers, individually and collectively, have done admirable service in bringing up ammunition.

Many instances of acts of heroism by individual men are detailed below.

PIPERS ON THE MARCH

Playing the pipes in action, though essentially the most important, is, for obvious reasons, only one of the duties of the soldier piper. Every unit of an army is not always in close touch with the enemy, and every battalion puts in a good many miles of marching in a year in conditions which are rarely ideal and very often acutely miserable. It is here that the pipes have rendered such conspicuous service as the marching instrument *par excellence*; and the cult of the bagpipe has spread to units and nationalities which, before the war, would never have thought it possible that the company piper would become one of their most cherished institutions.

That Irish regiments should again adopt the national instrument that had played their ancestors on to the battlefields of France in 1286 is so natural as to need no comment; but when we find English and Australian units, battalions of the United States army, and ships of His Majesty's Navy, to say nothing of field ambulances and transport units, adopting the bagpipe, no further evidence is required to substantiate its claim to be a highly important feature of modern military organisation.

It is indeed to a recognition, in the very early days of the war, of the great value of the pipes in "exciting alacrity and cheerfulness in the soldier" that is due the fact that so many units have deliberately tried to keep their pipers out of harm's way, and have only allowed them, under protest, to accompany their companies into action, and then only in limited numbers. Commanding officers have appreciated that, as a stimulus to tired men, to men marching weary miles to take up a position, to men returning worn out from a spell of duty, the music of the pipes has proved invaluable.

Instances of this stimulating effect are too numerous to mention, but a few, taken from contemporary accounts of the war, may be regarded as typical.

The following incident in the retirement from Mons has frequently occurred elsewhere. "I shall never forget how one General saw a batch of Gordons and K.O.S.B. stragglers trudging listlessly along the road. He halted them. Some more came up, until there was about a company in all, with one piper. He made them form fours, put the piper at the head of them, 'Now lads, follow the piper and remember Scotland,' and they all started off as pleased as Punch, with the tired piper playing like a hero." [1]

The Rev. Dr. Maclean, C.M.G., describes a case of the effect of the pipes on tired men :

"It was a sweltering hot day, and the road was deep with dust. The long snaky khaki column came marching steadily down the hill, silent under the weight of their accoutrements with the grinding heat of an April sun. . . . As the Scots came by he gave the sign to the piper. He stepped forward and struck up one of the great battle marches of our race. The scene that followed baffled description. A roar of cheering burst from the ranks."

Another instance,[2] by one who was himself in the ranks, may be regarded as typical. The regiment concerned was the Glasgow Highlanders, but the description is applicable to every Scottish regiment in the Army List :

"Kilometre after kilometre we marched, through the hottest hours of the middle day, and our feet and backs ached under the weight of all we carried, our faces were dabbled and streaked with dust and perspiration, and in our mouths was only dust to chew. . . . .

"Walking had become a purely mechanical exercise, our limbs controlled, as it seemed, by some power outwith us ; our brains were numb and dazed with fatigue and the maddening persisting pain that was our every step. Blindly, dumbly, helplessly we staggered on . . . in infinite weariness we dragged ourselves to the beginning of the street, and then—

"Then the pipes suddenly set the heavens and the earth dancing to the strains of 'Highland Laddie,' the regimental march of the Glasgows. And at the skirl of the pipes, and before the eyes of those critical spectators, every man braced himself, his step assumed as much of jauntiness as he could put into it, and he had a laugh and a jesting answer ready on his lips for every outsider who spoke to him. . . . It was something more potent than wine that put the boldness into their step, it was the sense

[1] *The Adventures of a Despatch Rider.* Major W. H. Watson.

[2] *More Adventures in Kilt and Khaki.* Thomas Lyon.

of the tradition and honour of their regiment : the feeling that on no account must they present other than a brave front to the world, that the one unpardonable offence would be to let the battalion down."

Examples could be multiplied indefinitely, but the best tribute to the value of the pipes as a marching instrument and in keeping the men cheery is, after all, the fact that regiment after regiment felt constrained to keep them out of action entirely—whether as pipers pure and simple or in other military capacities.

Statements to this effect have been received from nearly all the regiments whose views have been asked, commanding officers being almost unanimous in their opinion that, only where it is imperatively necessary, should a pipe band be exposed to the chances of annihilation inseparable from modern shell fire.

And in just the same manner as the pipes have helped battalions along the " via dolorosa " into action so they have, time and again, played them back to rest and comparative security. In some cases they had shared in the action itself, in others they waited until their services were required. Many commanding officers and observers have referred to this as one of the most important of their duties. In describing the return of a battalion, or what remained of it, from Longueval, Philip Gibbs writes :

" There was a thick summer haze about, and on the ridges the black vapours of shell bursts. . . . It was out of this that the Highlanders came marching. They brought the music with them and the pipes of war playing a Scottish love song, ' I lo'e na a laddie but ane.' Their kilts were caked with mud, they were very tired, but they held their heads up, and the pipers who had been with them played bravely . . . and the Scottish love song rang out across the fields."

An officer of an Argyll battalion, writing of the days of trench fighting, says : " They have done much to hearten us on long marches. They came out of Bethune after Loos and played what was left of us back to billets." Another, in the Royal Scots, referring to the return of the battalion from Kemmel, says : " I shall never forget the effect on the men ; as they struck up they fairly shouted themselves hoarse with delight."

"Wonderful pipes! The men get tired and would fall out, but the pipes make a unity of them. Invisible tendons and muscles seem to connect the legs of all files, and all move as one, mechanically, rhythmically, certainly. The strong are reduced to the step, the weak are braced up to it. All bear the strain and share the strain. So we go on, and the miracle is in the power of the music." [1]

A final quotation—one of a very great number received—reflects the opinion of all ranks:

"I have often seen a company just out of the trenches straggling along the road too weary to think of keeping in formation, let alone in step. On the first sound of the pipes these same men would double up to their place and march along with the best of them."

The ubiquity of the pipes on the Western front has been remarked by all observers. "The music of the pipes is now as much a part of the great orchestra of this war as the incessant rumbling of distant guns, as the swirl of traffic along the transport lines, as the singing of birds above No Man's Land. . . . And where there are pipes there are Scotsmen—Scots everywhere from the sea to St. Quentin, in old French market towns, and in Flemish villages . . . and in camps behind the fighting line not beyond the reach of long range shells, and up in the trenches where death is very near to them. . . . As long as history lasts the spirit of France will salute the memory of these kilted boys and of all the Lowland Scots who have gone into the furnace fires of this war to the music of the pipes, and have fallen in heaps upon her fields. A thousand years hence, when the wind blows softly across the ground where they fought, old Scottish tunes will sound faintly in the ears of men who remember the past, and all this country will be haunted with the ghosts of Scotland's gallant sons." [2]

Nor has it been on the Western front alone that the value of the pipes has made itself appreciated. In every other theatre of war as well has "the tune with the tartan of the clan in it" been heard at the head of columns toiling through the dust and heat, or through pitiless rain. In Egypt and Gallipoli and the Holy Land, in Mesopotamia and the Balkans,

[1] Stephen Graham.—*The Times*, 16th January, 1919. [2] Philip Gibbs.

the pipes have been the prelude to great happenings. " Bundle and Go " in the early dawn of an Eastern day, " Soldier lie down " at night—these have been the preliminaries which led up naturally to " Cabar Feidh " in a hail of machine gun fire, or " Horo mo nighean donn bhoídheach " in the streets of captured Bagdad.

" Many a soldier sadly misses his pipe, which of course may not be lit on a night march ; but to me a greater loss is the silence of those other pipes, for the sound of the bagpipes will stir up a thousand memories in a Highland regiment, and nothing helps a column of weary foot soldiers so well as pipe music, backed by the beat of a drum." [1]

When the British army advanced into German territory the pipers had an opportunity to play with an abandon that had never been felt before.

" Next day, with the skies still streaming, we made the longest continuous march, some 36 kilometres, and by that effort got well into Germany. The roads improved as we got farther on, but the tramp through the forest of Zitter was long, marshy, and melancholy. Our company was first after the pipers, and had the full benefit of the music all the way. And we wandered inward ; inward, with our seeking and haunting Gaelic melodies, into the depths of the hanging, silent wood. It was strange how aloof nature seemed to these melodies. In Scotland, or even in France, all the hills and the woods would have helped the music. But in this German land all were cold toward us, and those endless pine trees seemed to be holding hands with fingers spread before the eyes to show their shame and humiliation. There was a curious sense that the road on which we trod was not our road, and that earth and her fruits on either hand were hostile.

"And how tired the men became, with half of them through the soles of their boots and with racking damp in their shoulders and backs from their rain-sodden packs. But we listened still whilst voluminous waves of melody wandered homeless over German wastes and returned to us,

> I heard the pibroch sounding, sounding,
> O'er the wide meadows and lands from afar.

[1] " The battle beyond Baghdad.—'A Highland Officer.'"—*Blackwood's Magazine.*

or to the stirring strains of the 'March of the Battle of Harlaw,' or to the crooning, hoping, sobbing of 'Lord Lovat's Lament,' and so went on from hour to hour through the emptiness of Southern Germany. When we thought we had just about reached our camping ground for the night, we came to a guide post which showed it still to be seven kilometres on. But that was at the top of a long hill, and the road ran gently down through woods the whole way. The colonel sent a message to play 'Men of Portree.' The rain had stopped, and an evening sky unveiled a more cheerful light. So, with an easy inconsequent air, we cast off care and tripped away down to the substantial and prosperous bit of Rhineland called Hellenthal, well on our way to Cologne." [1]

The interminable marches are over and their goal has been attained; and the instrument which has a tune for every human emotion can now play "The Desperate Battle" in German towns with a safety which has been long unknown. To many a man, however, as he fingers his chanter, the feeling will come, as he thinks of the good men and true who never reached the 11th November, 1918, that the tune that is most appropriate is "Lochaber no more."

PIPE TUNES

Pipe tunes—as every piper knows—have local associations, associations with particular incidents, particular emotions; and in military piping this is never overlooked. In war everything has changed—everything but the elemental courage and passions of the men who are engaged in it; and, as *piob mhor* is essentially the instrument on which those elemental passions can be best expressed, it is not uninteresting to observe how individual pipers have resorted to particular tunes, to suit particular occasions. In many, perhaps in most, cases there were traditional or regimental reasons for playing one tune rather than another, and such tunes were often in the highest degree appropriate; but in other cases the individuality of the performer determined the choice.

Of a selection based on tradition the best authenticated instance is that of the Gordon piper who played Cogadh na Sith, "War or peace,"

[1] Stephen Graham.—"A Private in the Guards."

during the Somme fighting. The tune itself, a piobaireachd composed by the great M'Crimmon some 400 years ago, was played by the Gordons at Waterloo and by a Cameron piper, Kenneth M'Kay, at Quatre Bras.

"[1] About the middle of June a draft of about a hundred and twenty men arrived in camp for the Gordons—the finest draft the commanding officer declared he had ever seen. On the 18th, they were ordered to the front. I found they had a piper with them, and immediately laid hold on him to play the men down to the station. I brought him up to my tent and provided him with a set of pipes which I had reserved for my own particular work. . . . I found something more interesting than that. His great-grandfather had been a piper in the regiment in the days of the Napoleonic war, and at the Battle of Waterloo he stood within the square and played the ancient Highland challenge-march 'Cogadh na Sith,' as the French cuirassiers hurled themselves upon the immovable ranks in vain.

"'John,' I said, 'this is the anniversary of Waterloo, and you will lead the men out to that very tune which your great-grandfather played on that great day.' I told the colonel, and his eyes gleamed as he said to me, 'Ah! padre, we'll do better than that. You will tell the men about it, and I will call them to attention, and your piper will play his tune in memory of the men of Waterloo.'

"And so it was done, and a thrilling incident it was as the men stood rigid and silent in full marching order, and the piper strode proudly along the ranks, sounding the wild, defiant challenge that stirred the regiment a hundred years before."

Regimental tunes appeal enormously to the men who hear and know them; it was probably as much the sound of "Blue Bonnets over the Border" as the sight of Piper Laidlaw piping along the parapet that made the men, shaken with shell fire and gas, go straight forward; and red hackles have followed "Highland Laddie" in circumstances when another tune might have failed to exert the same extraordinary influence. But, having played his regulation onset, the piper has an opportunity of suiting his own taste and selecting a tune appropriate musically and emotionally, as well as in name, to the occasion.

[1] *With the Gordons at Ypres.*—Rev. A. M. Maclean, C.M.G.

On many occasions when the choice of a tune has not been restricted by regimental custom or tradition, individual performers have made selections which indicated the remarkable mentality of the British soldier.

At Loos, where Pipers Simpson and M'Donald of the 2nd Black Watch played their company over the top and through the attack, the tune they commenced with was " Happy we've been a' thegither,"—only later changing into the ceremonial onset " Highland Laddie." To men in a trench who have suffered untold nerve strain waiting for Zero and who happen—as do most men in Highland regiments—to know one tune from another, no more appropriate combination of " onsets " could have been selected.

At Beaumont Hamel, when the 17th H.L.I. took the German trenches and had an opportunity of bombing out the occupants, Pipe Major Gilbert played another popular and very suitable tune, " The muckin' o' Geordie's Byre," and greatly encouraged the men in their task. This same tune has done duty on many similar occasions.

It was to " We'll tak the guid auld way " that the 16th Canadians attacked at Vimy, and many Cameron pipers have played the " Piobaireachd Dhomhnuill Duibh " in similar circumstances.

Another very favourite tune was " The Macgregor's Gathering " which was played with great effect in the capture of many villages during the Somme fighting.

A curious coincidence was the selection by the pipers of the 1st H.L.I. of " I'll gang nae mair tae yon toun " as they marched out of Marseilles on 1st November, 1914, on their way to the front. During the first six months they lost seven pipers killed, eight wounded and two taken prisoner, and the band ceased to exist.

" Baile Inneraora,"—otherwise " The Campbells are Coming "—was the tune to which the first Highland regiment of the Expeditionary Force, the 2nd Argylls, landed in France ; from that time onward it has immortalised on every front, if that were necessary, the town of which Burns wrote :

> " There's naething here but Highland pride
> And Highland scab and hunger.
> If Providence has sent me here,
> 'Twas surely in his anger."

The Argylls long ago took Burns' song and treated it with the contempt it deserves when they adopted " Baile Inneraora " as their " onset." It was played at the taking of Longueval, in the attack at Loos, and at the subsequent rally after that glorious disaster, and in many other actions.

During the fighting on the Somme for the heaps of ruins which had once been a French village, an incident occurred which takes us back to the legend connected with the pibroch " A Cholla, mo run." Long ages ago, when the Campbells heard they were going to be attacked by Coll Kiteach at Dunivaig, they set an ambush and captured the advance guard. All were hanged except the piper, who was given permission to play a lament over his comrades. The piper at once started the warning, which was heard and understood by his comrades,

> " Coll of my love avoid the strait, avoid the strait, avoid the strait,
> Coll of my love, go by the Mull, gain the landing place."

The poor piper was instantly stabbed by the infuriated Campbells.

It is a far cry from those days, when men could converse to each other in pibroch, to 1916; but another tune—not " A Cholla, mo run "—was played by another piper in a French village when his party was cut off. Two officers, a sergeant, and a piper of an Argyll battalion, got separated from the main body, and found themselves unable to get away when the village was again attacked by our men. The small party at once started bombing the enemy from the rear, but the piper, appreciating the unpleasant possibility of their own presence not being recognised, struck up the regimental onset. This alarmed the Germans, who thought they were being attacked from a fresh quarter, and materially contributed to the success of the operation.

INDIVIDUAL ACHIEVEMENTS.

"Agus bha iad am measg uam fear treuna 'n an luchd-cuideachaidh 's a' chogadh."

To attempt to compile a complete record of the achievements of individual pipers or of the pipe bands of units is an impossible task; it would involve a review of the whole course of the war. A long time must elapse before the histories of battalions are completed, and even then we shall probably never know fully the extent to which their pipers have contributed to the attainment of success.

Throughout the war correspondence has been carried on with individuals who, in spite of their appalling environment, have found time to supply information. They at least have the satisfaction of knowing that to them is largely due the fact that brave acts have been saved from oblivion.

Such a review as follows is but a fragmentary one, based on information obtained from officers, N.C.O.'s and men of the battalions concerned—but almost never from individual pipers. Among these men there appears to have been a conspiracy of silence, and attempts to obtain fuller information as to the reason for the granting of awards or the names of pipers whose identity disappeared under the blue pencil of the Censor have proved in very many instances unavailing.

The omission from these pages of mention of achievements of pipers of many battalions must be regarded as indicating lack of space to record them, or of failure to obtain the desired information.

The original Expeditionary Force landed in France with seven Scottish battalions possessing pipe bands; when the armistice was signed the number of such units exceeded a hundred. Although on mobilisation the number of "full" pipers in a battalion is only six it must be remembered that there are always "acting pipers" serving in the companies who are available—until that source of supply is exhausted—to take the place of casualties; and it is safe to reckon that the 100 battalions have had more than 2500 pipers at various times.

The numbers that served in various units during the campaign varied enormously; in some, which freely utilised their pipers in the front line—in the ranks, as bearers, and as pipers in action—as many as seventy or eighty have been borne on the strength at different times; in others, which kept these men invariably behind the front line, the casualties were negligible and comparatively few were used up.

This difference in method of employment largely explains the variations in the casualty lists and honours of different units; and, in some cases, it has been found impossible to obtain anything like complete information.

8543 Piper JAMES MACKENZIE, 1st Scots Guards.

During the desperate fighting about Ypres in October, 1914, Piper Mackenzie greatly distinguished himself bringing up ammunition to the firing line. He was killed while doing so. Awarded a mention in despatches.

8081 Piper CHARLES SCOTT MAGUIRE, 2nd Scots Guards.

On the 27th October, 1914, near Ypres, an advanced trench was blown to pieces by shell fire, most of its occupants being killed or wounded. Hearing calls for help, Piper Maguire went forward from the support trench to report. He crawled 15 yards on hands and knees to the wrecked trench and found several men had been buried by the explosion. Although without any protection from enemy fire he dug out a man and found he was dead; he continued his task and got out another, placing him for safety under cover of the dead body. He then crawled back to his trench. The N.C.O. in charge had been killed meantime, and no official report of his conduct was possible. Maguire himself was wounded shortly after, his back being broken; he died of paralysis some seven months later.

11002 Piper J. McMILLAN, 1st Royal Scots.

Was awarded the D.C.M. for conspicuous gallantry as a battalion scout.

10123 Corpl. E. COLLINS,
10754 Piper J. CLANCY,
10639 ,, J. SMART,
10032 ,, P. MALLIN,
} 1st Royal Scots.

During the operations on the Salonika front the battalion had to capture Karadzakot Zir. The men had to advance over open country to the attack. These pipers played over three successive charges to the enemy's position, and the commanding officer considered their gallantry on this occasion was to a large extent instrumental in bringing about the success of the attack. In spite of their exposed position they all got through without being touched.

11065 Piper H. M'LEOD, 2nd Royal Scots.

Was repeatedly mentioned in despatches for gallantry in attending wounded under fire, and was recommended for the D.C.M.

1235 Piper W. SINCLAIR, 5th Royal Scots.

Shortly after the original landing on the Gallipoli Peninsula, a critical retirement took place. Piper Sinclair, on his own initiative, gathered together a handful of stragglers, and, taking up a favourable position, covered successfully the withdrawal of the battalion. He was killed.

Pipe Major JOHN BUCHAN, 4th Royal Scots.

Just before the attack on Achi Baba on 28th June, 1915, Pipe Major Buchan played along the line as the battalion went over; he was killed.

7271 Pipe Major J. M'DOUGALL, 8th Royal Scots.

Was awarded the Distinguished Conduct Medal " for gallant conduct under very trying circumstances " as a stretcher bearer at Festubert in May, 1915.

Corpl. ALEXANDER FORSYTH, 9th Royal Scots.

At Arras in April, 1917, this man, who was a highly skilled bomber, volunteered to bomb the Germans out of a position in which they were covered by machine guns. He crawled up and succeeded in his object, but was killed. He was given the Distinguished Conduct Medal.

13283 Pipe Major A. COLGAN, 12th Royal Scots.

In the Loos attack the pipe major played the battalion over the top and was wounded. Subsequently, in the great German offensive in 1918, when pipers had to serve in the ranks, he got the Military Medal " for good leadership and courage."

Pipe Major JOHN MOUAT, 13th Royal Scots.

During the final advance in 1918 the pipers were employed as bearers, and suffered heavy casualties. Pipe Major Mouat received a mention in despatches.

Pipe Major MURDOCH MACDONALD, 13th Royal Scots.

A heavy shell burst among a company and buried a number of men. Pipe Major Macdonald went out alone, under very heavy shell fire and brought in six wounded men unaided.

Pipe Major DAVID ANDERSON, 15th Royal Scots.

In the opening attack on the Somme front on 1st July, 1916, the battalion was played forward by the pipe major, to the old regimental tune " Dumbarton's drums." He was hit shortly after going over the top, but continued playing; he was again wounded after crossing the third line of trenches and fell to the ground. He tried to go on playing while sitting on the ground, but his pipes were shattered by a shell bursting near him. He managed to get up and was at once attacked by a German, but succeeded in knocking him out with his fists, and then continued fighting with a rifle until overcome by his wounds.

Pipe Major Anderson was given the one Croix de Guerre allotted to his Division for the most conspicuous act of bravery. The pipes he was playing on this occasion were of historical interest as they had been taken to the Antarctic by a member of Scott's expedition, and had been played also in the Arctic expedition of 1907.

Another interesting feature of Anderson's achievement was that several Germans surrendered to him as he played on the parapet of one of their trenches.

Pipe Major DAVID CAMPBELL, 1st Royal Scots Fusiliers.

Although he had been wounded in the arm on the previous day Pipe Major Campbell played his battalion to the attack on the German position at Hooge on June 16, 1915.

He played on right up to the German wire entanglements when, throwing his pipes aside, he caught up the bayonet of a comrade who had just been shot by a German officer and at once attacked the latter. He captured the officer.

9884 Piper HIGGINSON, 1st K.O.S.B.

The initial engagement of the battalion was the landing on Gallipoli. During the first few days the pipers were fighting in the ranks, and the gallant exploit of Piper Higginson is eloquent indication of the fact that they played the part of the fighting man right well. All the officers and N.C.O.'s of his Company having been killed or wounded during the heavy fighting of 26th April, 1915, Piper Higginson rallied the remainder, and organised and led a bayonet charge with such dash and bravery that the Turks were swept back from a line they had captured earlier in the day. Just as success was attained Piper Higginson was mortally wounded, and died some hours later. Had he survived he was to have been recommended for the D.C.M.

1315 Piper MAITLAND,
8248 Pipe Major W. MACKENZIE, } 1st K.O.S.B.

During most of their stay on the Gallipoli peninsula the pipers had to bring up ammunition, rations, stores, etc., a job which was at all times most trying and often extremely hazardous. For conspicuous bravery in charge of these carrying parties the Pipe Major and Piper Maitland were awarded the Military Medal.

556 Piper A. ERSKINE, 5th K.O.S.B.

Was mentioned in despatches for gallantry as a stretcher bearer in Gallipoli.

14851 Pipe Major ROBERT MACKENZIE, 6th K.O.S.B.

At the battle of Loos 25th September, 1915, when the battalion went forward to the attack in which it was decimated, the first over the top was the Pipe Major, who started playing at once. He was wounded and fell after a comparatively short distance, but managed to crawl back. His leg had to be amputated, and he died of shock shortly afterwards. Mackenzie was a man of nearly sixty years of age, and had forty-two years' Army service. He was awarded a mention in despatches. Before the action he had been detailed, on account of his age, to be postman, but insisted on going into action.

15851 Piper DANIEL LAIDLAW, V.C., 7th K.O.S.B.

Just before the attack on Hill 70 and Loos on 25th September, 1915, the battalion, which was under heavy shell fire, was exposed to a cloud of poison gas. Many of the men succumbed to this gas, and the remainder were shaken by what they were going through. The commanding officer, seeing Laidlaw standing waiting with his pipes for the order to advance, called to him, "Pipe them together, Laidlaw, for God's sake, pipe them together," and he immediately climbed out on to the parapet, and marched up and down, regardless of danger, playing "Blue Bonnets over the Border." The effect on the men was magical; at the same moment the order came to advance, and the officer shouted "Come on, the Borderers, who'll be the first to reach the German trenches?" The survivors of the company swarmed up and over to the assault following the piper. The men were falling all round him, but Laidlaw continued to advance until he got near the German line, when he was wounded and the officer, who was alongside of him, was killed. As he lay on the ground he tried to go on playing, and then managed to get up and hobble after the battalion.

He was awarded the Victoria Cross "for most conspicuous gallantry," and the French Croix de Guerre.

The sobriquet "Piper of Loos" was commonly applied to Piper Laidlaw; though, in fairness to two other men, it must be admitted that he only shared that distinction with them.

Pipe Major DOUGLAS TAYLOR, 7th K.O.S.B.

During the attack on Loos when Piper Laidlaw got the V.C., the other pipers were chiefly employed in bringing in the casualties. There were large numbers of men lying about who had been gassed. Pipe Major Taylor, though himself wounded in the hand, continued bringing in these men for thirty-six hours, until he was himself shot down with a bullet in the heart. He recovered ultimately—one of the surgical miracles of the war.

Pipe Major W. ROBERTSON, 2nd Scottish Rifles.

Was awarded the Military Medal for gallantry in the field.

Pipe Major NEIL MACLEOD, 8th Scottish Rifles.

Greatly distinguished himself in the Dardanelles fighting in attending on the wounded. He was killed in the attack on 12th July, 1915.

40631 Corpl. WHITELAW,
17806 Piper M'GURK, } 9th Scottish Rifles.

In a daylight raid at Arras in February, 1917, these two men played their companies over, standing on the parapet, and then followed them up to the German position.

Pipe Major J. M'COLL, 10th Scottish Rifles.

Was awarded the Military Medal for gallantry during the Somme fighting.

14631 Piper ALEXANDER STEVENSON, 11th Scottish Rifles.

On 20th April, 1917, Piper Stevenson observed a comrade, who had been out on a night patrol, lying wounded in No Man's Land, and calling for help. He at once went over the parapet in broad daylight and brought him in, although the Germans brought a machine gun to bear on him as soon as he exposed himself. While assisting the medical officer to dress the wounded man he was killed. His name was mentioned in despatches for gallantry. He had previously done excellent work carrying messages in action.

Piper ANDREW WISHART,
9430 Piper W. STUART, } 1st Black Watch.

After the failure of the first attack on Richebourg, 9th May, 1915—the attacking battalions simply melting away under a sheet of lead—a second attack on the position was ordered for midday; the leading battalions on this occasion being the 1st Black Watch and 1st Camerons. The men went over the top with a tremendous dash, and each company was led by its pipers. Two at least actually reached the German trenches and continued playing—9430 W. Stuart, and Andrew Wishart of the Black

Watch. They were under very heavy fire, and both got wounded. Wishart fell into a shell hole and lay there for four days before he succeeded in crawling back to our trenches. When he fell there were loud shouts "The piper's down," and the men made frantic efforts to get into the enemy's trenches; but the machine gun fire was too heavy, and they had to withdraw. Piper Stuart was awarded the D.C.M.

Piper GEORGE GALLOWAY, 7th Black Watch.

On one occasion Piper Galloway rescued five men who had been buried by a shell explosion. Subsequently, when employed as a runner, he was called on to deliver an important message under very heavy fire. This he accomplished in almost impossible conditions, and was given the Military Medal.

L/Corpl. G. SWAN, 7th Black Watch.

Served in the ranks during the Somme fighting. He was killed in action, and was awarded the Military Medal.

1919 Piper ALEXANDER PRATT, 2nd Black Watch.

Pipers throughout the war have been employed in a great variety of ways besides piping. Piper Pratt was reported in Mesopotamian Force Despatches as "one of the bravest and most intelligent bomb sergeants in the regiment; on three occasions he has proved his high capacity for leadership in the attack. He has been twice wounded. His power of training grenadiers and his influence over his men are quite exceptional." He was promoted in the field to Sergeant and awarded a D.C.M.

941 Piper PETER MACNEE, 2nd Black Watch.

Also distinguished himself greatly as a bomber. He won the D.C.M. at Neuve Chapelle. In France he was twice wounded, but went to Mesopotamia with the battalion. In the fighting at Sheikh Saad in January, 1916, he was mortally wounded.

1839 Piper ALEXANDER MACDONALD,
736 Piper DAVID SIMPSON,
365 Piper R. JOHNSTONE,
699 Piper DAVID ARMIT,
187 Piper J. GALLOWAY,
} 2nd Black Watch.

In the attack by the 2nd Black Watch at Mauquissart, 25th September, 1915, the pipers took a prominent part, playing their companies up to and through the German first and second lines. After three lines had been captured the order to attack the fourth was given. 736 Piper David Simpson at once dashed forward playing, followed by his company; he was killed just as they reached the objective. His bravery earned him the title, for long after, of "The Piper of Loos." He was recommended for the Victoria Cross. Further on, 1839 Piper Alexander Macdonald alternately played from one trench to the next and assisted in bombing the enemy out of their dugouts. In the third trench he marched, playing "Macgregor's Gathering," down the trench at the head of the bombers, and then climbed on to the parapet and continued playing. He was ultimately wounded and lost his leg. For his gallantry he was given the D.C.M., but did not long survive to enjoy the honour as he died soon after his discharge. At the same time 365 Piper R. Johnstone went on playing until he fell gassed. As pipers fell out wounded others took their places, and the battalion was played continuously into and through the action. It appears to have been a tradition among the pipers of this battalion that they were always to play whenever an opportunity occurred. Pipers David Armit and J. Galloway also played right up to and through the German support trenches.

1198 Pipe Major D. M'Leod, 4th Black Watch.

Piper M'Leod played his company into action at Loos.

During this action the commanding officer was mortally wounded; he was brought in, under intense fire, by Pipe Major—then Corpl. Piper—M'Leod, who received the Military Medal for his gallantry. He subsequently got a bar to the Medal for repeated acts of gallantry during the great advance of 1915.

410 Pipe Major Alexander Low, 4th Black Watch,

Received the Military Medal for devoted attendance to the wounded at Neuve Chapelle.

1568 Piper Alexander Howie, 5th Black Watch.

At Neuve Chapelle Piper Howie greatly distinguished himself in bringing in casualties. He was killed while performing this duty. Mentioned in despatches.

Piper R. Pirnie,
Piper A. Forbes,
Piper A. Tainsh,
Piper R. Mapleton,
} 6th Black Watch.

These men played the battalion in to the attack on High Wood, 14th July, 1916. Though much exposed they escaped unwounded.

Piper Ferguson, 6th Black Watch.

At Laventie this man marched from one end of the line to the other playing "Johnny Cope," which aroused the enemy, who, expecting an immediate attack, at once started a barrage. No attack was ever intended.

2126 Piper Alasdair M'Donald, 6th Black Watch.

Near Laventie in July, 1916, a small patrol of four men operating in No Man's Land ran into some Germans, with the result that two of them were badly wounded and could not get back to our lines. Volunteers were asked for, and M'Donald and another man went out. They met a German patrol and dipersed it, but this at once brought hostile machine gun fire on to them. They had to hunt about for a considerable time in high grass full of barbed wire before finding the wounded men, and, in bringing them back, had to make use of part of a German communication trench. Piper M'Donald was mentioned in despatches.

290056 Pipe Major Thomas Macdonald,
292440 L/Corpl. G. Swan,
200509 Piper A. Mands,
Piper George Galloway,
} 7th Black Watch.

All these men received the Military Medal for gallantry in carrying despatches during the Somme actions. On several occasions they performed quite invaluable service in this way.

7671 Piper ALEXANDER HENDERSON, 1st Cameron Highlanders.

On October 22nd, 1914, Piper Henderson went out to an officer of the battalion who was lying wounded in a very exposed position, and applied first field dressings. He then helped this officer back to our position under heavy machine gun fire and then returned to his duty in the ranks. He was awarded the Distinguished Conduct Medal.

Sergt. JOHNSON, 2nd Cameron Highlanders.

Received the Military Medal for conspicuous gallantry on the night of 11th March, 1917, when on a reconnoitring patrol on the Struma. He killed the enemy's sentry before he had time to warn his group, thus enabling the party to account successfully for five out of seven of the enemy. Also for continuous good work as sergeant in charge of regimental scouts.

As scout sergeant he subsequently still further distinguished himself, and by his initiative and daring in incessant patrol work, materially assisted in gaining complete ascendancy over all the ground between our own and the Bulgar trenches. " His display of daring, initiative and courage has been a splendid example to all the men under him."

56 Pipe Major JOHN ROSS, 4th Cameron Highlanders.

Played the battalion to the attack at Festubert on 17th May, 1915, along with the other pipers of the battalion.

17128 Piper J. SCOBIE, Cameron Highlanders.

Obtained the M.M., D.C.M. for gallantry in action.

9158 Acting Pipe Major J. MACLELLAN, 1st Seaforth Highlanders.

During the advance in Mesopotamia ammunition happened to run short at a point only 50 yards removed from the Turk trenches. MacLellan at once volunteered to fetch some, and was killed as he was bringing it up.

8391 Pipe Major D. MATHIESON, 1st Seaforth Highlanders.

Was awarded the Distinguished Conduct Medal " for gallant conduct on many occasions in conveying messages under heavy fire, and also for gallantry in attending on the wounded on an exposed part of the line."

9446 Pipe Major NEIL M'KECHNIE, 1st Seaforth Highlanders.

During the engagement at Sheikh Saad on 7th January, 1916, the battalion had to advance for a long distance over perfectly flat country under very heavy fire. Casualties among our men were very numerous. The pipe major and Pipers Colin M'Kay and Alex. M'Kay at once started playing " Caber Feidh," and continued to do so for some time. M'Kechnie and Alex. M'Kay were both wounded.

At Neuve Chapelle M'Kechnie had distinguished himself as a bomber, and was mentioned in despatches and awarded the Russian Order of St. George.

766 Pipe Major MACKENZIE, 1st Seaforth Highlanders.

Was mentioned in despatches for gallantry in Palestine.

412 Piper WILLIAM BARRY, 1st Seaforth Highlanders.

Went out into No Man's Land under heavy machine gun fire to the assistance of a wounded comrade who was lying unable to move, and whose clothing had caught fire. Piper Barry was recommended for the D.C.M.; he was mentioned in despatches.

529 Piper COLIN M'KAY, 1st Seaforth Highlanders.

During the advance at Sheikh Saad some of the pipers had to bring up ammunition. The Turkish barrage was generally late and missed the advancing battalion, but came down behind it; this resulted in severe casualties among ammunition parties. Piper M'Kay was specially promoted on the field for gallantry in performing duty as an ammunition carrier.

201307 Piper P. STEWART, 4th Seaforth Highlanders.

A company on the Ypres sector in September, 1917, had to advance a distance of nearly two miles over flooded ground badly cut up by our artillery. The men were very heavily laden with extra ammunition, bombs, etc.; Piper Stewart played them along until he fell and damaged his pipes. When they reached their position volunteers were called for to go out and try to establish communication with the brigade on the left, whose position was not known. Piper Stewart went out and performed this task, but was badly wounded in the arm. He had previously done excellent work in collecting casualties and putting them in an abandoned gun emplacement. He was awarded the Military Medal.

599 Piper DONALD M'KAY, 5th Seaforth Highlanders.

Was killed at Beaumont Hamel when carrying despatches. His C.O. said of him, " It was by devotion such as his that victory was bestowed on us that day."

21629 Piper D. FRASER,
4661 Piper B. HAMILTON, } 7th Seaforth Highlanders.

In the attack at Loos, when the battalion was played in by their pipers, most of these men were killed or wounded. At one time the position became very serious and the advance was checked. Pipers Fraser and Hamilton at once got up into the open and started playing "Caber Feidh"; the effect was very marked as their companies dashed forward after them. They were both killed.

8535 Piper D. DAVIDSON, 7th Seaforth Highlanders.

This man, when serving in the ranks, showed such gallantry and initiative that he received both the Distinguished Conduct Medal and the Military Medal.

8112 Pipe Major ALEXANDER MACKENZIE, 8th Seaforth Highlanders.

At Loos, when the battalion was played into action, there were very heavy losses among the pipers. Pipe Major Mackenzie distinguished himself greatly, and was given the Distinguished Conduct Medal.

8119 Pipe Major G. GORDON, 9th Seaforth Highlanders.

Played the battalion into action at Longueval on 14th July, 1916, and was awarded the Belgian Croix de Guerre.

5745 Piper CHARLES M'LELLAN, 9th Seaforth Highlanders.

At the battle of Loos he was acting as orderly to his captain; as they got over the parapet the officer was hit, and died a few minutes afterwards. Piper M'Lellan then reported himself to another officer who sent him back, under heavy fire, for reinforcements. Having done this several times, he went to look for his captain and brought in his body. He was awarded the Military Medal.

10744 Corporal A. GODSMAN, 1st Highland Light Infantry.

During the action at Neuve Chapelle he repeatedly brought up ammunition to the firing line under the heaviest fire, until he was wounded. He was awarded the Distinguished Conduct Medal and the Russian Order of St. George.

11480 Piper JOHN BRODIE, 2nd Highland Light Infantry.

This man was one of the party with the late Col. W. L. Brodie when that officer won the V.C.

240881 Piper WILLIAM MACKENZIE, 6th Highland Light Infantry.

In the action of 12th July, 1915, in which the battalion captured three lines of Turkish trenches in Gallipoli, Piper Mackenzie went into action armed with a revolver and a shovel, displaying great gallantry and doing great execution with both these weapons until he was wounded.

1914 Piper KENNETH MACLENNAN, 7th Highland Light Infantry.

Was awarded the Distinguished Conduct Medal "for playing the pipes during the attack (on the Turkish trenches, 12th July, 1915) and advancing with the line after his pipes had been shattered by shrapnel, and heartening the wounded under fire" (*London Gazette*). After his pipes had been broken he continued to play on his chanter for some time. He then made several journeys across the open to fetch water for the wounded under heavy fire; and also brought up boxes of ammunition.

1901 Piper D. CAMERON, 7th Highland Light Infantry.

In the attack on the Turkish trenches on 12th July, 1915, Piper Cameron played his company right up to the captured trenches and was awarded a special mention in Divisional Orders (52nd Division). On this occasion, while playing, he had a revolver hanging from his wrist, and on reaching the trenches started using it with good effect.

Piper DONALD MACFARLANE, 7th Highland Light Infantry.

In the same action in Gallipoli on 12th July, 1915, Piper Macfarlane played his company through a bayonet charge and continued doing so until a shell burst shattered his pipe drones. He then devoted himself to giving water to the wounded.

Corpl. Piper ALLAN M'NICOL, 12th Highland Light Infantry.

During the fighting at Loos and Hill 70 Corpl. M'Nicol was employed carrying an artillery observation flag, and signalling successive positions to our guns as they were captured. For his gallantry in action he was awarded the Military Medal.

15006 Pipe Major WILLIAM M'COMB, 16th Highland Light Infantry.

On 14th February, 1916, the Pipe Major, though stunned and sick from a blow by a branch of a tree which had been hit by a shell, went forward and dug out several men who had been buried. There was heavy shell fire at the time. He was given the Military Medal.

12095 Piper (Pipe Major) THOMAS RICHARDSON, 16th Highland Light Infantry.

Was awarded the Military Medal for gallant conduct at Roupy in the night of 2nd April, 1917, when the company in support was heavily shelled and casualties were heavy. "Pipe Major Richardson organised carrying parties and showed an utter disregard of danger under the continuous fire of heavy guns."

Pipe Major B. M'DONALD, Highland Light Infantry.

An ammunition dump having caught fire he went in under heavy machine gun and shell fire and succeeded in dragging out boxes of bombs and throwing them into a shell crater full of water. By this means he stopped the conflagration. At the time he had just been given a commission, and he received for this action the Military Cross.

16094 Pipe Major YOUNG GILBERT, 17th Highland Light Infantry.

On the 1st July, 1916, the battalion crawled up to within 100 yards of the Leipzig redoubt and rushed the latter when the barrage lifted, and held on. The position was a very perilous one, and the C.O. called on the Pipe Major to play to the men. This he at once did and continued doing so, with the most stimulating effect on the battalion. For this action he was awarded the Military Medal.

5495 Piper JAMES RITCHIE, 2nd Gordon Highlanders.

On the 14th July, 1916, the battalion had to attempt the capture of the road from High Wood to Longueval. Advancing beyond the first objective they advanced further and tried to dig in, but came under deadly fire from flank and rear. Of the two leading platoons only one wounded officer and five men ever got back. Piper Ritchie volunteered to carry a message to regimental headquarters and bring up reinforcements. He did this twice. He was awarded the Military Medal.

6349 Pipe Major CHARLES ANDERSON, 2nd Gordon Highlanders.

Was awarded the Military Medal. His C.O. writes: "Has done splendid work throughout; his cheerfulness and gallantry have been at all times most marked, and he was a splendid example to all until he was severely wounded at Hulluch on 25th September, 1915."

6863 Piper R. STEWART, 2nd Gordon Highlanders.

From the commencement of the war Piper Stewart's gallantry was repeatedly brought to notice and especially during the fighting in October and November, 1914, and at Ypres. He was specially promoted to Sergeant and awarded the D.C.M. and the Russian Order of St. George for bringing up ammunition under particularly trying circumstances at Ypres. He was killed at Loos.

Pipe Major (Sergt. Major) ANGUS MACLEAN, 2nd Gordon Highlanders.

Rejoined his old battalion on the outbreak of war and was transferred from the pipes to a company as sergeant major. He was awarded the Military Medal for "conspicuous courage and ability in organising work under very dangerous conditions."

THE 2ND GORDON HIGHLANDERS IN ITALY.

In the summer of 1918 the pipers, during the offensive, were attached for duty to the 23rd Field Ambulance. All the wounded had to be carried across a deep and very rapid burn, which was difficult to get across for a single man. These pipers, however, with four men to a stretcher and four more to steady them, and without their kilts and hose, succeeded in getting large numbers of casualties over. They stood in the water for many hours. Subsequently they went out to look for wounded and brought in many more. " But for the work of the pipers and drummers it would have been impossible to evacuate the wounded that night."

Piper GEORGE PATERSON, 4th Gordon Highlanders.

In the fighting outside Cambrai in November, 1917, Piper Paterson played the battalion into action and charged in three successive waves ; he also played it into Cantanig under heavy fire. Here he was wounded. He was awarded the Military Medal.

Piper WILLIAM WEBSTER, 4th Gordon Highlanders.

In the face of heavy fire during the retirement in March, 1918, repeatedly brought up ammunition to men in the front line. Was awarded the Military Medal.

Piper P. BOWIE,
Piper P. PATERSON,
Piper R. PRENTICE,
Piper G. DAVIDSON, } 4th Gordon Highlanders.

In the Ypres fighting on 31st July, 1917, Piper Bowie rallied the men at a time when things were looking very bad. He was awarded the Military Medal. At the Marne, too, he and Pipers P. Paterson, R. Prentice, and G. Davidson played their companies into action " and the example set by them roused the troops to further efforts to force the enemy from a difficult position and enabled them to gain a great victory."

1985 Piper CHARLES THOMSON, 5th Gordon Highlanders.

At Festubert Piper Thomson showed great courage as an observer, and repeatedly crossed a heavily shelled zone, which was also under fire by snipers, carrying messages to battalion headquarters.

Piper H. LUNAM, 5th Gordon Highlanders.

In the action at High Wood on 18th July, 1916, Piper Lunam " very heroically played his company into action in face of heavy machine gun fire and a heavy enemy barrage. He got no official recognition, but the thanks and respect of his comrades who followed him."

10115 Pipe Major J. HOWARTH, 6th Gordon Highlanders.

During the fighting at Loos Pipe Major Howarth was acting as orderly to the commanding officer, and, in the course of the advance, was wounded in the feet. A shell had burst and knocked over a dozen of our men and he at once went off to give first aid. On the way he saw Captain —— of the 2nd Gordons lying wounded. As, on account of his own wound, he was unable to carry the wounded officer in, he took off his own puttees, wound them round his knees as a protection, took Captain —— on his back and crawled back on hands and knees to our own line.

Pipe Major Howarth had already received the D.C.M. for his gallantry in tending the wounded at Neuve Chapelle. For his action on this occasion he was awarded a bar to the medal.

10700 Piper W. BANNERMAN, 6th Gordon Highlanders.

In the fighting at Givenchy on 2nd June, 1915, some of the pipers were employed in the ranks. Piper Bannerman was mentioned in despatches for great gallantry in leading a bayonet charge.

Piper (Sergt.) PETER DEAN, 2nd Argyll and Sutherland Highlanders.

When serving in the ranks as a machine gun sergeant he worked his gun alone in an exposed position when the rest of the gun team had all been killed or wounded. He was awarded the Distinguished Conduct Medal.

3162 Piper WILLIAM CARLYLE, 6th Argyll and Sutherland Highlanders.

After a bayonet charge at Festubert on 16th June, 1915, the battalion was lying on the ground under heavy fire. Near the enemy's line was a wounded man. Piper Carlyle crept out on hands and knees to try and bring him in ; just as he reached the man and had started to lift him, he was killed. Piper Carlyle was mentioned in despatches.

Piper JOHN WALLS, 7th Argyll and Sutherland Highlanders.

Was awarded the Military Medal for devotion to duty as battalion runner through the barrages on 23/24th July, 1915.

Pipe Major J. WILSON, 8th Argyll and Sutherland Highlanders.

On the 8th April, 1916, a German raiding party of considerable strength entered our trenches in the Labyrinth after the explosion of several mines which inflicted heavy casualties. Pipe Major Wilson at once organised a counter attack and drove out the enemy. He received a Divisional certificate of gallant conduct.

266 Piper GEORGE SHEARER, 9th Argyll and Sutherland Highlanders.

When employed as a bearer on 24th May, 1915, brought in a wounded man out of No Man's Land under particularly difficult circumstances, and was awarded the D.C.M.

4627 Pipe Major THOMAS AITKEN, 10th Argyll and Sutherland Highlanders.

During the fighting at Longueval in July, 1916, although a man of sixty years of age, Pipe Major Aitken, at his own request, acted as orderly to the commanding officer for the whole day ; he was ultimately wounded. He was awarded the Distinguished Conduct Medal " for conspicuous gallantry on this and many other occasions."

6191 Piper J. DALL,
2616 Piper D. WILSON, } 10th Argyll and Sutherland Highlanders.

When the battalion attacked Longueval it was met by heavy machine gun fire, which caused very severe casualties. Part of the enemy wire had been left uncut by our bombardment, and this caused momentary confusion in the ranks, as it was very dark. The advance was held up by some ruined dwellings in the streets of the village which had been turned into machine gun nests. Pipers Dall and Wilson at once started playing, and in spite of the noise of shell fire all round them, they succeeded in rallying the men, and in leading an attack which proved to be irresistible. Piper Dall was wounded. Piper Wilson was awarded a mention in despatches.

569 Piper G. Gamack, 10th Argyll and Sutherland Highlanders.

Received the Military Medal for great gallantry in evacuating casualties during the storming of the St. Quentin Canal, Sept., 1918.

Pipe Major Donald Macfarlane, 11th Argyll and Sutherland Highlanders.

In the action of Loos the Pipe Major was employed as a despatch runner carrying messages back from Hill 70. He continued doing this though severely wounded in the arm. He was recommended for the Distinguished Conduct Medal.

Piper Charles Hoey,
Piper J. Barnett,
Piper T. Wallace, } 11th Argyll and Sutherland Highlanders.

In the attack at Loos these men all played their companies into action. Piper Barnett was killed while doing so.

Piper Charles Cameron, 11th Argyll and Sutherland Highlanders.

When the battalion attacked Hill 70 on 25th September, 1915, the pipers led their companies and suffered heavy casualties. The 15th Division hung on to the slope of the hill until next day, but ultimately had to fall back, being heavily counter-attacked. The men of different units got mixed up in the hand to hand fighting which ensued, and it was necessary to rally them in their own units. Piper Cameron stood under heavy fire playing, and rallied the men of the 11th. His bravery resulted in his being known in the division as " The Piper of Loos."

598 Corpl. Piper R. Stevenson, 12th Argyll and Sutherland Highlanders.

Many of the pipers of this battalion were employed as scouts, and Corpl. Stevenson rendered particularly good service in this capacity, especially in August, 1918, when, in spite of heavy enemy fire, he went forward and carried out a successful reconnaissance of the wire on the enemy's trenches. For this he got the Military Medal.

139 Corpl. Piper H. G. Latham, 1st London Scottish.

On account of heavy losses at Messines the pipers of this battalion during the early part of the war were employed in the ranks. Corpl. Latham was a crack shot and had got into the final stage of the King's Hundred at the Bisley Camp in 1914. He was accordingly employed as a sniper with much success. He took a prominent part in the bayonet attack at Messines. He was killed at Zillebeke 16th November, 1914. Was awarded a mention in despatches.

Piper Sydney Wilson, Liverpool Scottish.

This man served in the ranks. He was awarded the certificate for gallantry on three separate occasions.

290 Pipe Major JOHN WILSON,
1525 Piper GEORGE TAYLOR, } 1st Tyneside Scottish.

Both these men received the Military Medal for bravery in playing their battalion into action at La Boiselle on 1st July, 1916. The whole of the pipers of this and the 2nd Battalion took part in this, one of the most spectacular attacks on the Somme; and their behaviour was an inspiration to the men. They were exposed to very heavy fire and to every sort of obstacle on the ground, but went on playing after ten pipers had been killed and five wounded. 1525 Piper James Phillips of the 2nd Battalion, after having his pipes shattered, started bombing the German trenches. He was mentioned in despatches.

Sergt. JOHN MACDONALD, Princess Patricia's Canadian Light Infantry.

At Hooge on 8th May, 1915, after a front trench had been obliterated by shell fire, Sergt. Macdonald dug out two wounded men who had been buried, and carried one on his back and assisted the other to a place of safety under very heavy shell and rifle fire. He was awarded the Distinguished Conduct Medal. In Sept., 1916, he died of wounds.

24011 Lance Corpl. J. DYCE, 13th Royal Highlanders of Canada.

During the Ypres fighting in April, 1915, Corporal Dyce was employed as a despatch runner and had to cross ground heavily bombarded by the enemy. While doing so he was shot through the chest, and became unconscious; on coming to, knowing the importance of the despatch he was carrying, he started crawling in to deliver it at battalion headquarters, collapsing when he arrived there. He was mentioned in despatches.

29327 Pipe Major JAMES GROAT, 16th Canadian Scottish.

In the attack on the Vimy Ridge Pipe Major Groat and the pipers of the battalion played them to the attack, Groat accompanying the commanding officer. They had to advance over a mile under terrific fire. On this occasion he received the Military Medal.

Subsequently, in the attack on Hill 70 on 15th August, 1918, he again led the battalion and was awarded a bar to the Medal; and on 2nd September, 1918, at Arras, he got the Distinguished Conduct Medal for a similar action. He had played the battalion through five successful attacks when he was finally wounded.

28930 Piper JAMES RICHARDSON, V.C., 16th Canadian Scottish.

At Festubert in May, 1915, he showed the greatest gallantry in carrying despatches, and also saved a wounded comrade's life. In the attack on the Regina trench on 8th October, 1916, he played his company to the attack. When they got near the enemy's position very heavy wire entanglements were encountered, which took a considerable time to cut through; while this was being carried out Piper Richardson marched up and down outside the wire playing, while the men were falling all round him. When the wire had been cut he continued at the head of his company, and played the "Reel of Tulloch" on the German parapet, followed by the "Deil in the Kitchen" as the battalion started bombing the dugouts. At this moment the Company

Sergeant Major was dangerously wounded and Richardson volunteered to take him out. He successfully accomplished this and then said he must go back to fetch his pipes which he had left behind in the captured trench. He never returned and must have been killed. The Commanding Officer[1] writes of him : " I really think his V.C. performance was one of the great deeds of the war. The conditions were those of indescribable peril and terror. The lad's whole soul was bound up in the glory of piping, and he was only taken into action after imploring his colonel with tears in his eyes. Altogether a most wonderful example of high souled courage and enthusiasm."

A year after Piper Richardson's death he was awarded a posthumous Victoria Cross.

28557 Piper Alexander M'Gillivray,
29048 Piper Allan Cameron M'Nab,
429603 Piper George Paul,
466703 Piper John M'Allister,
603174 Piper Gordon Cruickshank,
467573 Piper Alexander Robertson,
737176 Piper John M'Lean,
633179 Piper Archibald M'Dowell.
} 16th Canadian Scottish.

The whole of these men received the Military Medal for playing their companies into action on different occasions. No man was ever recommended for reward unless he had played into action on three different occasions, and every man had to volunteer for the duty. As a matter of fact so keen was the competition that lots had to be drawn to decide who should play.

429603 Piper George Paul, 16th Canadian Scottish.

After winning the Military Medal for his gallantry in playing his company to the attack on Hill 70 on 15th August, 1918, Piper Paul went into action at Amiens playing on top of the tank " Dominion." While doing so he was killed. His action on this occasion roused the wildest enthusiasm among his comrades and contributed greatly to the success of the operation.

59224 Corpl. William Currie, 21st Canadians.

On several occasions Corpl. Currie showed extraordinary gallantry in bringing in wounded men from positions in which any attempt at rescue appeared hopeless, on account of the heavy fire brought to bear on any one trying to approach. The last man rescued by Corpl. Currie had been shot by a sniper and was lying in a trench only a foot deep. Currie succeeded in getting him away although he was badly wounded in the process. He was several times complimented officially and was finally specially promoted and awarded the Military Medal. He subsequently got a Commission and won the Military Cross for gallantry.

60115 Piper Hugh Mackenzie, 21st Canadians.

At Hill 70 volunteers were called for to bring in a man who was lying wounded in

[1] Lieut.-Col. Cyrus Peck, V.C., D.S.O.

No Man's Land. Mackenzie was one of three who volunteered to get him; two of these men were killed. Mackenzie was given the Military Medal.

Piper W. BRAND,
Piper WALTER TELFER, } 25th Canadians.

In the attack on the Vimy Ridge 9th April, 1917, these two pipers played their companies into action. Telfer was so badly wounded that his leg had subsequently to be amputated, but continued playing, until he fell. Both of them were awarded the Military Medal.

1246 Piper JOHN MACDONALD, 1st Canadian Machine Gun Corps.

During an action the attack was held up and most of the teams of the machine guns were killed. Piper Macdonald succeeded in pushing forward to the objective with a gun and held on until dark. He was the last to leave, carrying the gun on his shoulders. For this he was promoted Quartermaster Sergeant, and was awarded the Military Medal.

Pipe Major ALEXANDER GRIEVE,
Piper J. WATERHOUSE,
Piper A. GRAY, } South African Scottish.

When the Germans advanced on the Cambrai front in March, 1918, the pipers were frequently called upon to serve in the ranks in various capacities. At Houdincourt they were suddenly required to reinforce a position and piled their pipes on the ground. A shell burst destroyed the whole of the pipes. For gallantry when acting as despatch runners Pipe Major Grieve got the D.C.M. and Pipers Waterhouse and Gray the Military Medal.

Pipe Major J. ROBERTSON, 2nd Auckland Regiment.

The pipers served in the ranks. Pipe Major Robertson received the D.C.M. for conspicuous gallantry at Bapaume.

Piper A. AITKEN,
Piper R. GILLESPIE, } 42nd Australians.

These men were employed as scouts and both received the Military Medal for valuable observation work prior to the action at Messines in June, 1917.

FOREIGNERS AND THE PIPES

Brought in contact as Scottish troops have been with those of our Allies it is not surprising that military pipers have attracted the attention of observers and writers who, before the war, knew nothing of their existence. From the early days of the war the pipes, the tartan and the kilt aroused the liveliest interest in France ; and perhaps the sincerest tribute to them is the fact that, in their caricatures of the nations, the Germans usually depicted the British soldier as a particularly unattractive Highlander.

At first the French writers were mildly sarcastic about the players of the "cornemuse," and regarded them as an amiable weakness of the comrades of the "auld alliance" ; but gradually they discovered that pipes and tartan were the outward and visible signs of a spirit which won their whole-hearted admiration, and then their attitude changed.

Describing an attack by the 51st Division a French observer wrote :

"Resolutely they crossed what seemed to be impossible ground . . . they charged to the shrill sounds of the bagpipes . . . they charged like heroes of Walter Scott—*leurs bonnets à rubans et leur jupes de danseuses.*"

Though the Breton bignon, the cornemuse, the German dudelsackpfeife are no longer—if they ever were—instruments of war, the instinctive admiration for the pipes remains in the most unexpected quarters ; and in France, Flanders, Italy, the Balkans, and even the occupied portions of Germany, "*piob mhor*" has aroused race memories long dormant. One effect of this is the demand which has recently arisen in Italy for pipes from this country ; another is the fact that the French Government have added a painting of a piper by a French artist to the official collection of war pictures.

American observers were often very ignorant of the mysteries of the bagpipe. A writer in the *Boston Evening Transcript*, after eulogising the piper as a military institution, informs his readers that in the hands of a really skilled performer the strains of the pipes can be heard for a distance of six miles against the wind or ten miles if the conditions are favourable. The writer may have been of M'Crimmon descent, but his enthusiasm exceeded his powers of observation.

One thing is quite certain, viz., whatever their inmost feelings regarding the musical qualities of the pipes, foreigners generally appreciate their military value in war and share the opinion of the court-martial in 1746 that they must be regarded as an " instrument of war."

The Germans certainly were not slow in forming an estimate of the military value of the piper. From a very early stage in the war they learned to associate the instrument with a type of troops for whose mentality, as exhibited in the attack, they had more respect than sympathy, and the piper at once became a marked man whenever he went over the top. The casualties among pipers while playing would of themselves suggest that this was the case ; but the statements of officer prisoners show that orders were given to pick off pipers for precisely the same reason as officers commanding platoons or companies.

THE PIPES IN CAPTIVITY

Even pipers fall into the hands of the enemy occasionally, but they were never allowed to take their instruments with them into captivity. Gradually, as " comforts," pipes were sent out to individual officers and men ; and the following letter from an officer of the Gordon Highlanders who was at Friedberg Camp, indicates how popular pipe music became among his fellow-prisoners of the Allied armies.

" FRIEDBERG, 11/1/1917.

Though only a young player I play here every day and do not find people too hostile to me. The Russians, French and even the Germans greet me with great interest and seem to find pleasure in listening to me—though as I said I am no great player ; the most unsympathetic are always to be found among the ranks of the " Sassenach." I learnt to play in 1911, on joining my Regiment, under George MacLennan, who was Pipe-Major at that time. While on leave in Edinburgh I used to have lessons with his father—Jno. MacLennan. Up till now I have only attempted " The Glen is mine " and " Struan Robertson " in Piobaireachd, but having been thoroughly taught by the MacLennans I naturally follow their way

PIPER KENNETH MACKAY, CAMERON HIGHLANDERS
AT QUATRE-BRAS

From the Painting by Lockhart Bogle, by kind permission of the Officers of the 1st Cameron Highlanders

of thinking. Yesterday I played to a Russian who is a very good player of the piano. He was delighted with the Pipes and I could not play too many tunes for him. Strathspeys and Reels are greatly appreciated by all our Russian friends. Last St. Andrew's Day we organized an Exhibition of dancing which was a complete success. As the Scottish Colony here is so small we asked the Russians to come and help us. This they did right well with dances and songs, the music being provided, in both cases, by " Balalaika," or Russian national instrument. For our part we danced two foursome Reels (dancing two different sets of steps), a Sword Dance and a Highland Schottische. In the latter dance we each took a Russian as a partner, they having been trained up for the event. We sang " Bonnie Dundee," " Lassies of Scotland," " MacPherson," and finished up with " Auld Lang Syne." For the Reels my Russian friend provided the music on the piano. Our costume was of course improvised. Kilt, shoes and hose we had, we wore white shirts with lace cuffs, a strip of tartan fastened with a brooch at the shoulder to do duty as a plaid and a black velvet band with a lace ruffle, falling down in front, round our necks. Our sporans, with the exception of one which was made out of a local rabbit, all came from home. I had several pretty compliments paid to me by the Russians and French, both on our costume and dancing. Five of us took part altogether. I wonder if it would be too much to ask you to send me instructions for dancing the " Lochaber Broadswords " and the " Seann Triubhas," in case we have the misfortune to pass another St. Andrew's Day here in Germany. If we do we shall give another Exhibition and I would like to be able to vary it. I only know 12 Strathspey steps and 8 Reel steps. Since I have been a prisoner I have taught over 30 people to dance the Reel—including two Frenchmen and one Russian, and at present I have five pupils on the chanter. We are 16 Scots here, so can you say we are losing our national distinctions ? I have only told you this because I thought it would interest you."

In Holland, in the internment camps, an organised pipe band was instituted by the writer of the above letter, and consisted of thirteen pipers of whom two were pipe majors.

MILITARY PIPE BANDS, AND REFORM

In preparing this record of the pipe bands of our Armies during the war the opportunity has been taken of consulting pipe presidents and pipe majors as to the present condition of military piping and the manner in which obvious defects might be remedied. Like other experts they exhibit divergences of opinion, sometimes as regards the nature of the defects, sometimes as to the best method of remedying them. In certain matters, however, there is absolute unanimity, and these are deserving of attention by the military authorities.

"*Sergeant piper.*"—Throughout the Army there is, and has always been, a strong objection to the title of "sergeant piper," which in official parlance is employed instead of "pipe major." No one ever calls a pipe major a sergeant piper, except in returns; and withdrawal of this modern and indefensible title could result in nothing but good. As there is no financial aspect involved in the change, it would be a graceful and inexpensive concession to a body of men to whom the Army and the nation owe much.

Rank of the Pipe Major.—On another point there is absolute unanimity of opinion, viz., the rank of the pipe major. As responsible for a band possibly numbering twenty or more pipers, the pipe major ought to have the same rank as a bandmaster. To limit the career of a piper to the possibility of becoming a pipe major with the rank of sergeant is to prevent good men accepting the position; and many a man, seeing he can hope for no advancement, leaves the pipes and returns to the ranks, thus getting a chance of rising to warrant rank.

This question of rank has a most important bearing on the interests of piping generally, and is therefore a national one. As instructor to his men the pipe major should be a first-class performer himself, and this—although the public appear to be unaware of the fact—involves long and assiduous training. It is useless asking a man to attain the necessary standard of excellence for this purpose and to offer him the pay of a sergeant in return. The consequence is pipe majors are not always the best pipers—from the professional point of view—in their units; and this ought to be remedied, even though it does cost the nation the difference between the emoluments of a warrant officer and of a sergeant in each unit.

The Appointment of " Piper."—Another necessary reform, which also has the merit of costing nothing, is the official recognition of " piper " as an appointment. In the Army " drummer " is an appointment, but a piper is a private.

One result of this is that, on mobilisation, all pipers revert to the ranks, excepting six (including the sergeant piper) per battalion. Apart altogether from the special liability to casualties among the " full pipers " when playing in action, it is evident that so small a band may, under the ordinary conditions of modern warfare, be put out of action ; and then great difficulty is experienced in raising another band. In many battalions during the war this happened, sometimes more than once ; and it is these battalions which are most insistent on the strength being twelve instead of six pipers.

Lowland regiments.—A grievance which cries for remedy at the hands of the War Office is the treatment of pipers in Lowland regiments. The official view appears to be that the existence of the pipes in regiments such as the Royal Scots, the K.O.S.B.'s and others is an unreasonable concession to a sentiment which is vulgarly called " Scotch," but which, though believed to be nebulous, happens to be too strong for the military reformers to ignore altogether. This view indicates ignorance of the history of the pipes and of the Lowland regiments ; the one may be pardoned, the other is inexcusable.

It is absolutely certain that Lowland regiments had pipers before the existing Highland regiments were raised at all ; and the pipes were a national instrument all over the Lowlands for centuries before there was any Regular Army at all.

This being so it is quite illogical that the maintenance of their pipe bands should be a greater financial burden on officers of a Lowland than of a Highland regiment. The value of the institution, from a military point of view, is the same in both ; and pipe bands should be treated as part of the recognised establishment in one as in the other.

Standardisation of military pipe music.—There is one grave defect in military piping which is capable of being remedied quite easily. Anyone who knows anything of piping knows that each individual piper learns his tunes after the setting of some well-known authority, and is for ever after prepared to maintain that that version alone is the correct one. Unfortunately every battalion has its own setting for every tune played in the band and declines to admit the possibility of any other setting being used in any circumstances. Even in the case of distinctively regimental tunes, *e.g.* "*Cabar Feidh,*" the two Regular battalions of the Seaforth Highlanders play—or used to play, just before the war—different settings of that tune, and a man transferred from one battalion to another had to learn the slight differences which his new unit preferred. The same remarkable individuality exists in every battalion and makes it very difficult indeed to get a number of pipe bands to play even the best-known tunes together without considerable practice.

This is quite wrong. By all means let the individual piper learn and adhere to the setting of piobaireachd by his favourite authority; but to have as many settings of an ordinary march as there are battalions in the Army is not to the advantage of piping.

The remedy is simple enough,—the standardisation of pipe tunes for military purposes, in precisely the same manner as obtains with the National Anthems and trumpet and bugle calls; and, just as no departure to meet regimental custom or prejudice is permitted in the case of these latter, so the setting laid down for the Army in the case of pipe tunes should be strictly defined and adhered to.

The superiority of one setting over another does not enter into the question; what is essential is uniformity.

Many pipe majors have pointed to this standardisation as one of the most important measures to be adopted after the war, in the interests of piping in the Army.

Neglect of Piobaireachd.—It is open to argument whether the military piper does or does not exert a determining influence on the cause of piping generally. Allowing fully for the great value of the recognised societies and the periodical piping meetings throughout Scotland, in keeping up the standard of the national instrument and offering inducements for its study, it will be readily admitted that, by their mere existence as permanent institutions, military pipe bands keep up the cult of the pipes, at home and abroad, to so marked a degree that any decline in their standard must have a deleterious effect on piping generally.

To what extent, then, if at all, is military piping conducted to the best advantage of the cause of piping, and is there room for reform ?

It may be taken as generally the case that, in so far as a military pipe band is regarded as designed for duty on the march, and for various routine military musical duties, it fulfils its functions to the satisfaction of all concerned. It is too much to expect the War Office—or even individual commanding officers—to accept the view that neglect of "ceol mor" is not compensated for by a high standard of excellence in the "middle music" and in dances and marches. Individual pipers in every battalion are players of "piobaireachd"; but any one with experience of regimental or garrison piping competitions knows how small is the number of men who enter for that class of event, as compared with performers of the march, strathspey and reel.

The explanation is simple enough—the men play what their audience demands, and "Leaving Glen Urquhart" or "Duntroon" appeals to more people, military or civil, than the finest piobaireachd. Pipe majors, even when themselves anxious to teach their pipers the higher class of music, recognise that to attempt to do so would often be wasted labour—men come to them too old to make piobaireachd players, and, in any case, the opportunities for playing it in the Army are too few to make it worth while trying to get men to go through the initial drudgery. Being human they naturally turn to march and dance music; and the result is that, except in the case of professional pipers who have enlisted, the soldier piper generally ignores altogether the classical side of his music.

This is a defect in military piping, and it should be remedied by insisting that, before promotion to pipe major, a piper should pass an examination in every branch of pipe music.

A school of piping.—The time has come to establish a school of piping for the army at which likely pipers could undergo refresher courses of instruction in all classes of pipe music, in the correct writing of music—a subject which is lamentably ignored, in the theory of music, and in methods of instruction of recruit pipers. In other words it should fulfil the same functions as regards the training of future pipe majors, and the improvement of the standard of playing in the army, that Kneller Hall does in the case of bandmasters and military musical education generally.

No piper should be promoted pipe major until he has undergone a complete course lasting at least six months, and has passed an examination at the end of it.

Such a school should be open to civilian pipers and should become the Macrimmon school of to-day.

The Piobaireachd Society have already decided to institute a memorial to fallen pipers which shall take this form, and to the necessary endowment the proceeds of this book will be devoted. But the army must contribute towards its maintenance.

REGIMENTAL RECORDS

THESE Records are not based on military returns, and are therefore not, in all cases, complete. They have been obtained by correspondence with commanding officers, pipe presidents, pipe majors and many others, but the exigencies of war have prevented the information so obtained being absolutely accurate.

In many cases, units, reduced by fighting to mere cadres, have been absorbed into other units and their pipers scattered; in others, the field records of the units themselves have been lost or have ceased to be available; and, in several, correspondence has been abruptly terminated by the correspondent himself being killed or wounded.

In the circumstances it is satisfactory that so much information has been obtained.

THE SCOTS GUARDS

1st Battalion.

During the first few months of the war there were very heavy casualties among the pipers, and the band soon ceased to exist in consequence. It was reconstituted in 1916, but was not again utilised in the front line.

REG. NO.	RANK.	NAME.	RECORD.
	Pipe Major	Alex. Ross	
3707	Sergt.	Samuel Richardson	Died of wounds, Battle of Aisne, 14/9/14.
6495	Lance-Cpl.	David Smith	Wounded, the Aisne, 14/9/14.
6926	Piper	Kenneth M'Kay	Wounded, Ypres, 31/10/14.
6999	,,	Bruce Hobson	Wounded, Ypres, 31/10/14; taken prisoner.
991	,,	Alexander Martin, D.C.M.	Won D.C.M.; killed 19/2/16.

REG. NO.	RANK.	NAME.	RECORD.
8543	Piper	JAMES M'KENZIE	Killed, Ypres, 31/10/14; despatches.
7529	,,	MURDOCH M'DONALD	Wounded.
8423	Corporal	JAMES CARSTAIRS	Wounded, Ypres, 26/10/14.
6456	Piper	ROBERT PATON	Wounded, Ypres, 31/10/14.
5437	,,	A. M'RURY.	
11150	,,	CHRISTOPHER M'PHERSON	
9456	,,	ALAN M'PHEDRAN	
	,,	HECTOR M'NAIR	
	,,	J. SMITH	Wounded.
	,,	THOMAS ANDERSON	
	,,	MALCOLM M'KENZIE	Killed, Oct. 1914.
	,,	J. M'DONALD	Wounded.
	,,	E. KENNEDY	
	,,	J. ORMISTON	
	,,	D. M'INNES	
	Corpl.	D. HOWISON	
	Piper	A. CARMICHAEL	Killed, 1915.
	,,	T. BROWNLOW, D.C.M., M.M.	Military Medal, D.C.M.
	,,	D. TAYLOR	
	,,	D. MARSHALL	
	,,	C. M'PHERSON	
	,,	J. COVENTRY	
	,,	R. PATON	Wounded.
	,,	J. JOHNSTONE	
	,,	W. M'LEOD	Wounded.
	,,	C. M'RAE	Wounded.

2ND BATTALION

There were heavy casualties in the Ypres fighting in Oct. 1914, and by the end of March, 1915, practically no pipers remained. The band was subsequently reconstituted, but like that of the sister battalion, was as far as possible saved from further decimation.

REG. NO.	RANK.	NAME.	RECORD.
	Pipe Major	WILLIAM ROSS	Invalided.
7743	Sergt.	ANDREW M'INTOSH	
	,,	DONALD M'INTOSH	
3681	Lance-Sgt.	ARCHIBALD M'KIMM	Wounded and taken prisoner, Zonnebeke, 26/10/14.
	Lance-Cpl.	HECTOR M'KIMM	Killed, Zonnebeke, 26/10/14.
5539	Piper	ALEXANDER RUSSELL	Wounded, Ypres, 21/10/14.
7281	,,	WILLIAM GRANT	Wounded, Gheluvelt, 28/10/14.
8053	,,	JOHN CONNOR	Wounded, 28/10/14.

REG. NO.	RANK.	NAME.	RECORD.
7725	Piper	James Welstead	Wounded and taken prisoner, Zonnebeke, 26/10/14.
8341	,,	William M'Donald	Wounded; invalided, 26/10/14.
8349	,,	Archibald M'Pherson	Wounded, Neuve Chapelle, 11/3/15.
	,,	M. M'Pherson	
8081	,,	Charles M'Guire	Died of wounds at Ypres, 29/10/14.
8852	,,	Colin Livingstone	Wounded, Ypres, 27/10/14; burned with liquid fire, Neuve Chapelle, 13/3/15.
11148	,,	James Coventry	
7039	,,	James M'Donald	Wounded, 13/3/15.
	,,	T. Marshall	
	,,	C. Munro	
	,,	D. Marshall	
	,,	W. Craig	
	,,	D. M'Phedran	Wounded, Ypres, 27/10/14.
	,,	J. M'Phedran	
	,,	D. M'Arthur	
	,,	J. Walker	

These two battalions, in the first year, had 7 pipers killed and 17 wounded.

THE ROYAL SCOTS

1st Battalion

In the capture of Karadzakot Zir, in the Salonika operations, the battalion was played to the attack by Pipers Collins, Clancy, Smart and Mallin, and the C.O. considers that their services on this occasion "were of inestimable value; it was largely due to the presence of the pipers with the leading wave that the enemy evacuated their trenches and retired in disorder." Besides their value on the march and in billets "they were invaluable in inspiring *esprit de corps* under fire."

Pipers were also employed as observers, messengers, scouts, etc.

REG. NO.	NAME.	RANK.	RECORD.
10369	Pipe Major	G. J. Allan	
8473	Sergt.	J. M'Nab	Promoted Pipe Major, 1st R.S.F.
10122	Corpl.	R. Softley	Wounded, May 1915, France.
10123	,,	E. Collins	
10183	Piper	J. Clancy	Invalided.
10754	,,	J. Burns	

REG. NO.	RANK.	NAME.	RECORD.
11002	Corpl.	W. M'MILLAN, D.C.M.	
10032	Piper	P. MALLIN	Invalided.
9885	„	W. M'ARTHUR	Invalided.
	„	E. DUGUID	
10639	„	J. SMART	
8450	„	R. DRUMMOND	Wounded, May 1915, France.
39291	„	H. THOMSON	
10273	„	R. ARMOUR	Wounded, Karadzakot, Sept. 1916.
13859	„	D. WHITE	
43315	„	H. M'WILLIAMS	Wounded, Aug. 1918.
32844	„	J. NOBLE	
48594	„	D. M'DONALD	Died in hospital, Bulgaria.
16443	„	A. ALVES	
200297	„	W. HOVAN	

2ND BATTALION

The 2nd battalion took part in the original fighting of the war. During the retirement from Mons the pipers were chiefly employed as despatch-runners and orderlies. They went out with 16 pipers and lost 6 during the first few weeks. Four pipers, including Pipe Major Duff, were taken prisoner at Audincourt on 26th August, 1914.

During the Somme fighting they were employed as stretcher-bearers and suffered severe casualties. On one occasion they did invaluable service in bringing water up to the battalion. At Ypres in September, 1916, the pipers were carrying barbed wire up to the front when a shell wounded three. After that the band was withdrawn from the front line and employed in playing the battalion to and from the trenches. By the end of 1918 there had been 7 pipers killed, 16 wounded and 4 taken prisoner, and, to quote the pipe major, "I have seen 3 bands disappear and the fourth is now on German soil."

Apart from the difficulty of replacement of casualties one of the reasons why pipers were not used in attacks was because it was felt "when the men heard the pipes they would lose control of themselves and, in their eagerness to get forward would be apt to rush into their own barrage."

REG. NO.	RANK.	NAME.	RECORD.
8696	Pipe Major	J. Duff	Wounded, taken prisoner, Audincourt, 26/8/14.
5815	Pipe Major	J. A. Dunbar	
9357	Lance-Cpl.	G. M'Donald	Wounded, taken prisoner, Audincourt, 26/8/14.
325127	Corpl.	J. MacKay	Wounded, 23/11/17.
10535	Piper	D. Wheelan	Wounded, taken prisoner, Audincourt.
9865	,,	A. Smart	Wounded, taken prisoner, Audincourt.
9867	Lance Cpl.	Groves	Wounded, Kemmel, Nov. 1914.
11161	Piper	J. Steele	Wounded, Kemmel, Nov. 1914.
9356	Piper	J. Hunter	Wounded, Ypres, 28/5/15.
10541	,,	F. M'Ewan	Wounded, 23/5/15, 12/4/18, 8/10/18.
11065	,,	H. M'Leod	Recommended for D.C.M.; wounded, Ypres, 28/5/15.
11484	,,	D. Lindsay	Killed, 4/5/17.
	,,	A. Mackinlay	Killed, 9/4/18.
4918	,,	A. Cruickshanks	Killed, 27/9/18.
9356	,,	R. Hunter	Wounded, 23/5/15.
13459	,,	William Fisher	Wounded, Loos, 25/9/15; killed, 15/4/16.
250240	,,	William Black	Wounded, 12/11/17.
8516	,,	J. Robertson	Killed, Croix Barbes, 13/10/14.
325547	,,	R. Robertson	Wounded, 9/4/18.
8450	,,	J. Drummond	Killed, The Bluff, 23/1/16.
8906	,,	J. Henry	Wounded, Somme, 13/7/16.
9787	,,	J. Youngson	Wounded, The Bluff, 4/3/16.
9061	,,	J. Johnston	Wounded, 13/9/14.
7929	,,	J. Anderson	Wounded, Kemmel, April, 1915.
3190	,,	J. Thompson	Died, 30/8/15.
10536	,,	E. Duguid	Killed (gas), 10/5/18.
270014	,,	J. Sinclair	Wounded, 9/4/17.
32553	,,	W. Hutcheson	Wounded, 26/3/18.
11613	,,	A. Macdonald	Wounded, 12/4/18.
8899	,,	R. Scholes	
10178	,,	J. Scott	
11486	,,	J. Clark	
270037	,,	J. Paul	
270045	,,	A. Stocks	
325080	,,	R. Johnstone	
250240	,,	W. Black	
270821	,,	D. Shane	
11437	Lance Cpl.	A. Swinney.	

4TH BATTALION (QUEEN'S EDINBURGH RIFLES)

This battalion served in Gallipoli, and took part in the attack on Achi Baba on 28th June, 1915. On this occasion the Pipe Major John Buchan was killed when playing along the line as the regiment commenced their advance.

REG. NO.	RANK.	NAME.	RECORD.
	Pipe Major	ANDREW BUCHAN	Killed, Gallipoli, 28/6/15.
	Piper	C. RUTHERFORD	Died of dysentery, June, 1915.
	,,	E. ALEXANDER	Wounded on Achi Baba, 28/6/15.
	,,	J. CHRISTIE	
	,,	A. MURRAY	
	,,	J. DUNCAN	
	,,	W. ARMSTRONG	
	,,	J. HUGHES	
	,,	P. LAIDLAW	

5TH BATTALION (QUEEN'S EDINBURGH RIFLES)

During the Gallipoli fighting the whole of the pipers became casualties, some of them while acting as pipers, others while serving in the ranks. Shortly after the landing, 1235 Piper Sinclair gathered together some stragglers and successfully covered the retirement of his battalion at a critical period. He himself died of his wounds. The band ceased to exist until again started in 1916. Writing of their subsequent experiences the commanding officer says " they gloriously upheld the traditions achieved by their predecessors."

REG. NO.	RANK.	NAME.	RECORD.
1417	Pipe Major	JAMES PEDEN	
1303	Piper	G. HARDIE	Killed, 2/5/15, Gallipoli.
1235	,,	W. SINCLAIR	Died of wounds, 8/5/15, Gallipoli.
766	,,	A. LAWSON	Killed, 28/4/15.
1824	,,	G. W. DOWNIE	Killed, 7/5/15.
471	,,	J. UNCLES	Wounded, April, 1915 , Gallipoli.
1885	Corpl.	D. SWAN	Wounded, 7/5/15.
1156	Piper	J. G. SCOTT	Wounded, May, 1915.
1364	,,	N. M'ELHINNY	Wounded, 4/6/15 ; and again, Gallipoli.
1539	,,	W. M'IVOR	Wounded, 28/6/15, Gallipoli.
8109	,,	DAVID ROSS	Killed, July, 1916.

6th Battalion

Pipers were almost entirely employed behind the front line owing to the difficulty of replacement.

The battalion was ultimately merged with the 5th Royal Scots.

REG. NO.	RANK.	NAME.	RECORD.
	Pipe Major	R. Anderson	
	Corpl.	J. Greer	
	,,	R. Rough	
	Piper	T. Leake	.Died, Egypt.
	,,	A. M'Kenzie	
	,,	R. Bremner	
	,,	J. Fisher	
	,,	R. Irvine	

5/6 Battalion

REG. NO.	RANK.	NAME.	RECORD.
	Pipe Major	J. A. Gordon	
	Corpl.	A. Jack	
	Piper	R. Davidson	
	,,	R. Martin	
	,,	R. Fletcher	
	,,	J. Marshall	
	,,	J. Hannah	

7th Battalion

This battalion lost the pipe major and 2 pipers in a railway accident before going overseas. While in Gallipoli they were employed in the ranks. After the Gallipoli operations the band was brought up to strength and played the battalion into Palestine to the old air of "Blue Bonnets over the Border."

REG. NO.	RANK.	NAME.	RECORD.
	Sergt. Piper	James Gear	Killed in train in England.
	Piper	George Smeaton	Killed in train in England.
	,,	Alex. Nicol	Killed in train in England.
	Lance-Cpl.	James Campbell	Wounded.
	Piper	James Pearson	Wounded in train smash.
	,,	Fred Turner	Killed, 12/7/15.
	,,	Thomas Clachers	
251141	,,	Peter M'Neill	Killed, 6/11/17, Palestine.

8th Battalion

At Festubert and elsewhere the pipers were employed as stretcher-bearers, and Pipe Major J. M'Dougall was awarded the D.C.M. "for gallant conduct under very trying circumstances." After the first two years it was decided to keep the band out of action as far as possible.

REG. NO.	RANK.	NAME.	RECORD.
7271	Pipe Major	J. H. M'Dougall, D.C.M.	Wounded, 22/5/15; D.C.M.
7124	,,	J. Sterrick	Time expired, 6/5/16.
335120	,,	J. Stevenson	
325119	Lance-Cpl.	S. Thomson	
335062	Piper	D. Sheills	
335113	,,	A. Euman	
7059	,,	J. Stirling	Wounded, 20/5/15.
594	,,	J. Martin	Wounded, 21/12/14.
335118	,,	R. A. Dodds	
7112	,,	A. Sterrick	Invalided, Dec., 1914.
7132	,,	R. Crawford	Invalided, May, 1915.
819	,,	G. Darling	Wounded, 13/10/16.
4244	,,	T. Forrest	Invalided, 26/2/15.
4467	,,	A. Notman	Invalided, 13/10/16.
330041	,,	W. Brown	
335074	,,	F. Confrey	Invalided, 10/8/18.
330347	,,	J. Dickson	
330400	,,	G. Reid	
10027	,,	A. Methven	
9885	,,	R. M'Arthur	
42591	,,	H. Cameron	
302447	,,	J. O'Donnell	

9th Battalion

The band was kept out of action as far as possible as it was regarded as an invaluable asset on the march and in billets.

REG. NO.	RANK.	NAME.	RECORD.
	Pipe Major	C. M'Kinley	Wounded, 17/5/15.
	,,	William Reid	
	Lance-Cpl.	A. L. Forsyth, M.M.	Wounded, 17/5/15; awarded Military Medal; killed, 23/4/17.
	Piper	J. M'Ewan	Wounded, 7/4/15; and again 23/5/15.
	,,	R. Houston	
	,,	J. Urquhart	

REG. NO.	RANK.	NAME.	RECORD.
	Piper	W. B. Martin	Invalided.
	,,	J. Charge	
	,,	H. C. Clark	
	,,	C. Manderson	
	Corpl.	G. Lauder	Killed, 23/5/17.
	,,	James Robertson	
	Lance-Cpl.	E. M'Donald	
	Piper	William Ritchie	Wounded, 25/3/18.
	,,	William Legg	(Lieut. Royal Air Force).
	,,	A. Cannon	Invalided.
	,,	J. Tully	
	,,	G. Cockburn	
	,,	J. Robertson	
	,,	J. Clark	Wounded, Soissons, 29/7/18.
	,,	P. M'Lean	
	,,	J. Armstrong	
	,,	W. Duffy	
	,,	W. Ross	
	,,	D. Ross	
	,,	R. Connolly	

11th Battalion

In spite of their frequent requests to be allowed to play in action the pipers were not permitted to do so, as the band was regarded as too valuable.

REG. NO.	RANK.	NAME.	RECORD.
3451	Pipe Major	J. Clark	
227629	Sergt.	W. Sinclair	
27230	Piper	Robert Marshall	Wounded, 7/7/16.
8906	Lance-Cpl.	W. Henry	
200521	Piper	W. Christie	
29304	,,	G. Combe	
29519	,,	J. Harper	
29331	,,	T. Hermiston	
41216	,,	R. Johnstone	
40063	,,	G. Muir	
20857	,,	W. Stewart	
40057	,,	W. Bruce	
40787	,,	A. Young	Wounded, 23/3/18.
27237	,,	A. Potts	
	,,	J. Kane	Killed, 14/7/16.

12th Battalion

During the advance of the 26th Brigade at Loos in September, 1915, the companies were played to the attack by their pipers, and suffered heavily.

Normally they were kept out of the front line owing to the difficulty of replacement. During the German offensive of 1918 they were in the ranks, and Pipe Major Colgan got the Military Medal "for good leadership and courage." The casualties among them were heavy, two having been killed and nine wounded.

REG. NO.	RANK.	NAME.	RECORD.
13283	Pipe Major	A. Colgan, M.M.	Military Medal.
10122	,,	R. Softley	Wounded, 25/9/15.
12991	Piper	Thomas Hislop	Killed, 25/9/15.
200737	Lance-Cpl.	P. West	Killed.
13459	,,	William Fisher	Wounded, Sept., 1915; killed, 15/4/16.
270322	Pipei	H. Barrie	
31137	,,	D. Bowes	Wounded, 25/9/15.
16036	,,	C. Campbell	
13530	,,	W. Cowe	Wounded, 25/9/15.
43280	,,	J. Gray	
12991	,,	D. M'Donald	Wounded, 25/9/15.
270099	,,	J. M'Intyre	
3404	,,	N. M'Intyre	
270324	,,	J. M'Knight	
	,,	G. M'Phee	
43345	,,	A. Robertson	
6392	,,	J. Robertson	Wounded four times.
270326	,,	D. Ross	
40300	,,	D. Thomson	Wounded, 1916.
18516	,,	G. Watson	Wounded, 1916.

13th Battalion

At Loos, 25th September, 1915, and in subsequent actions, the pipers were employed as bearers. There were heavy casualties among them in the last advance in 1918, when 2 were killed and 5 wounded.

RANK.	NAME.	RECORD.
Pipe Major	Murdoch Macdonald	Invalided; died, 9/2/16.
,,	John Mouat	Mentioned in despatches, 27/12/18.
Sergt.	Robert M'Kay	
,,	Thornton	Invalided, 1917.
Corpl.	F. Dalgleish	
Piper	John Ford	Wounded, Loos, 25/9/15.
,,	John Marr	Wounded, 26/8/18.
,,	William M'Neill	Wounded, 26/8/18.
,,	Peter Campbell	Wounded, 26/8/18.

RANK.	NAME.	RECORD.
Piper	THOMAS FLOOD	Killed, 26/8/18.
,,	ROBERT CAMPBELL	Wounded, 25/9/15 ; taken prisoner and died.
,,	JOHN CROWBOROUGH	Wounded, April, 1918.
,,	JOHN FALCONER	Invalided.
,,	JOHN FERRIER	
,,	JOHN KILPATRICK	Invalided.
,,	JOHN MACMILLAN	Invalided.
,,	JOHN RANKIN	Invalided.
,,	JOHN ROUGH	Invalided.
,,	ROBERT NORRIS	Wounded, 27/1/16.
,,	ANGUS MACDONALD	
,,	WILLIAM TWEEDIE	Wounded, 28/3/18.
,,	ROBERT MITCHELL	Died of wounds, 26/8/18.
,,	J. FINDLAY	
,,	F. GRAY	
,,	G. GUILD	
,,	M. M'LENNAN	
,,	F. MORRIS	
,,	J. M'LEAN	
,,	W. WHITEHEAD	
,,	J. CLUNIE	

15TH BATTALION

The battalion was played to the attack on Fricourt on the 1st July, 1916, by Pipe Major David Anderson, who was subsequently awarded the Croix de Guerre. Only one decoration was available for the Division, and his was considered the most conspicuous act of bravery.

16TH BATTALION

After suffering heavy losses this battalion was absorbed by the 9th Royal Scots.

RANK.	NAME.	RECORD.
Pipe Major	W. DUGUID	
Corpl.	D. SINCLAIR	
Lance-Cpl.	P. GOLDIE	
Piper	W. ADAMS	Invalided.
,,	M. BETHUNE	Killed, Somme, July 1916.
,,	H. GREY	Killed, Arras, April 1917.
,,	D. HENDRY	
,,	A. JACK	
,,	A. LOCH	Wounded, 1918.

RANK.	NAME.	RECORD.
Piper	A. Noon	Killed, Arras, April 1917.
,,	G. Philp	Invalided.
,,	D. Ross	
,,	J. Thomson	
,,	H. Tuohy	Wounded, Somme, 1916; invalided.
,,	E. Tuohy	
,,	A. Wilson	

17th Battalion

The pipers, when employed in action at all, went as bearers.

RANK.	NAME.	RECORD.
Pipe Major	M'Donald	Invalided.
,,	Donald M'Lean	Became Lieut. 1st Gordons; killed, July 1918.
,,	A. M'Phedran	
Corpl.	C. M'Kinnon	
Lance-Cpl.	Lawrie	Prisoner of war.
,,	J. Moon	
Piper	Ramage	Wounded; invalided.
,,	Calder	
,,	Swanson	Wounded; invalided.
,,	Wilson	Invalided.
,,	Douglas	Invalided.
,,	M'Anulty	
,,	Peebles	
,,	M'Garvie	
,,	Brennan	
,,	J. Thomson	
,,	A. Collins	
,,	Jas. Hogg	
,,	P. Mack	

THE ROYAL SCOTS FUSILIERS

1st Battalion

The battalion was played to the attack on the German trenches at Hooge on 16th June, 1915, by the Pipe Major David Campbell.

RANK.	NAME.	RECORD.
Pipe Major	David Campbell	Wounded, Hooge, 15/6/15.
,,	J. M'Nab	From 1st Royal Scots, 20/11/15.

2nd Battalion

After the first battle of Ypres only one piper remained, but a small band was made up from such acting pipers as could be spared from the trenches. Drafts from other battalions ultimately brought the band up to strength. The pipers who were taken prisoner, along with one of the officers, started a band in a German prison camp.

RANK.	NAME.	RECORD.
Pipe Major	A. Meikle	Prisoner of war.
Sergt.	D. Duncan	Prisoner of war.
,,	J. Jamieson	Wounded.
,,	D. Bryce	Wounded.
Corpl.	H. Ellis	
,,	A. W. Richardson	Killed.
,,	J. Duff	Wounded.
,,	A. Jennings	Killed.
Piper	W. Cruickshank	Prisoner of war.
,,	J. Urquhart	Prisoner of war.
,,	J. Verrall	Wounded.
,,	W. Butterworth	Killed.
,,	A. M'Garva	Prisoner of war.
,,	W. Stewart	
,,	G. Gillespie	Three times wounded.
,,	J. Hunter	Wounded.
,,	H. Fullstone	Wounded.
,,	W. Moore	Wounded ; invalided ; died.
,,	D. M'Lean	Killed, Messines, 1917.
,,	M. Watt	
,,	G. Lawrie	
,,	G. Prattis	
,,	T. Alston	
,,	G. Withers	Invalided.
,,	C. Connor	Invalided.
,,	J. Bain	
,,	A. Lees	
,,	F. Coutts	
,,	G. Greig	
,,	W. Sinclair	
,,	A. Mathieson	

4th Battalion

Pipers in Gallipoli were originally employed as duty men in their companies, and in the action on 12th July, 1915, three of them were killed.

The band was gradually reduced to vanishing point, and was reconstituted in France in 1918 from men of the 7th R.S.F. In France they were kept out of the front as they were regarded as too valuable an institution to be lost again.

RANK.	NAME.	RECORD.
Pipe Major	M'QUEEN	Invalided, Nov. 1915.
,,	N. SHAW	Died of wounds, Palestine, 21/4/17.
,,	C. M'INNES	
Lance-Cpl.	J. W. M'ALLISTER	Killed, Gallipoli, 12/7/15.
Piper	P. GREIG	Killed, Gallipoli, 12/7/15.
,,	J. MILNER	Killed, Gallipoli, 12/7/15.
,,	A. GORDON	Invalided, Nov. 1915.
Lance-Cpl.	W. HIGHET	
Piper	W. BATCHELOR	Transferred from 6/7 Battalion to 4th Batt. on return to France from Palestine.
,,	J. SMITH	,,
,,	J. RAE	,,
,,	R. STORRIE	,,
,,	J. KIDDIE	,,
,,	J. CREWS	,,
,,	J. K. STEPHEN	,,
,,	R. CURRIE	,,
,,	J. WOODS	,,
,,	D. INNES	,,
,,	H. HOGGAN	,,
,,	R. HOGGAN	,,

5TH BATTALION

In Gallipoli the pipers served in the ranks. The C.O. considers, however, their value in keeping the men cheery, and on the march, so great that they should not be allowed in the front line at all. "When the men were exhausted and inclined to straggle the effect of the pipes was most marked, the men at once pulled themselves together."

REG. NO.	RANK.	NAME.	RECORD.
6909	Pipe Major	ANDREW THOM	Invalided
241387	,,	JOHN MACPHEE	
7797	Lance-Cpl.	JOHN MURDOCH	Killed, 13/7/15.
7613	Piper	HUGH DICK	
6348	,,	ALEXANDER CALDWELL	Wounded, 12/7/15.
7107	,,	ANDREW HOPE	
5726	Lance-Cpl.	WILLIAM JOHNSTONE	
241579	Piper	WILLIAM LENAGHEN	

REG. NO.	RANK.	NAME.	RECORD.
9806	Piper	JAMES M'CONNELL	
240011	,,	ROBERT MAGIE	
240190	,,	THOMAS SHANKS	
240834	,,	H. SAMSON	

7TH BATTALION

When the battalion went out it was found necessary to put the pipers in the ranks. After the amalgamation of the 7th with the 6th Battalion they were kept out of the front line for a time.

RANK.	NAME.	RECORD.
Pipe Major	WATSON	
Piper	T. MARR	Killed, Loos, 25/9/15.
,,	W. MARR	Wounded.
,,	R. ROMMIE	Killed, Loos, 25/9/15.
,,	BALSILLIE	
,,	DAVIDSON	
,,	W. BARCLAY	
,,	M'ARTHUR	Invalided.
,,	FINLAYSON	Wounded, Loos, 25/9/15.

6TH AND 7TH BATTALION.

RANK.	NAME.	RECORD.
Pipe Major	D. INNES	
Piper	J. KIDDIE	
,,	W. CRAIG	
,,	J. WOOD	
,,	J. STEPHENS	
,,	J. CREWS	
,,	R. CURRIE	
,,	D. TUNES	
,,	J. JAMIESON	
,,	CLAYDON	
,,	BALSILLIE	
,,	DAVIDSON	

The combined battalions were ultimately broken up, and the pipers transferred to the 4th Battalion, which had returned from Palestine with its pipe band no longer in existence.

8th Battalion

Owing to the difficulty of replacing casualties the pipers were not allowed to go into action.

REG. NO.	RANK.	NAME.	RECORD
	Pipe Major	H. Peters	
	,,	W. M'Cormick	Invalided.
	,,	J. Duff	
	Corpl.	G. Gray	
	Lance-Cpl.	A. Alves	
	,,	J. Noble	Invalided.
	Piper	J. M'Nab	
	,,	A. M'Kay	
	,,	P. M'Guinness	
	,,	J. Blaylock	
	,,	G. Glendinning	
	,,	F. Morrison	
	,,	W. Murray	
	,,	J. Ferguson	Invalided.
	,,	A. Lave	Invalided.
	,,	B. Paterson	Invalided.
	,,	R. Storie	Invalided.
	,,	J. M'Farlane	Invalided.
	,,	W. Haran	Invalided.
	,,	P. Abernethy	Invalided.

11th Battalion

REG. NO.	RANK.	NAME.	RECORD
26522	Pipe Major	T. Porteous	
59663	Sergt.	R. Hailstones	
265732	Piper	A. M'Donald	
59415	,,	D. M'Bain	
265763	,,	A. Forbes	

THE KING'S OWN SCOTTISH BORDERERS

1st Battalion

In the landing on Gallipoli the pipers of the battalion had to take their places in the ranks in the first line fighting; here they distinguished themselves. During the subsequent operations in the Peninsula the pipers were employed in miscellaneous duties behind the front line.

Of the 10 pipers who landed only 4 remained to accompany the battalion on its evacuation.

In France they were employed in any and every capacity; "as bearers and ammunition carriers they had tasks to carry out that were almost superhuman, but as a band they ceased to exist until May 1917, when they were reconstituted. It was then decided to keep them out of the front line altogether."

The opinion of the officers is that pipers are far too valuable an institution to be employed in action in any capacity. The C.O. considers the band "plays no inconsiderable part in promoting the efficiency of a fighting force."

REG. NO.	RANK.	NAME.	RECORD.
8248	Pipe Major	W. MACKENZIE, M.M.	Military Medal.
6863	Sergt.	F. PURGAVIE	Wounded, Flers, 25/11/16, while in charge of a Dump.
8400	Corpl.	H. M'DONALD	Wounded, Suvla Bay, 10/8/15.
11412	Piper	COLGAN	Wounded, Gallipoli, 4/6/15.
9884	,,	HIGGINSON	Killed while leading bayonet charge, Gallipoli, 26/4/15.
7936	,,	LILLIE	
11315	,,	MAITLAND, M.M.	Killed at Paschendaele, 27/4/17; awarded Military Medal.
8629	,,	R. SCOTT	Wounded, Gallipoli, 4/6/15.
9545	,,	TURNBULL	
10884	,,	TROTTER	Wounded, Gallipoli, 1/6/15; Cambrai, 28/11/17.

2ND BATTALION

The officers of the battalion regard the pipers as a most necessary adjunct to a unit on active service, but consider that owing to the difficulty of replacement they should not be employed in action.

REG. NO.	RANK.	NAME.	RECORD.
	Pipe Major	J. MACINTYRE	Wounded, Givenchy, 27/9/15.
11537	,,	W. MACKIE	
9059	Corpl.	T. HOPE	
10340	,,	L. RODGERS	
10693	,,	F. CAIRNS	Wounded twice.
6342	Piper	W. WOODS	
8401	,,	J. BLACK	

REG. NO.	RANK.	NAME.	RECORD.
10632	Piper	W. MACDONALD	Wounded.
11893	,,	M. HALLIDAY	
11172	,,	F. MARR	Wounded twice.
40089	,,	G. LOCKIE	Wounded.
44039	,,	A. BRUCE	
23492	,,	R. M'ROBERTS	
202225	,,	A. LENNOX	
201229	,,	J. CAIRNEY	
44069	,,	J. CASSIDY	
9876	,,	J. BLACK	
8274	,,	J. RIDDLE	
8366	,,	J. ROACH	Prisoner.
7152	,,	ROBB	Wounded twice.
22122	,,	J. HALL	

4TH BATTALION

In Gallipoli the pipers were principally employed as messengers and bearers, and most of them became casualties. When the band was reconstituted the pipers were kept out of the front line.

REG. NO.	RANK.	NAME.	RECORD.
28	Pipe Major	C. FORBES	
6074	Piper	J. YOUNG	
179	,,	W. SCOTT	
729	,,	F. WOOD	Wounded.
478	,,	J. LOCKHART	
593	,,	B. MOWATT	Wounded.
778	,,	T. LUNHAM	Died of wounds.
779	,,	J. KERR	Died of wounds.
306	,,	C. STREET	Missing.
822	,,	A. HENDRY	Missing.

5TH BATTALION

In Gallipoli the pipers were mostly employed as stretcher-bearers, and nearly all of them became casualties.

REG. NO.	RANK.	NAME	RECORD.
1163	Lance-Sgt.	PORTER	
1333	Corpl.	J. PRIESTLY	Wounded, 12/7/15.
554	Piper	A. ERSKINE	Congratulated for bravery.
686	,,	R. T. ARRALL	Wounded, 22/6/15.
308	,,	R. BROWN	Killed, 12/7/15.
833	,,	J. CLINT	

REG. NO.	RANK.	NAME.	RECORD.
1760	Piper	T. E. Martin	Killed, 12/7/15.
1762	,,	H. C. Burnett	Wounded, 30/6/15.
995	,,	J. Dickson	
556	,,	J. Erskine	
1489	,,	J. Jackson	
1622	,,	D. M'Minn	
799	,,	M. Stewart	Wounded, 12/7/15.
1377	,,	D. Wilson	Wounded, 12/7/15.
	,,	Jas. Gorman	Killed.

6th Battalion.

In the attack on the Hohenzollern redoubt in September 1915 the battalion was played over the top by the Pipe Major, Robert Mackenzie. The casualties in this action, 4 killed and 3 wounded, resulted in the temporary disappearance of the band. At Arras, Ypres, and in later engagements, the men were employed as bearers.

REG. NO.	RANK.	NAME.	RECORD.
14851	Pipe Major	R. Mackenzie	Loos, 25/9/15; died of wounds; despatches.
	,,	T. Richardson	Transferred to Depôt.
	,,	J. Day	
	Corpl.	J. Wallace	
	Lance-Cpl.	J. Lomas	Killed, Loos, 25/9/15.
	,,	J. Marshall	
	,,	A. M'Kenna	Invalided.
	Piper	J. Sime	Killed, Loos, 25/9/15.
	,,	J. Bloomer	
	,,	P. Moffat	Killed, Loos, 25/9/15.
	,,	D. Hanlon	Wounded, Loos, 25/9/15.
	,,	G. M'Gregor	Wounded, Loos, 25/9/15.
	,,	J. Pringle	Missing; killed, Somme, October 1916.
	,,	J. Ferguson	
	,,	D. Barry	Wounded, Gallipoli, 1915.
	,,	J. Gray	Wounded, Hill 60, 1915.
	,,	H. Stott	
	,,	J. Jenkins	Invalided.
	,,	W. Little	
	,,	H. Sherry	
	,,	J. Phillips	
	,,	G. Stevenson	Wounded, Loos, 25/9/15.
	,,	W. H. Smith	
	,,	T. Rankine	

7TH BATTALION.

Just before the attack at Loos when there was a very heavy bombardment and gas discharge, Piper Daniel Laidlaw got up on the parapet and played the men over the top and continued until he fell wounded. For this act he was awarded the V.C. Another piper, Douglas Taylor, who had been wounded in the hand and could not play, went out and brought in several wounded men who had been gassed; he continued until he was dangerously wounded.

During the first eighteen months of the campaign the whole of the pipers were wounded.

The enormous value of pipes to a battalion returning from the front line is recognised by all ranks.

REG. NO.	RANK.	NAME.	RECORD.
	Pipe Major	DOUGLAS TAYLOR	Loos, wounded, 25/9/15.
15851	Piper	DANIEL LAIDLAW, V.C.	Loos, 25/9/15, wounded; V.C.
	,,	J. MILLIGAN	Loos, 25/9/15, wounded.
	,,	G. STEVENSON	Loos, wounded, 25/9/15.
	,,	G. DUTTON	Wounded.
	,,	W. IRVINE	Wounded Hulluch; invalided.
	,,	J. M'DONALD	Wounded, Arras.
	,,	W. LAMONT	Wounded, Dardanelles.
	,,	J. TAYLOR	Died of wounds, Arras.
	,,	G. BLACK	Invalided.

8TH BATTALION

This battalion, on account of its losses, was absorbed into the 7th K.O.S.B. The casualties among the 23 pipers of the two battalions were heavy, viz. 4 killed and 10 wounded.

REG. NO.	RANK.	NAME.	RECORD.
8352	Pipe Major	J. BALLOCH	Invalided; Meritorious Service Medal.
14875	Lance-Sgt.	J. BROADWOOD	Invalided.
8365	Corpl.	R. HALLIDAY	Promoted Pipe Major of 7/8th K.O.S.B.
14277	Lance-Cpl.	A. M'VITTIE	Killed, Arras.
	Piper	D. BALLOCH	
	,,	A. SIMPSON	

RANK.	NAME.	RECORD.
Piper	C. Reid	Killed, Somme, July 1916.
,,	P. Ogilvie	Wounded, Ypres.
,,	J. Young	Wounded, Arras.
,,	W. Buchanan	Wounded, Ypres.
,,	G. Swinton	Killed, Arras.
,,	J. Cairney	
,,	D. Reid	

THE CAMERONIANS (THE SCOTTISH RIFLES)

1st Battalion

During the early part of the campaign the casualties among pipers were so heavy that it was found necessary to keep them as much as possible out of the front line. By the end of 1915 the band had practically ceased to exist. Of 25 pipers who have served during the war 3 have been killed and 9 wounded.

REG. NO.	RANK.	NAME.	RECORD.
6062	Pipe Major	J. Alexander	Wounded.
265008	,,	D. M'Gruer	
8453	Corpl.	R. Gordon	
10873	,,	G. Peters	
6740	Lance-Cpl.	W. Smith	
9429	Piper	T. Best	Killed.
9441	,,	R. Black	Killed.
10786	,,	T. Brodie	
8899	,,	D. Cameron	Invalided.
8890	,,	W. Cattanach	Wounded.
10688	,,	W. Dick	Wounded.
10006	,,	R. Fleming	Wounded.
9209	,,	C. Gullan	Prisoner of war.
8883	,,	C. Henderson	
8254	,,	J. Hamilton	Wounded.
10641	,,	W. Kingsman	Invalided.
7739	,,	R. Menzies	Discharged.
36628	,,	G. Miller	Wounded.
8809	,,	A. M'Culloch	Invalided.
10924	,,	P. Robertson	Killed.
10326	,,	R. Stewart	Wounded.
10765	,,	W. Shane.	Prisoner of war.
22436	,,	J. Strachan	Wounded.
8393	,,	G. Whitehead	Discharged.
53509	,,	J. Williamson	

2nd Battalion

Pipers during the first part of the war were chiefly in the ranks, and the casualties among them were so heavy they had to be withdrawn. The band was reconstituted, and the pipers were then kept out of the front line. In March 1918 they again had to be employed as rifles.

REG. NO.	RANK.	NAME.	RECORD.
	Pipe Major	W. Robertson, M.M.	Military Medal; gassed, Lens, Sept. 1918.
	,,	D. Macdougall	
	,,	A. Cameron	Killed, 4/2/15, Laventie; acting platoon sergeant.
	Corporal	A. Wyllie	Wounded, 10/3/15, Neuve Chapelle.
	,,	J. Campbell	Killed, La Bassée, 16/5/15, while leading section.
	,,	A. Horne	Killed, 31/7/17.
	,,	D. M'Culloch	Wounded; promoted P.M. 13th Scottish Rifles.
6703	Piper	Ian Macpherson	Wounded, Nesle.
	,,	A. Macdonald	Killed, Laventie, Jan. 1915.
	,,	Forsyth	Killed, Bois Grenier, July 1915.
	,,	Nicol	Invalided.
	,,	Fleming	Wounded, 23/10/16.
	,,	Ferguson	Wounded, Dec. 1914.
	,,	Parker	Invalided.
	,,	Stark	Wounded, 10/3/15; Neuve Chapelle; invalided.
	,,	Clark	Killed, 10/3/15, Neuve Chapelle.
	,,	E. O'Neil	Invalided.
	,,	Lauder	Died of wounds, March 1918.
	,,	A. M'Donald	
	,,	C. Barclay	
	,,	J. Ingram	
	,,	C. Robertson	
	,,	G. Latham	
	,,	W. Campbell	

5th Battalion

The original pipers served in the ranks and became casualties, and from early in 1915 to the end of 1916 the band ceased to exist. Since the reconstitution the men have been employed behind the front line as far as possible.

In April 1917 they played the battalion back out of the Hindenburg line which had just been captured. During the last phase of the war they had to be employed in the ranks.

REG. NO.	RANK.	NAME.	RECORD.
5476	Pipe Major	C. G. Taylor	Invalided, 1/10/15.
	,,	Paterson	Accidentally killed.
5515	Piper	D. M'Phee	
5474	,,	C. Robertson	
6408	,,	J. Sloan	Wounded 3 times; invalided.
6240	,,	F. Watt	Invalided.
6471	,,	A. Mackay	Invalided.
6595	,,	M. Dunbar	
6572	,,	K. Sutherland	
6696	,,	R. M'Gregor	

6th Battalion

This battalion was merged into the 5th in July 1916. The pipers were employed in the ranks.

REG. NO.	RANK.	NAME.	RECORD.
201124	Pipe Major	J. C. Purdie	Killed.
	Lance-Cpl.	Jas. Kirk	Wounded, Festubert, 16/6/15.
202159	Cpl.	D. M'Dougall	
	Lance-Cpl.	A. M'Donald	Transferred to 2nd S.R.
202140	,,	D. Gardiner	
201213	Piper	H. M'Gregor	Wounded, 24/2/16; invalided.
240869	,,	J. Begg	
6435	,,	D. M'Gregor	Wounded; invalided.
202162	,,	J. Graham	
202161	,,	L. M'Dougall	
202051	,,	M. M'Intyre	Invalided.
202160	,,	T. Pollock	
240024	,,	J. Potter	
202164	,,	W. Sweeten	
240653	,,	R. Kerr	
290665	,,	P. MacCulloch	
39875	,,	A. Ferguson	
54252	,,	S. Bell	
291284	,,	D. Lamont	
39693	,,	A. M'Phee	

7th Battalion

In the Dardanelles and Palestine the pipers were employed as bearers and suffered heavy casualties. It was then decided to keep them out of the front line.

REG. NO.	RANK.	NAME.	RECORD.
152	Pipe Major	E. J. M'Pherson	Invalided.
166	,,	Louis Beaton	
1103	Piper	W. Jamieson	
1106	,,	Archibald Ramage	Killed, 28/6/15, Dardanelles.
868	,,	Archibald Shearer	Killed, 23/7/15, Dardanelles.
1178	,,	William Deans	Killed, June 1915.
1260	,,	J. Campbell	
404	,,	W. Taylor	Wounded, 28/6/15 ; invalided.
1095	,,	J. Paterson	
266069	,,	J. M'Donald	Wounded, 23/11/17, Palestine.
265902	,,	A. Thomson	
265858	,,	D. M'Kenzie	
265803	,,	R. M'Intyre	Wounded, 2/11/17, Palestine.
265958	,,	J. M'Iver	Killed, 12/11/17, Palestine.
1817	,,	J. Strachan	Killed, 4/11/17, Palestine.

8th Battalion

Pipers were principally employed, when in Gallipoli, as bearers, and suffered very heavily. On the 28th June, 1915, three were killed, and from Jan. 1916 for a year only one piper remained. There were also heavy losses in Palestine. They were chiefly employed in the ranks.

RANK.	NAME.	RECORD.
Pipe Major	Neil Macleod	Killed, Dardanelles, 12/7/15.
Corpl.	Alexander Stenton	
Piper	D. Macdougall	Transferred to 2nd Batt. as Pipe Major.
,,	G. Latham	
,,	John Macintyre	Killed, Gallipoli, 28/6/15.
,,	James Ferguson	Killed, Gallipoli, 28/6/15.
,,	Robert Whitelaw	Killed, Gallipoli, 28/6/15.
,,	John Mackenzie	Wounded, Gallipoli, 28/6/15.
,,	James M'Indoe	Killed, France, 29/7/18.
Lance-Cpl.	James Middleton	
Piper	William Dickie	Wounded, Gaza, 19/4/17.

RANK.	NAME.	RECORD.
Piper	JAMES ANDERSON	Wounded, Gaza, 19/4/17.
,,	ROBERT CAMERON	Wounded, Gaza, 19/4/17.
,,	A. F. CLARK	
,,	T. RAE	

9TH BATTALION

The whole band went into action at Loos, and suffered so heavily it took months to restore it. In a daylight raid at Arras in February 1917 Corpl. Whitelaw and Piper M'Gurk played their companies over the top.

During the Somme fighting pipers were employed in bringing up ammunition.

REG. NO.	RANK.	NAME.	RECORD.
1886	Pipe Major	M. FERGUSON	
40631	Lance-Cpl.	R. WHITELAW	
30503	Piper	HUGH MACARA	Killed, March 1917.
40643	Lance-Cpl.	W. JOHNSTON	
11619	Piper	A. MACPHERSON	
43338	,,	H. LENNOX	
16458	,,	J. M'KENNA	
11113	,,	W. MILLAR	Wounded.
267072	,,	H. BAIRD	
12094	,,	T. MACFARLANE	
17806	,,	M. M'GURK	
10542	,,	J. NICOL	
12325	,,	T. STEWART	
11797	,,	G. MUIR	
11839	,,	J. THOMPSON	Wounded.
11064	,,	J. SHIELDS	Invalided.
28525	,,	H. CAMERON	Invalided.
10588	,,	J. GILCHRIST	Wounded.
	,,	G. NAPIER	Gassed.

10TH BATTALION

The pipers were used as stretcher-bearers. Pipe Major M'Coll won the Military Medal when in charge of the stretcher party on the Somme.

RANK.	NAME.	RECORD.
Pipe Major	J. M'COLL, M.M.	Military Medal.
Piper	ROBERT BLACK	Wounded, Loos, 15/9/15; killed, 28/1/16.
,,	DUNCAN MACKENZIE	Killed, 17/11/15.
,,	ALEX. HARRIS	Killed, 27/1/16.

11th Battalion

Pipers were frequently employed as runners, orderlies, and to bring up stores and ammunition.

REG. NO.	RANK.	NAME.	RECORD.
15515	Pipe Major	A. Finlayson	Invalided.
14786	Corpl.	W. Reid	Wounded, 8/5/17.
16195	Piper	W. Robertson	Invalided, 29/9/16.
14631	,,	A. Stevenson	Killed, 28/4/17; despatches, 29/11/17.
14324	,,	W. Lewis	
15174	,,	R. M'Kay	
14595	,,	R. Tull	
14597	,,	G. Currie	
14687	,,	A. Tait	Wounded, 8/5/17.
11839	,,	J. Thomson	Wounded, 8/5/17.
11505	,,	D. Hunter	
30547	,,	J. Coull	
35462	,,	J. Richmond	
18176	,,	W. Hewitt	

THE ROYAL HIGHLANDERS (THE BLACK WATCH)

1st Battalion

During the opening stages the pipers were necessarily mostly employed in the ranks, and, within the first three months, practically the whole of the 13 pipers were casualties. During the Somme fighting the companies were repeatedly played to the attack by their pipers; on one of these occasions the pipe major, M'Leod, was killed. At Rue des Bois in May 1915, when the battalion attacked the German positions near Festubert, every company was played up, and Pipers Stuart and Wishart distinguished themselves, and Stuart was awarded the D.C.M.

REG. NO.	RANK.	NAME	RECORD
4621	Pipe Major	T. Clark	Invalided.
7068	,,	Hugh Maxwell Thom	Pipe Major, 22/8/16.
635	Lance-Cpl.	J. Reid	Invalided.
9617	Piper	D. M'Leod	Promoted Pipe Major; killed, 21/8/16.
7820	,,	H. Bruce	Wounded; missing, 9/5/15.

REG. NO.	RANK.	NAME.	RECORD.
2053	Piper	W. Burns	Wounded, 26/1/15; invalided.
2487	Lance-Cpl.	R. Knowles	Wounded, 26/10/14.
1314	Sergt.	R. Smith	Wounded, 8/9/14.
2190	Piper	T. Cardownie	Wounded, 24/10/14.
1956	,,	T. M'Intyre	Killed, 14/8/14.
1738	,,	B. Bain	Wounded, 26/10/14; invalided.
1771	,,	T. Peters	Wounded, 14/9/14; invalided.
1186	,,	G. Robertson	
943	Lance-Cpl.	J. Brown	Transferred as Pipe Major 8th Batt.; 3 times wounded.
740	Piper	R. Jaap	
	,,	J. Lees	Wounded, 25/1/15.
	,,	N. M'Leod	
	,,	A. Stewart	Wounded, 9/5/15.
	,,	P. M'Ginn	
	,,	A. Wishart	Wounded, 9/5/15.
9430	Lance-Cpl.	W. Stuart, D.C.M.	Wounded, Rue des Bois, 9/5/15 awarded D.C.M.
	Piper	T. Hardy	
9088	,,	David Wemyss	
43115	,,	Robert Muir	
699	,,	David Armit	
779	,,	Andrew Hadden	
40034	,,	Andrew Sime	
40154	,,	John Carmichael	
43114	,,	Alex. Sheriff	
1892	,,	Dugald M'Dade	
15895	,,	James Higgins	
2045	,,	John Neill	
7099	,,	George Wilson	
13291	,,	William Harley	
12194	,,	Edward Tatton	
2106	,,	William Hardie	
9723	,,	John Dawson	
16186	,,	George Martin	

2nd Battalion

At Neuve Chapelle, March 1915, and at many other subsequent engagements, the pipers lost heavily. At Mauquissart on 25th September, 1915, when the companies were played to the attack, one piper, Robert Johnstone, played on until he fell gassed; and another, Armit, on reaching the enemy trenches, started bombing. On the same occasion, Pipers David Simpson and A. Macdonald stood on the parapet under very heavy fire playing their company over ; Simpson was killed and Macdonald, who lost his leg, received the D.C.M. The pipers were also employed as bombers, and in this capacity Lance-Corpl. Peter MacNee obtained the D.C.M. at Neuve Chapelle.

On another occasion Pipers Gordon and Crichton played from one end of the line to the other out in the open, and similar feats were subsequently performed by other pipers.

While the battalion was in France, out of 22 pipers 4 were killed and 13 were wounded, during the first year of the war.

The battalion subsequently went to Mesopotamia. Here again the pipers were employed, sometimes in miscellaneous duties in the ranks, sometimes as pipers. The pipe major, John Keith, was awarded the D.C.M. Piper Pratt was promoted and given the D.C.M. for " high capacity in leadership " when acting as sergeant.

REG. NO.	RANK.	NAME.	RECORD.
6830	Sergt.	JOHN KEITH, D.C.M.	Wounded, Rue de Bacquerat, 15/7/15.
7184	Corpl.	DONALD MACMASTER	Wounded, Rue des Bois, 5/3/15.
8358	,, (Sgt.)	ANGUS MACLEOD	Wounded, Neuve Chapelle, 10/3/15.
9908	Lance-Cpl.	JAMES WANN	Died of wounds, Neuve Chapelle, 10/3/15.
365	Piper	ROBERT JOHNSTONE	Wounded Neuve Chapelle, 9/5/15 ; and again at Mauquissart, 25/9/15 ; finally gassed.
9476	,,	JOSEPH GORDON	Wounded, Neuve Chapelle, 9/5/15.
1165	Lance-Cpl.	PETER CRICHTON	
65	Piper	JOHN DUTHIE	Invalided.
699	,,	DAVID ARMIT	Wounded, Givenchy, 8/10/15.
1449	,,	JAMES DAVIS	Missing, Mauquissart, 25/9/15 ; believed killed.
1871	,,	JAMES GALLOWAY	Wounded, 3/11/14 ; killed, Givenchy, 8/10/15.
1838	,,	JAMES BRADLEY	Wounded, November 1914, and invalided.
1350	,,	THOMAS LOGAN	Invalided.
736	,,	DAVID SIMPSON	Killed, Mauquissart, 25/9/15.
1539	,,	ALEXANDER M'DONALD, D.C.M.	Wounded, Givenchy ; awarded D.C.M. ; died.
1478	,,	THOMAS PHINN	
1919	Lance-Sgt.	ALEXANDER PRATT, D.C.M.	Wounded, La Gorgue, 2/8/15 ; Mesopotamia, 22/4/16.

REG. NO.	RANK.	NAME.	RECORD.
941	Lance-Cpl.	PETER M'NEE, D.C.M.	Gassed, Mauquissart, 25/9/15; Mesopotamia, 13/1/16; D.C.M.; subsequently died of wounds.
779	Piper	ALEXANDER HADDEN	Wounded, 18/5/15, and again, 4/7/15.
467	,,	JOHN KIDD	Wounded, 1/11/14, and again Mauquissart, 25/9/15, and again Mesopotamia, 7/1/16.
1358	,,	WILLIAM MACKAY	Died of wounds, Neuve Chapelle, 10/3/15.
1314	,,	A. SMITH	
1998	,,	JOHN JORDAN	
288	,,	WILLIAM THOMSON	Wounded, Ypres.
S/17486	Corpl.	NEIL YOUNG	
	,,	WM. MATHIESON	Killed.
3/3422	,,	JOHN BENZIE	Invalided.
3/8973	Piper	JOHN BROWN	Invalided.
3/8570	,,	DAVID STORRAR	
487	,,	JAMES ANGUS	Wounded, Aisne, 14/9/14.
S/17639	,,	DAVID DRUMMOND	
S/19965	,,	JAMES DUNN	
S/17691	,,	JAMES GREIG	
336	,,	DAVID KIDD	Wounded, Le Cateau, Aug. 1914.
S/4372	,,	WILLIAM ROBERTSON	Wounded, Loos, 25/9/15, and San-i-yat, April 1916.
S/18525	,,	DAVID STARK	
1171	,,	THOMAS TALLON	
8875	,,	ALEXANDER THOMSON	Wounded, Sheikh Saad, 7/1/16; again, 20/4/16; again, 22/4/16.

4TH BATTALION

The pipers were employed principally as bearers, and were highly complimented for their gallantry at Neuve Chapelle in March 1915; at Loos they were similarly employed, and Piper M'Leod was awarded the Military Medal for gallantry in bringing in his colonel, who was mortally wounded, under very heavy fire. On 3rd September, 1916, the battalion was played in to the attack, but, as a rule, they were kept back behind the front line. Pipe Major Alex. Low got the D.C.M. for attending wounded, and Piper M'Leod got a bar to his Military Medal.

REG. NO.	RANK.	NAME.	RECORD.
210	Pipe Major	ALEXANDER LOW, D.C.M.	Recommended for D.C.M., Neuve Chapelle.
1198	,,	D. M'LEOD, M.M.	Awarded Military Medal, 25/3/15; and bar in 1918.
263	Corpl.	J. NICOLL	Wounded, 10/3/15.
1914	Piper	J. REID	Wounded, 9/5/15.
1403	,,	J. LYALL	Wounded, 6/9/15.
1301	,,	R. SWORD	Wounded, 9/5/15.
832	,,	J. DONALDSON	Wounded, 10/3/15.
663	,,	J. SOUTER	
714	,,	J. DEWAR	
1039	,,	G. SCOTT	
1160	,,	J. MERCHANT	
1887	,,	T. CAMERON	
1678	,,	F. MITCHELL	
2204	,,	A. FINDLAY	
4029	,,	C. GIBSON	
1717	,,	J. MYLES	
2177	,,	A. SANGSTER	
769	,,	H. MITCHELL	
	,,	THOS. PATERSON	Transferred to Wireless Service, R.N., as Sub-Lieut.

5TH BATTALION

Pipers were employed, during the trench fighting, as observers, messengers and stretcher-bearers, and in the ranks, and suffered heavy casualties.

The battalion was subsequently merged into the 4th Black Watch.

REG. NO.	RANK.	NAME.	RECORD.
668	Pipe Major	A. M'DONALD LAMOND	Wounded, 9/5/15, Fromelles.
1053	Sergt.	A. E. CROWE	
1163	Piper	J. CARSTAIRS	Invalided.
729	Lance-Cpl.	J. STEWART	Invalided.
826	Piper	J. DUNCAN	
1150	,,	A. NICOLL	Wounded, 25/8/15, while sniping.
1053	,,	A. LUNDIE	Wounded, 9/5/15.
1689	,,	J. WHITTON	
1051	,,	J. BEGG	
1568	,,	A. HOWIE	Killed, 10/3/15, Neuve Chapelle; mentioned in despatches.
406	Lance-Cpl.	F. REID	Killed, 13/3/15, Neuve Chapelle.
382	Sergt.	P. M'KAY	
719	Piper	W. WEBSTER	
1719	,,	J. MYLES	
751	,,	A. C. SCOTT	
1017	,,	A. BRAND	

6th Battalion

Pipers were employed in many ways, but chiefly as stretcher-bearers. The band was regarded by the men as the best stretcher-bearers they came across. At High Wood in July 1916 the battalion was played over by Pipers Pirnie, Forbes, Mapleton and Tainsh.

Since September 1916 they have been kept out of the front line as far as possible.

In December 1917 four pipers were killed and one wounded by a bomb during an aeroplane raid at Fromicourt.

REG. NO.	RANK.	NAME.	RECORD.
	Pipe Major	W. Galloway	
	,,	J. Sinclair	
	,,	D. Anderson	
	Lance-Cpl.	D. Berry	
2126	Piper	Alasdair M'Donald	Despatches.
	,,	P. Fallon	Killed, May, 1915.
	,,	R. Pirnie	
	,,	P. Davidson	
	,,	P. Irons	
	,,	W. M'Ewan	
	,,	J. Ferguson	Killed, La Boiselle, August 1916.
	,,	A. M'Donald	
	,,	P. M'Intosh	
	,,	R. Mapleton	Commission in Gordons.
	,,	MacCullen	Wounded, March 1917.
	,,	J. Harper	Killed, 23/12/17.
	,,	A. Tainsh	Killed, 23/12/17.
	,,	A. Forbes	Killed, 23/12/17.
	,,	J. Wyse	
	,,	J. Guthrie	
	,,	W. Peggie	
	,,	A. Paton	Transferred to R.E.; killed, June 1917.
	,,	W. Mason	
	,,	D. Stewart	
	,,	D. M'Beth	
	,,	T. Lyall	
	,,	A. Lees	
	,,	C. Mackenzie	
	,,	G. Gow	
	,,	J. Gow	

REG. NO.	RANK.	NAME.	RECORD.
	Piper	A. Myles	Killed, 23/121/7.
	,,	J. M'Beth	
	,,	A. M'Coll	
	,,	D. Leggat	
	,,	J. Burleigh	
	,,	J. Nicol	
	,,	F. Christie	
	,,	R. Low	
	,,	J. Condie	
	,,	E. Deans	
	,,	J. Stewart	
	,,	N. Beaton	
	,,	R. Spence	
	,,	H. Rattray	Transferred to 7th Gordons as Pipe Major.
	,,	C. Nisbet	
	,,	J. Simpson	
	,,	L. Massie	Killed, Somme, Oct. 1916.

7th Battalion

The pipers were employed in the ranks, as despatch runners, etc. Piper G. Galloway was awarded the Military Medal for performing this most hazardous duty under heavy fire during the Somme fighting; and Pipe Major Thomas Macdonald and Pipers Swan and Hands were rewarded with the same distinction.

Latterly the pipers were trained as anti-aircraft Lewis gunners, and proved extremely successful.

REG. NO.	RANK.	NAME.	RECORD.
290056	Pipe Major	Thomas M'Donald, M.M.	Military Medal, Somme.
	Lance-Sgt.	J. Chisholm	Invalided.
292440	,,	N. M'Donald	
	Lance-Cpl.	G. Swan, M.M.	Killed, Dec. 1916, Somme; Military Medal.
292435	,,	A. Chalmers	
	,,	A. Wilkie	
	Piper	H. Forker	
	,,	A. Wilkie	Killed, Dec. 1916, Somme.
	,,	B. Morris	
	,,	J. Johnstone	Killed, Dec. 1916, Somme.
	,,	George Galloway, M.M.	Wounded, April 1917; Military Medal.

REG. NO.	RANK.	NAME.	RECORD.
	Piper	J. Ross	Invalided.
	,,	W. Bridy	Killed, Dec. 1916, Somme.
	,,	E. Linn	Wounded, July 1916.
	,,	D. Leggat	Wounded, Dec. 1916.
	,,	J. Moodie	
	,,	J. Condie	Invalided.
	,,	R. Adamson	Invalided.
	,,	J. Robertson	Invalided.
	,,	J. Guthrie	Invalided.
	,,	W. Campbell	Invalided.
3/4470	,,	James Johnston	Killed, 7/1/17, Somme.
	,,	E. Archibald	Invalided.
	,,	A Mitchelson	Invalided.
41028	,,	J. Russell	
292434	,,	A. Chalmers	
293096	,,	D. Chalmers	
292406	,,	W. Fitzpatrick	
200509	,,	A. Mands, M.M.	Military Medal.
112084	,,	J. M'Kellar	
290127	,,	T. Archibald	
201553	,,	F. M'Leod	
42124	,,	D. Cameron	
	,,	J. M'Gill	

8th Battalion

The battalion was played into action at Loos and in many of the Somme engagements. After 1916, on account of losses among them, they were kept out of the front line as far as possible.

The band headed the State Entry of King Albert into Brussels in November 1918.

REG. NO.	RANK.	NAME.	RECORD.
2911	Pipe Major	R. Matchett	
8368	,,	E. Rennie	Wounded, Ypres, 1915; invalided.
943	,,	J. Brown	Wounded, three times.
4266	Corpl.	D. Sinclair	Wounded, Festubert, 1915.
6245	Piper	D. Ainslie	Wounded, Nieuport.
853	,,	J. Allan	Wounded, Aisne.
1738	,,	B. Bain	Wounded, Aisne.
7211	,,	A. Barclay	
9220	,,	A. Campbell	Wounded, Ypres, 1915.
11780	,,	R. Edmonston	
6365	,,	D. Glen	

REG. NO.	RANK.	NAME.	RECORD.
16987	Piper	W. Hosie	
3925	,,	W. Lockhart	Wounded, Somme, 1916.
40577	,,	J. M'Arthur	
3020	,,	A. M'Courtie	
266912	,,	J. M'Kay	
265912	,,	R. Menzies	Killed, Meteren, July 1918.
3281	,,	J. M'Leod	Wounded, Loos, 1915.
8832	,,	W. Nicholson	Wounded twice, Vermelles, Loos.
3375	,,	W. Reilly	Killed, Loos, 1915.
8659	,,	S. Reid	Wounded, Ypres, 1915.
299331	,,	G. Redpath	
265989	,,	J. Strang	
265715	,,	P. Stewart	
6366	,,	W. Strathie	
3019	,,	D. Simpson	Killed, Somme, 1916.
266055	,,	D. Winton	
3014	,,	D. Wilson	Killed, Loos, 1915.
3/1861	,,	J. Woods	

9th Battalion

The pipers played the battalion into action at Hill 70, and the whole band, except one man, was killed or wounded.

The battalion was ultimately absorbed into the 4/5th Black Watch.

REG. NO.	RANK.	NAME.	RECORD.
9005	Pipe Major	T. Harley	
4924	Lance-Cpl.	D. Cameron	
11463	Piper	J. Armour	Invalided.
40016	,,	J. Burleigh	Wounded, 18/5/18.
43236	,,	G. Fairweather	Wounded, 28/7/18.
	,,	J. Johnstone	Killed, March 1918.
40018	,,	D. Lamond	
43448	,,	J. Scott	
7814	,,	R. Napier	
43155	,,	A. Robertson	Wounded, 30/10/18.
16105	,,	J. Spence	
6563	,,	A. Stirling	Wounded, 18/5/18.
11195	,,	R. Thomson	
	,,	J. Wemyss	Invalided.
1350	,,	T. Logan	

THE HIGHLAND LIGHT INFANTRY

1st Battalion

During the first six months of the war 7 pipers were killed, 8 were wounded and 2 were taken prisoner. These casualties mostly occurred at Festubert in December 1914, and later at Neuve Chapelle. They were then withdrawn from the front lines. Subsequently they were employed as bearers, ammunition carriers, etc.

REG. NO.	RANK.	NAME.	RECORD.
11281	Pipe Major	R. Sutherland	
6894	Sergt.	D. Buchan	Killed, Festubert, 19-21/12/14.
10774	Corpl.	A. Godsman, D.C.M.	Wounded, Neuve Chapelle, 12/1/15; D.C.M. and Order of St. George.
7918	Piper	W. White	
9615	,,	C. Stewart	Killed, Ypres, 1/5/15.
10116	,,	J. M'Grory	Wounded, Festubert, 19-21/12/14.
10258	,,	H. Cater	
10107	,,	F. Burns	Killed, Festubert, 19-21/12/14.
11356	,,	C. Wilson	
9860	,,	T. James	Killed, Festubert, 19-21/12/14.
11782	,,	D. Sutherland	Wounded, Neuve Chapelle, 11-14/3/15.
11685	,,	A. Bain	Wounded, Neuve Chapelle, 14/3/15
9011	,,	J. Morrison	Killed, Festubert, 19-21/12/14.
10579	,,	T. Jackson	
11124	,,	J. M'Donald	Prisoner of war, Festubert, 19-21/12/14.
11718	,,	R. M'Leish	
11470	,,	J. Smith	Wounded, Festubert, 19-21/12/14; wounded, Richebourg, 6/10/15; died, 7/9/16.
11533	,,	J. Johnstone	Prisoner of war, Festubert, 19-21/12/14.
11499	,,	J. M'Naught	Killed, Festubert, 19-21/12/14.
10383	Corpl.	D. Chisholm	Wounded, Ypres, 23/10/14.
	Lance-Cpl.	Mitchell	Killed, Verneuil, 18/9/14.
10010	Piper	Gault	Wounded, Rue du Bois, 17/5/15.
11468	Corpl.	J. Smith	Wounded, Ypres, 22/10/14; died enteric.
12064	Lance-Cpl.	A. Craig	
12061	Piper	A. Mackay	
12106	,,	C. Bald	

2nd Battalion

Of the original band of thirteen men all but two were killed or wounded in the first few months of the war. While they lasted they acted as pipers as well as in the ranks. From May 1915 to May 1916 there was practically no band, and, when reconstituted, the men were kept out of the front line as far as possible.

Reg. No.	Rank.	Name.	Record.
9728	Pipe Major	W. Young	
10713	Lance-Cpl.	L. M'Kinnon	Wounded, 21/10/14.
11448	,,	J. Smith	Wounded, 21/10/14; died of enteric.
11480	Piper	J. Brown	
10478	,,	J. Bruce	
9029	,,	J. Campbell	Wounded, 2/11/14.
7721	,,	W. Haines	Wounded, 17/5/15, Ypres.
11945	,,	R. Henderson	Wounded, 18/5/15, Ypres.
10976	,,	J. Irving	Killed, 3/11/14.
11137	,,	A. Morrow	Wounded, 24/8/14; taken prisoner.
11614	,,	A. Macdonald	
11627	,,	J. Smith	Wounded, 3/12/17.
9272	Corpl.	J. Mackenzie	Killed, 21/10/14.
7885	Piper	J. Dale	
7943	Corpl.	J. Robertson	
7886	Piper	J. Gibson	
35100	,,	J. Morgan	
33119	,,	R. Morrison	
35123	,,	R. Macnaughton	
8515	,,	W. Peil	
6978	,,	A. Williamson	
7472	Sergt.	C. W. Johnstone	
9387	Piper	A. Macneilage	Twice wounded.
7270	,,	D. Macintyre	
9280	,,	R. Stein	
331117	,,	W. Gunn	
332186	,,	H. Campbell	
331230	,,	J. Menzies	
330068	,,	A. Ogilvie	
330070	,,	R. Wilder	Wounded.
327119	,,	W. White	
3970	,,	J. Macrae	
10264	Sergt.	T. Findlay	Killed, Neuve Chapelle, 14/3/15.
220217	Piper	J. Reid	
12302	,,	D. Bonnar	

5th Battalion

In Gallipoli, in 1915, practically all the pipers became casualties within a very short time, and, until the end of 1916, there was no band at all. It was then decided to keep the band out of the firing line as far as possible.

REG. NO.	RANK.	NAME.	RECORD.
306	Pipe Major	John Thomson	Killed, 12/7/15, Dardanelles.
3601	,,	A. Purdie	
201571	,,	A. Arthur	
309	Lance-Cpl.	J. B. Day	Invalided.
280313	,,	D. J. Cameron	
330041	,,	R. Agnew	
1596	Piper	J. Reid	
1233	,,	G. Cameron	Invalided.
1317	,,	J. Smith	Invalided.
201259	,,	J. Connelly	Invalided.
201330	,,	T. Clelland	Invalided.
203064	,,	A. Thomson	
12226	,,	C. Kennedy	
200170	,,	R. Reid	
200601	,,	J. Pithie	
18263	,,	A. Davie	
240633	,,	M. Watson	

6th Battalion

The pipers were employed in the ranks while the battalion was in Gallipoli, but, in attacks, the pipers played their companies. On 12th July, Piper M'Niven was killed while playing the charge, in an attack on the Turkish forts. Most of the original band were killed or wounded on the Peninsula, and, when reconstituted, it was decided to keep them out of action as far as possible.

REG. NO.	RANK.	NAME.	RECORD.
24001	Pipe Major	John Mackenzie	
55533	Sergt.	J. Braidwood	
240881	Piper	W. Mackenzie	Wounded, 12/7/15.
1237	,,	Peter M'Niven	Killed, 12/7/15, Gallipoli.
1190	,,	A. M'Coll	Wounded, 21/11/15.
240066	Lance-Cpl.	W. Francey	Wounded, 17/8/15.
1286	Piper	W. Finlay	Invalided.
240171	,,	W. Christian	
240235	,,	A. Cameron	Wounded, 12/7/15.

REG. NO.	RANK.	NAME.	RECORD.
	Piper	James Ross	Machine Gun Corps; gassed, Marne, March 1918.
240189	,,	James Nicoll	
240168	,,	C. M'Phedran	
240538	,,	P. Mulvey	
241426	,,	H. Climie	
243457	,,	J. M'Munn	Wounded, 12/6/18.
203070	,,	D. Sutherland	
355753	,,	F. Young	
29111	,,	J. M'Cormick	
64901	,,	W. Stringer	
201126	,,	W. Campbell	

7th Battalion

On several occasions in Gallipoli the battalion was played to the attack by pipers. Piper Maclennan was awarded the D.C.M. Piper Macfarlane had the drones blown off his pipes. The acting pipers served in the ranks or as bearers. Piper D. Cameron was mentioned in despatches for conspicuous bravery in playing his company over the top, and right on to the enemy trenches. These men also did great work in bringing up water for the wounded under heavy fire, and ammunition.

REG. NO.	RANK.	NAME.	RECORD.
	Pipe Major	William Ferguson	
1914	Piper	Kenneth Maclennan, D.C.M.	D.C.M., 12/7/15.
1901	,,	D. J. Cameron	Despatches, 12/7/15.
	,,	Donald Macfarlane	Wounded.
	,,	William Paterson	
	,,	Donald Lamont	
	,,	J. G. Mackenzie	
	,,	Ritchie Graham	
	,,	James Carruthers	
	,,	John Scott	

8th Battalion

The battalion was disbanded early in the war, and the pipers were distributed to other units.

9th Battalion

At first pipers were used as orderlies, ammunition carriers, and similar duties; and, after active operations, as bearers. As far as possible they were, however, kept out of the front line, as being too valuable to lose. On one occasion, when the battalion had to make a demonstration to test the strength of the enemy, pipers were sent up to the front line to play. Pipe Major MacDiarmid was awarded the Military Medal.

REG. NO.	RANK.	NAME.	RECORD.
	Pipe Major	T. Baillie	Discharged after 31 years' service.
330075	,,	A. B. MacDiarmid, M.M.	Awarded M.M.
330167	Lance-Sgt.	T. J. Kelly	Wounded, 25/1/15.
330115	Lance-Cpl.	G. C. Blackadder	
	Piper	R. Agnew	Invalided home.
331499	,,	D. Barrie	
331044	,,	W. Baird	
56645	,,	J. D. Buchanan	
330304	,,	R. Blackadder	
	,,	C. Brown	Wounded, May 1915.
333792	,,	T. Crawford	Died of wounds.
330310	,,	T. M. Fraser	Wounded, 24/3/18.
241138	,,	K. Fraser	Wounded, 22/3/18.
	,,	W. Gibson	Wounded, 24/3/18; discharged.
	,,	J. Hall	Invalided home.
1666	,,	J. Drummond	Killed in action, June 1915.
333118	,,	W. Imlay	Wounded, 13/4/18.
331077	,,	R. Johnston	
330834	,,	W. Kennedy	
333269	,,	P. M'Arthur	Invalided home, 17/4/15; discharged, 14/6/15; recalled, 1/9/16.
333138	,,	G. M'Creath	Died of wounds, Oct. 1918.
	,,	J. M'Donald	Wounded, 25/9/15.
333162	,,	J. B. M'Nee	
332318	,,	J. M'Gilvray	Wounded, 24/3/18.
330865	,,	G. M'Gregor	
	,,	A. Ogilvie	Wounded, July 1915.
331564	,,	W. Robertson	Wounded, 22/3/18.
333729	,,	R. Ross	
333137	,,	H. Stark	Wounded, 27/9/17.
331198	,,	H. Simpson	Wounded, 24/3/18; discharged.
331579	,,	J. Stewart	
	,,	H. Wilder	Invalided.

10th Battalion

Pipers were occasionally employed as bearers, but were usually kept out of the front line. Nearly all the original pipe band were killed or wounded at Cambrai on 25th September, 1915.

REG. NO.	RANK.	NAME.	RECORD.
7682	Pipe Major	E. Richardson	Transferred to 12th H.L.I.
2747	,,	C. Cameron	
9016	Piper	Charles M'Gregor	Gassed and wounded, Cambrai, 25/9/15.
12562	,,	Alex. Whitefield	Killed, Cambrai, 25/9/15.
17174	,,	J. Webster	Invalided.
902	Lance-Cpl.	David Donaldson	Killed, Festubert, 9/7/15.
1988	Piper	Andrew Thomson	Wounded, Cambrai, 25/9/15.
1991	,,	W. Currie	
9628	Lance-Cpl.	D. Sutherland	
19858	,,	J. Rose	
17805	Piper	P. M'Intyre	Gassed, Cambrai, 25/9/15. died, 8/11/18.
21233	,,	J. M'Lennan	
40166	,,	J. Duguid	
40091	,,	J. M'Kenzie	
240908	,,	J. Mackay	
	,,	J. Cunningham	
355667	,,	D. M'Nicol	

12th Battalion

During trench warfare the pipers acted as orderlies, stretcher bearers and the like ; in engagements, however, they took part as company pipers. So many casualties occurred in the Loos action in Sept. 1915 that there was only one survivor. The band ceased to exist until the following spring, and it was then decided to allow only half of the pipers to go up into the line or into action.

During the battles of the Somme, 1916, and Arras, 1917, the companies were played into action by one piper each ; casualties occurring among them, it was decided again to withdraw them from the front ; and they took no part in the fighting at Ypres, 1917.

During the last phase of the war, the attack in Flanders on 28th Sept. 1918, the pipers played their companies throughout their triumphant attacks on the Germans.

The C.O. of the battalion says : " I cannot speak too highly of the work done by the pipers of this unit. There is nothing I can think of which has added more to the *esprit de corps* of the men, which has enabled them to put up with misery and discomfort and which has given them the inspiration necessary to accomplish what had appeared at first sight an impossibility.

REG. NO.	RANK.	NAME.	RECORD.
	Pipe Major	E. Richardson	
	Sergt.	William Pierce	Killed, Somme, August, 1916.
	Corpl.	Allan M'Nicol, M.M.	Despatches, Loos, and Hill 70, 25/9/15; Military Medal.
	Piper	Thomas Spendlove	Wounded, Ypres, 8/10/14.
	,,	Jack Smith	Wounded, Cambrai, 5/12/17.
	,,	George M'Kay	Wounded, Somme, 1/7/16.
	,,	Peter Kennedy	
	,,	William Taylor	
	,,	Robert Comloquoy	
	,,	Robert Bell	
	,,	William Anderson	
	,,	Donald M'Pherson	
	,,	John M'Ghee	
	,,	David Robertson	
	,,	William Thompson	Killed, Arras, April 1917.
	,,	George Tullis	Invalided.
	,,	Malcolm M'Lean	Wounded, Arras, April 1917.
	,,	John Morrison	Wounded, Albert, 17/9/16.
	,,	William Barclay	Wounded, Albert, 17/9/16.
	,,	Robert Weir	Wounded, Albert, 17/9/16.
	,,	John M'Kean	Killed, Loos 25/9/15.
	Lance-Sgt.	Alex. M'Kay	Wounded, Loos, 25/9/15.

14th Battalion

Pipers played their companies into action on the Somme and at Bourlon Wood.

REG. NO.	RANK.	NAME.	RECORD.
	Pipe Major	A. Hynd	
	Sergt.	G. Taylor	
	Lance-Cpl.	J. M'Cormack	
	Piper	J. Connly	
	,,	J. Mann	
	,,	T. Kennedy	
	,,	J. Wilson	
	,,	Sutherland	
	,,	T. Pirie	
	,,	A. Phinn	
	,,	J. Gordon	
	,,	P. Thomson	Killed, 29/4/17.

15th Battalion

At Thiepval and Beaumont Hamel the pipers lost very heavily when leading their companies, and, as a consequence, it was found necessary afterwards to keep them in the reserve line. In April 1918, on account of heavy casualties in the battalion, they had to be employed in the ranks, and suffered very heavily; of 20 pipers all but 3 became casualties, mostly through being gassed at Ayette. Within a month, however, the band was reconstituted.

REG. NO.	RANK.	NAME.	RECORD.
973	Pipe Major	N. M'Lellan	Gassed, 13/4/18; invalided.
16084	"	T. Gilbert, M.M.	From 17th H.L.I.
13374	"	J. Park	Wounded, 14/10/17; gassed, 13/4/18; invalided.
14078	Piper	J. Kilpatrick	Wounded, 1/7/16.
1020	"	C. Logan	Gassed, 13/4/18; invalided.
13591	"	D. Keenan	Wounded, 10/5/16; invalided.
13356	"	R. Hough	
15497	"	J. Burleigh	Gassed, 13/4/18.
36456	"	T. Marr	Wounded, Loos, 25/9/15.
36455	"	W. Marr	Wounded, May 1916.
13601	"	J. Reid	
13706	"	R. Gillies	Wounded, 2/7/16; gassed, 13/4/18.
10010	"	J. Gault	Gassed, 13/4/18.
28093	"	A. J. Macdonald	Gassed, 13/4/18.
350254	"	T. Graham	
280889	"	A. Gray	Wounded, Aug. 1918.
281053	"	W. Brown	Gassed, 13/4/18.
280979	"	J. Bryson	Gassed, 13/4/18.
15719	"	H. M'Arthur	Gassed, 13/4/18.
14304	"	A. F. Watson	Wounded, 13/4/18.
353152	"	D. M'Kenzie	Killed, Ayette, 13/4/18.
15296	"	C. Galloway	Gassed, 13/4/18.
10108	"	W. M'Lelland	Invalided.
200601	"	J. Pithie	Gassed, 13/4/18.
54366	"	W. M'Nair	
58009	"	M. M'Lean	
50267	"	T. Orr	
56597	"	A. Millan	

16th Battalion

The pipers were employed chiefly as bearers.

On 1st July, 1916, at Thiepval the pipers played the battalion over with the loss of two killed and two wounded. The band was then withdrawn as far as possible from the front, except occasionally as stretcher bearers. It was felt by all ranks that pipers were too valuable an institution to lose.

REG. NO.	RANK.	NAME.	RECORD.
	Pipe Major	W. M'Combe, M.M.	
	,,	T. Richardson, M.M.	
	Lance-Cpl.	W. Orr	Killed, 1/7/16.
	,,	P. Murray	
	Piper	R. Alexander	
	,,	J. Watson	Wounded, 1/7/16.
	,,	R. Baird	
	,,	B. Fraser	Wounded, 1/7/16.
	Lance-Cpl.	L. Armourer	
	Piper	A. Rankine	Killed, 1/7/16.
	,,	R. M'Kay	
	,,	R. Watson	
	,,	R. Barclay	
	,,	J. Fogo	
	,,	R. Hunter	
	,,	J. Hoy	
	,,	J. M'Donald	
	,,	H. Barrie	
	,,	T. Porteous	
	,,	D. Bell	
	,,	D. Macintosh	
	,,	G. Bell	
	,,	W. Coutts	
	,,	J. Bruce	
	,,	A. MacPherson	
	,,	R. Hope	
	Lance-Cpl.	W. Hendry	
	Corpl.	R. Brown	

17th Battalion

In the attack on the Leipzig Redoubt on 1st July, 1916, when the battalion had to hang on unsupported to a part of the captured Leipzig Redoubt, the pipers played and did an immense deal in keeping the men's spirits up. Pipe Major Gilbert on this occasion won the Military Medal. The casualties in this attack put the pipe band out of action, and the pipers were thereafter kept, as far as possible, out of the front line. The battalion was subsequently merged in the 15th H.L.I.

REG. NO.	RANK.	NAME.	RECORD.
	Pipe Major	T. GILBERT, M.M.	Military Medal, July 1916; despatches, July 1917; transferred to 15th H.L.I.
	Corpl.	JOHN BURLEIGH	Gassed, April 1918; transferred to 15th H.L.I.
	,,	CHARLES GALLOWAY	Wounded, Nieuport, 10/7/17; promoted for gallantry, 1/7/16; gassed, Arras, April 1918.
	Lance-Cpl.	JAMES M'MUNN	Wounded, 1/7/16, Somme; again, in Egypt; transferred to 7th H.L.I.
	Piper	ARCHIBALD FORREST	Received Commission; died of disease, 1918.
	,,	HUGH M'ARTHUR	Gassed, Arras, April 1918; transferred to 15th H.L.I.
	,,	ARCHIBALD CARMICHAEL	Wounded, Nieuport, 10/7/17.

THE SEAFORTH HIGHLANDERS

1st Battalion

The casualties among the pipers of this battalion have been very heavy. At Richebourg in November 1914, 2 pipers were killed and 6 wounded, and the pipe major, Matheson, was awarded the D.C.M. for great gallantry in carrying messages. In December 1914, and again at Neuve Chapelle in May 1915, 3 more were killed and 4 wounded. Some of them were employed as pipers, others as bearers and in the ranks. At Neuve Chapelle the companies were played into action in May 1915, and Piper Pratt was killed while playing.

The battalion went to Mesopotamia, and in the action at Sheikh Saad on 7th January, 1916, Pipe Major M'Kechnie played the regimental charge at a most crucial moment and continued until he fell wounded. In this and other subsequent engagements pipers played their companies into action. Some of them did excellent work bringing up ammunition, and 529 Piper Colin M'Kay was specially promoted for this. This duty was particularly dangerous as the Turkish barrage was generally late.

The casualties continued to be heavy. Altogether 11 pipers have been killed.

REG. NO.	RANK.	NAME.	RECORD.
8391	Pipe Major	D. B. MATHIESON, D.C.M.	D.C.M.; wounded "Port Arthur," 7/11/14.

REG. NO.	RANK.	NAME.	RECORD.
10169	Lance Cpl.	J. TULLOCH	Wounded in trenches, "Port Arthur," 6/11/14.
9158	Sergt.	J. MACLELLAN	Wounded," Port Arthur," 9/5/15; subsequently killed, 21/4/17.
7900	Piper	W. F. COWANS	Killed, 7/11/14, "Port Arthur."
9291	,,	J. PRATT	Died of wounds, Neuve Chapelle, 9/5/15.
479	,,	D. BLACK	Killed, 3/11/14, "Port Arthur."
766	Lance Cpl.	Lance Sgt. J. MACKENZIE	Wounded, "Port Arthur," 9/5/15.
216	Piper,	Actg. P.M. W. PATON	Wounded, Givenchy, 6/4/15.
10457	Lance Sgt.	J. STEWART	Transferred to 2nd Batt.; killed, 1917.
412	Piper	WILLIAM BARRY	Despatches.
311	Lance-Cpl.	DONALD CAMPBELL	Wounded, Givenchy, 4/11/14; killed, Mesopotamia, 1917.
9458	,,	JOHN DUNBAR	Wounded, Mesopotamia, 7/1/16, while performing duties in attack.
9628	,,	ALEXANDER HAY	Transferred to R.E.
444	,,	ROBERT HILL	Wounded, "Port Arthur," 9/5/15.
262	,,	A. M'DONALD	
264	,,	ALEXANDER M'GILL	
433	,,	ANDREW MACKAY	Wounded, Mesopotamia, 21/4/17.
435	,,	JOHN M'VEAN	Wounded, Mesopotamia, 7/1/16; invalided.
564	,,	N. MORRISON	Wounded, Givenchy, 4/12/14.
366	,,	T. MUIR	Wounded, "Port Arthur," invalided.
284	,,	D. MURRAY	Wounded, Givenchy, 6/4/15; invalided.
768	,,	ADAM ROSS	Wounded, Givenchy, 17/11/14.
9419	,,	D. SKINNER	Wounded, Givenchy, 20/12/14 invalided.
10183	Lance Cpl.	J. HERON	
645	Piper	D. SMITH	Killed in France.
661	,,	J. STEIN	Wounded in trenches; invalided.
788	,,	T. URQUHART	Killed, Givenchy, 20/12/14.
	Corpl.	A. VINCE	Wounded, Neuve Chapelle, 9/5/15; transferred to R.S.F.
9446	Corpl.	Actg. P.M. NEIL M'KECHNIE	Acting Pipe Major when battalion went to Mesopotamia; wounded, 7/1/15; mentioned in despatches, 25/8/15.
10056	Piper	JOHN SHAND	Wounded, Mesopotamia, 21/4/17; and again Palestine.
7214	Lance Cpl.	JAMES HARDY	
543	Piper	NEIL MORRISON	

REG. NO.	RANK.	NAME.	RECORD.
529	Sergt. Piper	COLIN M'KAY	Died of wounds, Baghdad.
	Lance Cpl.	ALEX. ROBERTSON	Severely wounded, Sheikh Saad; pipes smashed, 7/1/16.
	Piper	JAMES ROBERTSON	
7184	Lance Sgt.	JAMES DUNCAN	
	Lance Cpl.	HEARNE	Died at home.
200300	Piper	WILLIAM M'DONALD	
16360	,,	J. CUTHILL	
9526	,,	GEORGE PATERSON	
	,,	WILLIAM M'LELLAN	
	,,	ALLAN	
709	,,	J. WILKINSON	Killed, France.
	,,	COOK	Killed, Mesopotamia.
204786	,,	A. HART	
8338	,,	J. WILSON	
7208	,,	J. KNOX	
22602	,,	REID	
8337	,,	M. JOHNSTONE	

2ND BATTALION

The pipers were largely employed as runners, orderlies, etc., and suffered very heavy casualties. On several occasions during the open fighting they were employed in the attack as pipers. Of 23 pipers who went to France with the battalion 6 were killed and 10 wounded in the first year of the war. The opinion of the officers is that only the difficulty of reinforcements limits the employment of pipers in action.

REG. NO.	RANK.	NAME.	RECORD.
6731	Pipe Major	JOHN HAYWOOD	Invalided, Dec. 1914.
577	,,	JAMES MACKENZIE	Wounded, 25/1/17.
6171	Corpl.	ANGUS MACLEAN	Wounded, May 1915.
9106	Lance Cpl.	WILLIAM ROSS	Killed, June 1915.
9223	,,	JOHN GRANT	Killed, October 1914.
283	,,	DOUGAL MACMILLAN	Died of disease, Feb. 1915.
9454	,,	JAMES RENNIE	Wounded, August 1914; killed, Loos, Oct. 1915.
70	Piper	HUGH KEIL	Gassed, May 1915.
625	,,	GEORGE THOMSON	Wounded, March 1915.
	,,	DAVID MACRAE	Killed, February 1915.
3	,,	ROBERT HALL	Killed, July 1916.
	,,	ALEXANDER THORNTON	
570	,,	ALEXANDER MACKENZIE	Wounded, February 1915.
	,,	RONALD MACKENZIE	
711	,,	JAMES URQUHART	Invalided, Dec. 1914.

REG. NO.	RANK.	NAME.	RECORD.
	Piper	Frederick Cook	Wounded, 13/10/14.
	,,	Albert Hunter	
	,,	Alexander MacAngus	
1096	,,	Gregor Mackenzie	Gassed, 2/5/15.
	,,	Kenneth Mackenzie	Killed, May 1915.
	,,	Alexander Angus	Wounded, April 1915.
	,,	Robert Rennie	Killed, May 1915.
	,,	Alexander Clark,	Killed, May 1915.
10670	,,	Alexander MacIntosh	Wounded, August 1914; prisoner of war.
10457	Lance Sgt.	James Stewart	Transferred from 1st Batt.; wounded, 1/7/16, Maillet (Somme); killed, 1917.
7635	Lance Cpl.	A. Ross	
8666	Corpl.	W. Lowlands	
7838	Piper	A. Calder	
9132	,,	N. Johnstone	Wounded, 25/4/15; killed, 26/1/17.
4255	,,	J. Robertson	Wounded, Nov. 1916.
10169	,,	J. Tulloch	Wounded, 20/11/14.
189	,,	A. Stein	
24729	,,	J. Murdoch	
	,,	A. Milne	
21630	,,	D. Macleod	
7366	,,	D. Macleod	
	,,	N. Maclean	
7126	,,	W. Maclean	
7603	,,	J. Mackay	
7206	Lance Cpl.	M. Maclean	
2886	Piper	G. Bell	Gassed, April 1915.
8134	,,	J. Grant	Wounded, April 1915 and August 1917.
204612	,,	P. Lamont	
9607	,,	J. Macarthur	Wounded, April 1917.

4th Battalion

In the early part of the war pipers were employed as such, and in many other capacities. Casualties, however, were exceedingly heavy, and it was decided in the later stages to keep them out of action as much as possible. Five pipers were killed and sixteen wounded.

REG. NO.	RANK.	NAME.	RECORD.
	Pipe Major	Murdo Mackenzie	Discharged, 1918.
	,,	John M'Kenzie	Wounded, Neuve Chapelle.
	Piper	D. M'Kenzie	Died of wounds in Germany.

REG. NO.	RANK.	NAME.	RECORD.
	Piper	J. KEMP	Died of wounds at Neuve Chapelle, 1915.
	,,	A. M'AULAY	Died of wounds at Valenciennes, 1918.
	,,	J. M'KENZIE	Died of wounds at Neuve Chapelle, 1915.
	,,	J. M'DONALD	Wounded at Cambrai, 1917; discharged.
	,,	A. J. M'KENZIE	Wounded at NeuveChapelle, 1915; discharged.
201307	,,	P. STEWART, M.M.	Wounded at Cambrai, 1917; discharged.
	,,	J. STEWART	Wounded at Marne, 1918.
	,,	W. M'KENZIE	Discharged, 1916.
	,,	M. SANDISON	Wounded at Cambrai, 1917.
	,,	H. FORBES	Wounded and gassed at Arras, 1918.
	,,	J. URQUHART	Wounded at Cambrai, 1918; discharged.
	,,	W. MARSHALL	Wounded and gassed at Cambrai, 1917.
	,,	D. M'RAE	Discharged.
	Lance-Sgt.	D. THOMSON	Invalided home.
	,,	F. FINDLAYSON	Invalided home.
	Piper	J. M'DONALD	Wounded at Aubers Ridge, 1915.
	,,	A. M'LENNAN	Killed at Neuve Chapelle, 1915.
	,,	W. ROSS	Transferred to Home Service.
	,,	H. ROSS	Transferred to Home Service.
	,,	H. M'LENNAN	Wounded at Aubers Ridge, 1915.
	,,	D. WILLIAMSON	Wounded and gassed, Arras and Cambrai.
	,,	W. M'DONALD	
	,,	W. CORBET	Wounded at Aubers Ridge, 1915.
	,,	W. M'LEOD	Wounded at Neuve Chapelle, 1915, and discharged.
	,,	H. R. M'KENZIE	Wounded.
	,,	R. HIGGINS	Invalided, 1918.
	,,	J. M'DONALD	Discharged.
	,,	J. M'LENNAN	
	,,	N. ROSS	Discharged.
	,,	J. ROSS	Wounded at Cambrai.
	,,	E. LEAMAN	Wounded at Cambrai.
	L/C. Piper	W. GRAY	
	Piper	J. M'KENZIE	
	,,	J. GUMM	
	,,	M. SANDISON	

REG. NO.	RANK.	NAME.	RECORD.
	Piper	W. Marshall	
	,,	J. A. Aird	
	,,	H. Forbes	
	,,	A. M'Leod	
	,,	J. Baird	
	,,	D. M'Millan	
	,,	W. Richardson	

5th Battalion

Pipers in action were employed as orderlies, despatch runners, etc.

REG. NO.	RANK.	NAME.	RECORD.
2026	Pipe Major	J. Sutherland	
	,,	A. Harley	Invalided.
97	,,	W. Grant	
422	,,	G. Ross	Killed, 21/7/15, Fauquissart.
41186	Corporal	H. Gammack	
450	Piper	A. M'Leod	
214	,,	W. Trussler	
240082	,,	R. M'Kay	
240578	,,	G. Stewart	
379	,,	R. M'Kenzie, M.M.	Wounded; Military Medal.
599	,,	Donald Mackay	Killed, 13/11/16, Beaumont Hamel.
242179	,,	D. MacInnes	
144	,,	H. Grant	
240137	,,	D. A. Matheson	Wounded.
426	,,	C. Rae	
8971	,,	A. Mackay	
560	,,	R. Mackay	
242212	,,	G. Urquhart	
2266	,,	W. S. Coghill	
3023	,,	A. Keith	
2392	,,	R. Stephen	
24227	,,	J. MacDonald	
2729	,,	A. Taylor	
251	,,	R. Ross	Killed, 21/7/15, Fauquissart.
242094	,,	D. Mackenzie	
669	,,	M. Murray	Wounded.
26	,,	R. Trussler	
25209	,,	J. Munro	
267336	,,	Jas. Sutherland	Transferred to 6th Seaforths; killed, 19/4/17.
42195	,,	D. Morrison	
24284	,,	J. Cullen	

6th Battalion

At Festubert, June 1915, the pipers did magnificent service as bearers, working day and night, and bringing in 170 wounded men. They were largely employed in the ranks as machine gunners. The casualties among them were heavy—8 killed and 6 wounded.

REG. NO.	RANK.	NAME.	RECORD.
	Pipe Major	G. Milton	
	Sergt.	W. MacLeod	Killed, May 1916, Labyrinth.
	,,	C. D. Macdonald	Killed, Beaumont Hamel, 13/11/16.
	,,	H. Mackie	Killed, Beaumont Hamel, 13/11/16.
	,,	J. Brown, M.M.	Killed, Arras, May 1917.
	,,	G. Gilbert, D.C.M.	Wounded, Beaumont Hamel, 13/11/16.
	Corpl.	W. Urquhart	
	Piper	J. Alexander	Killed, La Bassée, April 1918.
	,,	J. Bowie	
	,,	L. Cumming	
	,,	G. Fraser	
	,,	J. Gibb	
	,,	J. Grant	
	,,	G. M. Grant	
	,,	D. Grant	
	,,	D. Geddie	Invalided.
	,,	J. Logie	
265172	,,	W. Logie	Wounded, 9/4/17, Roclincourt.
	,,	J. Lumsden, M.M	Wounded, High Wood, July 1916.
	,,	A. Jenkins	Invalided.
	,,	A. Mitchell	
	,,	W. D. Mill	
	,,	A. Mackay	Killed, 9/4/17, Roclincourt.
	,,	W. Mackay	Wounded, Cambrai, Nov. 1917.
	,,	H. Mackenzie	
	,,	W. Macdonald	
	,,	J. Macdonald	Wounded, 9/4/17, Roclincourt.
	,,	W. Mackay	Invalided.
	,,	A. Paterson	Invalided.
	,,	J. Robertson	Killed, July 1915.
	,,	G. Rose	Wounded, Beaumont Hamel, 13/11/16.
	,,	W. Shervan	
	,,	W. Sutherland	Killed, 9/4/17, Roclincourt.
	,,	A. Thomson	

PIPE-MAJOR HOWARTH, D.C.M., 6TH GORDON HIGHLANDERS
AT NEUVE CHAPELLE

From the Painting by J. Prinsep Beadle

7TH BATTALION

At Loos the battalion was played to the attack, and had 5 pipers killed and 3 wounded. At one time, when the position was very serious, a piper rallied the men with "Cabar Feidh," and produced a tremendous effect. On the Somme, in 1916, a piper was always on duty with the battalion. At Arras, in 1917, the pipers acted as bearers, but in later operations they were kept out of the front line as far as possible.

REG. NO.	RANK.	NAME.	RECORD.
5111	Pipe Major	W. TAYLOR	Awarded Croix de Guerre and Meritorious Service Medal.
1536	,,	A. HARLEY	Invalided.
1689	Sergt.	W. FRASER, M.M.	Military Medal.
7765	,,	W. GORDON	Wounded, Loos, 25/9/15.
8822	Corpl.	T. JOHNSTON	Received Commission in Camerons.
711	Lance Cpl.	A. URQUHART	
40417	,,	O'KAIN MACLENNAN	Killed, 11/4/17.
6876	,,	M. M'LEAN	
8134	,,	J. GRANT	Wounded, 12/10/17.
13385	Piper	P. CALDER	
6892	,,	W. COOPER	
8535	,,	D. DAVIDSON, D.C.M., M.M.	D.C.M. and Military Medal; promoted Sergt. in his Coy.
21629	,,	T. EATON	
1456	,,	D. FRASER	Killed, Loos, 25/9/15.
40177	,,	R. FRASER	
4272	,,	W. GALBRAITH	Wounded, Loos, and again Arras, 9/4/17.
4181	,,	R. GALBRAITH	Killed, Loos, 25/9/15.
9070	,,	G. GRANT	Died in hospital.
2177	,,	B. HALLIDAY	Died of wounds received at Loos.
4661	,,	B. HAMILTON	Killed, Loos, 25/9/15.
9859	,,	J. HINTON	
10859	,,	A. J. MACKAY	
9488	,,	J. MACKAY	
570	,,	A. MACKENZIE	Wounded, 10/4/15, Messines; gassed, 23/6/18.
1487	,,	R. MACKENZIE, M.M.	Wounded, 12/3/18; Military Medal.
7366	,,	D. MACLEOD	Invalided.
201819	,,	M. MONTGOMERY	
12597	,,	M. MURRAY	
201991	,,	R. MURRAY	
825	,,	G. THOMSON	Wounded, Messines, 10/4/15.
3843	,,	K. THYNE	Killed, Somme, 14/7/16.

8th Battalion

There were heavy casualties at Loos, September 1915, when 5 pipers were killed and 5 were wounded; on this occasion the gallantry of these men won the wholehearted admiration of all ranks. The companies were played into action by the pipers.

REG. NO.	RANK.	NAME.	RECORD.
8112	Pipe Major	Alex. Mackenzie, D.C.M.	D.C.M.
	,,	John Haywood	
8119	Sergt.	George Gordon	Transferred 9th Seaforths as Pipe Major; Belgian Croix de Guerre.
8172	Lance Cpl.	John Munro	
3161	Piper	Andrew Hamilton	Wounded, Loos, 25/9/15.
5721	,,	Charles Anderson	Killed, Loos, 25/9/15.
6368	,,	Robert Clark	Wounded, Loos, 25/9/15, and taken prisoner.
	,,	Andrew Clark	Killed, Loos, 28/9/18.
7519	,,	John Matheson	
6567	,,	George Spence	Killed, Loos, 25/9/15.
3503	,,	James Cairns	Wounded, Loos, 25/9/15.
2897	,,	Robert Robertson	Wounded, Loos, 25/9/15, and taken prisoner.
2583	,,	James Morton	
	,,	Alexander Mackay	Wounded, Ypres, 31/7/17.
6400	,,	William Mackay	Killed, Loos, 25/9/15.
	,,	Robert Beaton	
6546	Lance Cpl.	Duncan MacGregor	Killed, Loos, 25/9/15.
3307	Piper	Donald Valantine	Wounded, Loos, 25/9/15.
	,,	Hugh Sutherland	Died of disease, 1917.
	Corpl.	R. Currant	
	Piper	James Harvey	Wounded, Arras, 21/2/18.
	,,	Alexander MacAulay	
25812	,,	Alexander MacDonald	
25825	,,	Alexander MacDonald	
	,,	Malcolm Mackenzie	
	,,	Robert Mackenzie	
	,,	Donald MacLeod	
	,,	George Macmillan	
	,,	James Matheson	
	,,	James Morton	
	,,	Robert Robertson	
	,,	Alexander Simpson	
	,,	George Spence	

REG. NO.	RANK.	NAME.	RECORD.
	Piper	P. Stewart	
	,,	Henry Sutherland	
	,,	J. Tait	
	Lieut.	Hector Ross	Formerly Piper 6th S.H.; killed, 23/4/17.

9th Battalion

Pipers were frequently employed as despatch runners. In the advance of the 26th Brigade at Longueval on 14th July, 1916, the battalion was played into action under very heavy fire. When attacking the village they met with a stout resistance and came under heavy machine gun fire from a flank as well as from the front. The pipers rallied the men who were thrown momentarily into confusion, and, at their head, charged down the street and over the wires into the German trenches.

The casualties were heavy throughout, 4 killed and 15 wounded.

REG. NO.	RANK.	NAME.	RECORD.
8119	Pipe Major	G. Gordon	Belgian Croix de Guerre.
4422	Lance Sgt.	D. M'Niven	
5745	Lance Cpl.	C. M'Lellan, M.M.	Military Medal, Loos, 1915.
261949	Piper	James Lumsden, M.M.	Wounded, Somme, 1916; Military Medal.
240018	,,	Robert Ross	Killed, 11/4/18.
267336	,,	James Sutherland	Killed, 19/4/17.
4394	,,	M. Ross	Wounded.
8264	,,	D. Mackenzie	Wounded.
4858	,,	J. Macdonald	Wounded.
5011	,,	A. Cheyne	
3949	,,	H. Arnott	Wounded.
9394	,,	W. M'Mahon	Killed.
4657	,,	W. Gray	Wounded.
5693	,,	D. Hunter	Wounded.
40497	,,	A. Mackenzie	
40502	,,	R. Watt	Wounded.
40547	,,	G. Davidson	
267049	,,	J. MacLeod	
13286	,,	J. Aitken	Wounded.
23879	,,	W. Duncan	Killed.
23889	,,	J. M'Lellan	Wounded.
26416	,,	P. Macdonald	
26426	,,	D. M'Kinnon	Wounded.

REG. NO.	RANK.	NAME.	RECORD.
5943	Piper	R. Lawson	Wounded and gassed.
24518	,,	A. Buchanan	
261313	,;	A. Mackenzie	
5570	,,	J. Barclay	Wounded three times.

THE GORDON HIGHLANDERS

1st Battalion

The battalion took out 18 pipers, and at the roll call at Cambrai on 26th August, 1914, only two remained. For a long time pipers had to be employed in the ranks. On several occasions in the Somme fighting they took their place at the head of their companies and played them into action.

REG. NO.	RANK.	NAME.	RECORD.
	Pipe Major	J. Henderson	
	Sergt.	J. Johnston	Wounded, 25/9/15.
	Piper	Geo. Cruickshank	Prisoner, Le Cateau, 26/8/14.
	,,	David Copland	Prisoner, Le Cateau, 26/8/14.
	,,	A. Thompson	Prisoner, Le Cateau, 26/8/14, but escaped and returned to duty; again captured, 24/10/14.
	,,	F. Paterson	Killed, Mons, 26/8/14.
	,,	J. Watt	Gone to 2nd Batt.
	Corpl.	F. Robertson	Prisoner, Le Cateau, 26/8/14.
	Lance Cpl.	W. M'Fall	Killed, October 1914.
	Piper	W. Fraser	Prisoner, Le Cateau, 26/8/14.
	,,	Geo. Mitchell	Prisoner, Le Cateau, 26/8/14.
	,,	Geo. Anderson	Prisoner, Le Cateau, 26/8/14.
	,,	N. Watt	
	,,	D. Weir	Prisoner, Le Cateau, 26/8/14.
	,,	P. Cran	Invalided.
	,,	F. Grant	Invalided.
	,,	P. Hair	Prisoner, Le Cateau, 26/8/14.
	,,	W. Cromarty	Wounded, 26/9/15.
	,,	W. Harvie	Killed, 24/10/141.
	Corpl.	A. Garden	
	Piper	A. M'Kay	Died of wounds, Jan. 1915.
	,,	W. Allan	Killed, 14/12/14.
	,,	J. Coutts	
	,,	W. Paton	
	,,	Eadie	

REG. NO.	RANK.	NAME.	RECORD.
	Piper	HAY	
	,,	M'KAY	Wounded.
	,,	GILLIES	Wounded.
	,,	HECTOR ROSS	Wounded, Loos, 25/9/15; killed, March, 1916.

2ND BATTALION

This battalion took 32 pipers out to France; by the end of the first year of the campaign 10 had been killed and 20 wounded. At Loos and in the Somme fighting the pipers of the 2nd Gordons repeatedly played the battalion into action and suffered heavily. The pipers were also employed as runners, bearers, etc., and in the ranks.

In March 1915, the battalion was played to the attack on the Aubers Ridge under heavy fire, and again at Mametz and Guichy.

In the Italian field of operations they did most excellent work in getting the wounded back across a swift river, work which their C.O. considered it would have been impossible to accomplish without their enthusiastic assistance.

REG. NO.	RANK.	NAME.	RECORD.
6349	Pipe Major	C. ANDERSON	Wounded; Military Medal, Loos, 1915.
10655	Piper	R. GRANT	Killed, Loos, 1915.
10639	,,	J. GRANT	Killed, Loos, 25/9/15.
110	,,	R. WILSON	Killed, Loos, 25/9/15.
219	,,	W. BRUCE	Killed, Loos, 25/9/15.
10653	Corpl.	J. M'KENZIE	Killed, Loos, 25/9/15.
205	Piper	J. LEDINGHAM	Killed, Loos, 25/9/15.
	,,	J. RAMAGE	Killed, Loos, 25/9/15.
	,,	A. CASSIE	Killed, Loos, 25/9/15.
	,,	J. BISSETT	Killed, Loos, 25/9/15.
10296	,,	W. SINCLAIR	Died of wounds, Loos, 25/9/15.
311	Lance Cpl.	A. M'DONALD	Wounded, Ypres, 1/11/14; invalided.
10113	Piper	J. GILLIES	Wounded, Ypres, 30/10/14.
175	Lance Cpl.	J. LIVINGSTONE	Wounded; prisoner of war, 30/10/14.
10243	Piper	J. MURRAY	Wounded, Ypres, 30/10/14.
8699	,,	C. MUNRO	Despatches; wounded, Loos, 1915.
349	,,	J. CRUICKSHANKS	Wounded, Neuve Chapelle, 1915.
10219	,,	J. TOPP	Wounded, Ypres, 30/10/14.

REG. NO.	RANK.	NAME.	RECORD.
297	Piper	J. Grant	Wounded and invalided.
120	,,	H. Adams	Wounded, Ypres, 1/11/14.
10072	,,	G. Tennent	Wounded, Ypres, 30/10/14.
233	,,	J. Watt	Wounded, Loos, 25/9/15.
7569	Sergt.	W. Smith	Wounded, Loos, 25/9/15.
606	Piper	A. Bruce	Wounded, Loos, 25/9/15.
192	,,	W. Hinnie	Wounded, Loos, 25/9/15.
429	,,	T. Macintosh	Wounded, Ypres, 1/11/14; invalided.
	,,	Fraser	Wounded; invalided.
543	,,	A. Holmes	Wounded, Ypres, 5/10/17.
10256	,,	B. M'Kay	Wounded, Ypres, 30/10/14.
430	,,	J. Robertson	Killed, Ypres, 30/10/14.
206	Lance Cpl.	J. Duguid	
6853	Sergt.	R. Stewart, D.C.M.	Killed, Loos, 1915; awarded D.C.M.
7641	Piper	J. M'Donald	
10486	,,	C. Taylor	Wounded, Somme, July 1916.
5614	,,	James Ritchie, M.M.	Military Medal, Somme.
7375	Corpl.	A. Smith	Killed, Loos, 1915.
8390	Piper	J. Scott	Killed, Somme, 1916.
335	,,	J. M'Crimmon	Wounded, Ypres, 1914; killed, Loos, 1915.
10139	,,	D. White	Killed, Loos, 1915.
747	,,	J. Lorimer	Wounded, Somme, 1916.
6994	Sergt.	A. Horne	Invalided.
7288	Piper	C. Orchard	
5495	,,	J. White	
10264	,,	D. Bowie	
7383	,,	P. Brown	Killed, Ypres, 5/10/17.
235745	,,	R. Innes	
240455	,,	J. Gow	
43479	,,	J. Graham	
2595	,,	D. Williams	

4th Battalion

During the trench fighting the pipers were mostly used behind the front line, and in marching the battalion to and from rest billets. Subsequently, in open fighting, the company pipers took their place at the heads of their companies. At the Marne, Pipers P. Paterson, R. Prentice, P. Bowie and G. Davidson played their companies into action, and their action immensely stimulated the troops "and enabled them to gain a great victory on that day"; at Ypres on 31st July, 1917, Piper P. Bowie "rallied the men at a time when fighting was very fierce," and was awarded the Military

Medal; on 17th November, 1917, Piper G. Paterson also got the Military Medal for playing the battalion through three successive charges and into Cantaing under heavy fire. The pipers were also employed as ammunition carriers.

REG. NO.	RANK.	NAME.	RECORD.
	Pipe Major	A. Chisholm	
201290	Piper	John Webster, M.M.	Military Medal.
	Lance-Cpl.	W. Cruickshank	
	Piper	T. Watson	Invalided.
200347	,,	G. Paterson, M.M.	Wounded; Military Medal.
	,,	N. Paterson	
	,,	W. M'Kay	Invalided.
	,,	E. Ewen	Wounded.
	,,	P. Paterson	Wounded.
	,,	D. Robbie	Wounded (twice).
	,,	G. Davidson	Gassed, Ypres, 31/10/17.
	,,	J. Wych	Prisoner.
	,,	C. Lawson	Prisoner.
	,,	J. Gray	
	,,	J. Gray	Wounded.
	,,	R. Sim	Wounded.
	,,	P. Bowie, M.M.	Military Medal.
	,,	E. Mather	
	,,	R. Prentice	
	,,	J. Oswald	
	,,	F. Wright	
	,,	J. Foote	
	,,	A. Thomson	Killed.

5th Battalion

The pipers were principally employed in the ranks and as observers, but in the attack on High Wood on the Somme front company pipers played at the head of their units. On this occasion Piper Willox was killed as he led his company, and several others became casualties. It was thereafter decided not to employ pipers in action again.

REG. NO.	RANK.	NAME.	RECORD.
302	Pipe Major	J. H. Clark	
1596	Cpl.-Piper	J. Harvey	
760	Piper	A. Stewart	
1985	,,	G. Thomson	
1586	,,	A. Willox	Killed, 31/7/16, High Wood.

REG. NO.	RANK.	NAME.	RECORD.
1156	Piper	W. GRAHAM	Killed, 3/6/15, Festubert.
	,,	W. ALLAN	
	,,	J. BIRNIE	
	,,	H. LUNAN	
	,,	J. M'DONALD	
	,,	G. MIDDLETON	Wounded, Bullecourt.
	,,	A. ROBINSON	
	,,	J. A. SCOTT	
	,,	J. STEWART	
	,,	R. WYNESS	
	,,	ANDREW BROWN, M.M.	Military Medal; killed, 31/7/16, High Wood.
	,,	G. LINDSAY	Wounded, Sept. 1917, Ypres.

6TH BATTALION

At Neuve Chapelle the pipers headed the charge of the battalion on the Moulin du Piètre, losing one piper killed and four wounded.

Pipers were mostly employed in action as stretcher bearers or in the ranks, and, while suffering heavily, won the highest reputation in their battalion. At Neuve Chapelle in March 1915 they lost one killed and six wounded; on this occasion Pipe Major Howarth won the D.C.M. At Loos in the following September, the casualties were again heavy, and the pipe major won a bar to the D.C.M. In later operations pipers were kept, as much as possible, out of the front line.

REG. NO.	RANK.	NAME.	RECORD.
10115	Pipe Major	J. HOWARTH, D.C.M. and Bar	Wounded, Loos, 25/9/15.
161	Corpl.	G. LOGIE	Wounded, Neuve Chapelle, 25/3/15.
728	Piper	A. SMITH	Wounded, Neuve Chapelle, 25/3/15.
62	,,	G. MILTON	Killed, Neuve Chapelle, 25/3/15.
1257	Lance-Cpl.	G. M'PHERSON	
104	Piper	A. COUTTS	Wounded, Neuve Chapelle, 25/3/15.
117	,,	G. GRANT	Wounded, Neuve Chapelle, 25/3/15.
10604	,,	A. MILNE	
967	Lance-Cpl.	J. BIRNIE	
10700	Piper	W. BANNERMAN	
806	,,	R. SCOTT	
961	,,	J. BIRNIE	
1561	,,	R. M'CAY	Wounded, Festubert.
	,,	H. DAVIDSON	Wounded, Loos, 25/9/15.
	Lance-Cpl.	T. KNOWLES	

8th Battalion

REG. NO.	RANK.	NAME.	RECORD.
	Pipe Major	W. J. Grant	Wounded.
	Corpl.	G. Flockhart	

9th Battalion

The great value of the pipers in action is recognised by the whole battalion, but it is considered it sometimes happens that the men get so overkeen under the influence of the music that they are liable to exceed orders. The employment of pipers as bearers, etc., is deprecated as resulting in casualties which cannot be replaced.

REG. NO.	RANK.	NAME.	RECORD.
	Pipe Major	K. MacLeod	Invalided, Dec. 1914.
S/7747	,,	G. Findlater, V.C.	Invalided, Dec. 1915.
S/4212	,,	D. MacLeod	
S/6827	Piper	A. M'Donald	
S/2772	,,	M. Murray	
S/9023	,,	C. Campbell	Killed in action, Somme, 10/7/16.
S/3068	,,	T. Turner	Invalided.
S/4057	,,	J. Miller	
S/4058	,,	H. Heeps	
S/4560	,,	J. Craig	Wounded, Somme, 1916.
S/9364	,,	J. Aitken	
348	,,	J. M'Donald	Wounded Neuve Chapelle, 1915; Loos, 25/9/15; Somme, 1/7/16.
560	,,	W. Watt	Wounded, Ypres, 1914.
S/17640	,,	H. MacLachlan	
9283	Lance-Cpl.	H. Adams	Wounded, Ypres, 1914.
S/3052	Pte.	J. Sharkey	

10th Battalion

REG. NO.	RANK.	NAME.	RECORD.
	Pipe Major	Horne	
	Corpl.	Orchard	Wounded.
5614	Piper	James Ritchie, M.M.	Transferred to 2nd Gordons; Military Medal.

THE QUEEN'S OWN CAMERON HIGHLANDERS

"A chlanna nan con
A chlanna nan con
Thigibh an so
S'ghaibh sibh feoil.'

1st Battalion

Pipers were not employed as such, but, during the early part of the war, they were in the ranks. At the battle of the Aisne and Ypres the casualties were heavy.

The value to the battalion of their pipe band is considered so great that the officers would like the establishment doubled.

REG. NO.	RANK.	NAME.	RECORD.
6720	Piper Major	G. Selby	Killed, 22/10/14.
6718	,,	W. Cruickshanks	
5210	Corpl.	W. Kinnear	Wounded, 5/11/14, Ypres.
5173	Piper	H. Barrie	Killed, 5/11/14, Ypres.
8445	,,	C. Maclachlan	
7671	,,	A. Henderson, D.C.M.	Taken prisoner, 11/11/14; D.C.M.
8535	Lance-Cpl.	G. M'Calman	Wounded, Langemarck, Oct. 1914; died after discharge.
8072	Piper	D. Ross	
8475	,,	M. Campbell	Wounded, Aisne, 14/9/14.
9575	,,	L. Johnstone	Wounded, Aisne, 14/9/14.
6726	,,	D. Cook	Wounded, Aisne, 14/9/14.
9345	,,	L. M'Bean	Died of wounds, Arras, Aug. 1918.
9444	,,	J. Coyle	Wounded, Aisne, 25/8/14.
14059	,,	J. Peders	
18921	,,	N. Ross	
5859	,,	A. Macdonald	
30748	,,	N. Smith	

2nd Battalion

There were heavy casualties among the pipers, who were employed in many ways throughout the war,—largely in the ranks. One, Lance-Corporal Johnstone, was awarded the D.C.M. and M.M. for his gallantry as a guide in 1915 and subsequently as scout sergeant. Throughout the war the pipers went into action with their companies. The opinion of the commanding officer is that they have been invaluable to the battalion. At the time of the advance into Bulgaria sickness had caused the disappearance of the band.

Altogether 14 pipers were wounded and 7 died or were killed during the war.

REG. NO.	RANK.	NAME.	RECORD.
	Pipe Major	DOUGALL MATHESON	Wounded, 1915, and in 1916.
	,,	JOHN STEELE	Wounded, 15/2/15.
	Sergt.	JAMES JOHNSON, D.C.M., M.M.	Wounded, 1918.
	Corpl.	ALEX. M'LEOD	
	,,	ALEX. THOMSON	
8479	Piper	DONALD DYCE	Wounded, Salonika, 30/9/16.
	Lance-Cpl.	ARCHIBALD ROBERTSON	
	Piper	WILLIAM BORTHWICK	
	,,	PETER EASSON	Wounded, 1915, Ypres.
	,,	JOSEPH ELLIOT	Wounded, 1916.
	,,	DONNACHIE	Killed, 1915.
	,,	ARCHIBALD FULTON	Prisoner of war, 1915; invalided.
	Lance-Cpl.	JAMES GILLON	Wounded, 10/5/15, St. Eloi.
	Piper	KEEBLE	Wounded.
	,,	JOHN LUMSDEN	Wounded, Struma, 1/10/16.
	,,	JAMES M'DOUGALL	Wounded, Hill 60; invalided.
	,,	JOHN M'CABE	Died, 1917.
	,,	DONALD M'RAE	
	,,	JOHN M'ASKILL	Killed, Hill 60, April 1916.
	,,	THOMPSON	Died.
	,,	ALEXANDER THOMPSON	Invalided.
	,,	WILLIAM HOPE	Wounded, Ypres, 1918.
	,,	HUGH CONNER	Wounded, 30/9/16, St. Eloi; invalided.
	,,	DONALD CAMPBELL	Wounded, 10/5/15, St. Eloi.
	,,	ARCHIBALD M'KENZIE	Killed, Hill 60, April 1916.
	,,	MURDOCH SCOTT	Wounded, Aug. 1915.
	,,	LACHLAN M'BEAN	Died of wounds, St. Eloi, 10/5/15.
	,,	MURDOCH SCOTT	Wounded, Aug. 1915.
	,,	ARCHIBALD LINDSAY	
	,,	ROBERT FERGUSON	Invalided.
	,,	WILLIAM STEWART	Died, Salonika, 18/10/17.
	,,	JOHN SMART	
	,,	JAMES CARSWELL	
	,,	ARCHIBALD SMITH	

4th Battalion

At Festubert on 17th May, 1915, the companies were played to the attack by their pipers, and these men came through unscathed but with their pipes rendered useless by mud and water. Of those who were serving in the ranks several were killed and wounded at Festubert.

Again at Loos the pipers were employed in action as such.

They were often employed as bearers. The battalion was disbanded as a separate unit.

REG. NO.	RANK.	NAME.	RECORD.
56	Pipe Major	J. S. Ross	
275	Lance Cpl.	J. Shirran	Wounded, Fanquinart, 9/5/15.
1090	Piper	A. Fullarton	
44	"	W. Fraser	Wounded.
519	"	R. Munro	
988	"	C. Milne	
528	Lance Cpl.	G. Forsyth	
53	Piper	K. Logan	Wounded.
1395	"	W. F. Macdonald	Wounded, Richebourg, 17/7/15.
1120	"	J. Cheyne	Killed, Festubert, 17/5/15.
1100	"	J. Munro	
645	Lance Cpl.	D. Paterson	Killed, Festubert, 17/5/15.
2670	"	T. D. Mackay	Wounded, Neuve Chapelle, 12/3/15.
200120	Piper	W. Macdonald	Died of wounds, 14/10/17.
	"	W. Maclean	Transferred as Pipe Major to 5th Camerons.

5th Battalion

At Loos the battalion was played into action, and practically all the pipers became casualties. Subsequently they were employed as bearers.

REG. NO.	RANK.	NAME.	RECORD.
4424	Pipe Major	A. Beattie	(Now Quartermaster.)
	"	John Macmillan	
	"	William Maclean	
3/5497	Piper	Alex. MacEachen	Died of wounds received 25/9/15.
3/5113	Lance Cpl.	A. J. M'Donald	Killed at Fosse 8, 27/9/15.
3/5096	"	Donald M'Lean	Wounded, Festubert, 1915.
3/5059	Piper	Alexander Boyd	
S/14504	"	Donald M'Intyre	
3/3931	"	Neil Wilson	Killed, 27/9/15.

REG. NO.	RANK.	NAME.	RECORD.
S/11755	Piper	James Butler	Wounded, 27/9/15; Loos, and again subsequently.
3/5636	,,	J. A. Macaskill	
3/3541	,,	Angus M'Donald	Wounded, 27/9/15, Loos.
3/5621	,,	Alex. M'Lennan	Wounded, 27/9/15, Loos.
S/10510	,,	John M'Lachlan	Wounded, 27/9/15, Loos; killed, Sorel, 21/3/18.
S/10311	,,	J. M'Gregor	Invalided.
S/12582	,,	Angus M'Pherson	Gassed, 25/9/15, Loos.
S/11605	,,	John Ross	Wounded, 25/9/15, Loos.
S/10026	,,	Joseph Scott	Wounded, 25/9/15, Loos.
	,,	Donald MacPhee	
	Corpl.	Donald Campbell	
	Piper	William Strachan	Invalided.
	,,	Angus Robertson	
	,,	Malcolm MacGregor	
	,,	Alex. Clunie	Killed, 3/5/17, Arras.
	,,	James Henderson	
	,,	Lachlan Maclean	
	,,	James Macdonald	Invalided.
	,,	Duncan MacLennan	
	,,	Archibald Crawford	Killed, Sorel, 21/3/18.
	,,	John MacLennan	
	,,	Donald MacLennan	
	,,	D. Bowes	
	,,	T. Fyffe	Invalided.
	,,	C. Grant	Invalided.
	,,	Allan Cameron	Invalided.
	,,	Charles Milne	
	,,	John Stavert	
	,,	Norman M'Killop	
	,,	James Porteous	Killed, Oct. 1918.
	,,	James Innes	
	,,	Finlay Martin	
	,,	James Ferguson	
	,,	James Richard	

6th Battalion

During trench fighting the pipers were employed behind the line. In the Loos attack, when they played the battalion into action, there were many casualties. On this occasion, when the 44th Brigade had to fall back, the men rallied on an extemporised flag of Cameron tartan at the foot of which stood the pipers of several battalions.

REG. NO.	RANK.	NAME.	RECORD.
5161	Pipe Major	A. Mathieson Macdonald	Gassed, 25/9/15.
12643	Lance Cpl.	William Fraser	Wounded, Loos, 25/9/15.
11347	Piper	William Whitehead	
12629	,,	Thomas MacCulloch	
10101	,,	Dugald Dow	Gassed, Loos, 25/9/15.
10210	,,	James Pitcairn	
10297	,,	Wilfred Morris	
12070	,,	J. Leckie MacLean	
14831	,,	David Roy Robertson	
27434	Sergt.	Campbell	From 1st Lovat's Scouts.
43268	Lance Cpl.	M'Neill	From 2/4th Cameron Highlanders.
10256	,,	M'Ready	Wounded, Somme, Oct. 1916.
40971	Piper	MacLennan	From 2/4th Cameron Highlanders.
43267	,,	MacNeil	From 2/4th Cameron Highlanders ; wounded, Oct. 1916.
43318	,,	Johnstone	From 2/4th Cameron Highlanders.
40715	,,	MacCormick	
43311	,,	M. M'Lennan	From 2/4th Cameron Highlanders.
22461	,,	James Walker	Killed, 26/4/17.

7th Battalion

In the historic attack at Loos the pipers took a prominent part, and helped to rally the men subsequently. They lost heavily, and in subsequent actions pipers were only employed singly in the attack.

REG. NO.	RANK.	NAME.	RECORD.
13845	Pipe Major	R. Macdougall	
	Piper	J. Maclean	Wounded, Loos.
14356	,,	J. Raeburn	Wounded, Loos, 25-27/9/15.
13291	,,	Dugald Scoular	
14059	,,	Peden	
	Corpl.	Ross	
	,,	R. M. Dewar	Gassed.
	Lance Cpl.	J. Levack	
200104	,,	H. R. Munro	
	Piper	G. Alves	Killed, Loos, 25/9/15.
21487	,,	G. Cowie	Wounded, Loos, 25/9/15.
9444	,,	J. Coyle	Wounded, Loos, 25/9/15.
	,,	A. Duncan	
	,,	J. Findlay	
	,,	T. Fraser	Gassed
14055	,,	W. Henderson	Wounded, Loos, 25/9/15.
200252	,,	J. Hunter	

REG. NO.	RANK.	NAME.	RECORD.
201253	Piper	A. M'Donald	
5545	,,	J. M'Donald	
	,,	J. M'Intosh	Wounded, Loos, 25/9/15.
13294	,,	R. M'Kenzie	
	,,	M. M'Killop	Invalided.
	,,	M. Mackinnon	
43209	,,	J. Munro	
13442	,,	A. Shand	
	,,	A. Smart	Killed, Loos, 25/9/15.
	,,	F. Stewart	Wounded, Loos 25/9/15.
14369	,,	W. Williamson	

THE ARGYLL AND SUTHERLAND HIGHLANDERS

1st Battalion

Early in the war pipers were used in action, but, on account of casualties being very heavy among them, the practice was given up.

REG. NO.	RANK.	NAME.	RECORD.
	Pipe Major	R. Macfarlane	
	Piper	M'Kay	Wounded.
	,,	Kenealy	Wounded.
	,,	Campbell	Wounded.
	,,	Woodside	Killed, St. Eloi, 16/2/15.
	Corpl.	F. Ross	
	Piper	W. M'Intosh	
	,,	C. Hay	
	,,	J. Beattie,	
	,,	W. Waddel	
	,,	Stevenson	
	,,	Lynch	
	Lance-Cpl.	Struthers	
	,,	Wilson	
	,,	Birrell	
	Piper	M'Fadyen	
	,,	Hanlison	
	,,	Bell	
	,,	Hardie	
	,,	M'Donald	

REG. NO.	RANK.	NAME.	RECORD.
	Piper	CAMPBELL	
	,,	FRASER	
570	,,	ROBERT KENNEDY	Killed, 30/7/16, Somme.

2ND BATTALION

During the first year of the war 3 pipers were killed, 3 were wounded and 3 were taken prisoner, and the band was broken up, the survivors being returned to the ranks. Throughout the war pipers have been employed as orderlies, ammunition and ration carriers.

REG. NO.	RANK.	NAME.	RECORD.
	Pipe Major	WILLIAM GRAY	
	,,	JOHN MACKINTOSH	
10719	,,	LAWRIE	
672	,,	JOHN GRAY	
8157	Piper	L. A. PLANNER	Killed, Oct. 1918.
	,,	ALEXANDER STEVEN	
188	,,	ALEXANDER SINCLAIR	
10313	,,	J. BLACK	
10295	Corpl.	J. P. M'DONALD	Invalided.
522	Piper	HENRY JONES	Invalided.
	Lance-Cpl.	MILNE	Missing.
567	Piper	PETER M'LINTOCK	Killed, Armentières, 27/11/15.
90	,,	M'KAY	Killed, Armentières, 27/11/15.
	,,	J. GARDNER	Wounded, Le Cateau, 26/8/14.
974	Lance-Cpl.	A. PATERSON	Wounded, Le Cateau, 26/8/14.
	Piper	PETER MURRAY	Wounded, Le Cateau, 26/8/14.
1153	Sergt.	P. DEAN, D.C.M.	D.C.M.
9901	Lance-Cpl.	A. MILLER	Prisoner of war; wounded, Le Cateau, 26/8/14.
660	Piper	R. SCOTT	Prisoner of war; wounded, Armentières, 27/11/15.
58	,,	S. DUFF	Prisoner of war; wounded, Le Cateau, 26/8/14.
9279	,,	ROBERT ORMISTON	Wounded, Somme, 13/7/16.
	,,	WILLIAM BLACK	
	,,	JOHN WATT	
	,,	DAVID BLAIR	
	,,	RICHARD ANSELL	Wounded, 19/11/15 and 21/6/15.
	,,	DONALD ANDERSON	
	,,	ALEXANDER M'DONALD	
	,,	JOHN MACCULLOCH	

BEN BUIDHE, ARGYLLSHIRE

From the Water-colour Drawing by George Houston, A.R.S.A.

REG. NO.	RANK.	NAME.	RECORD.
	Piper	Alexander Gray	
	,,	Gordon Innes	
	,,	Duncan Mackellar	

5th Battalion

When in Gallipoli the full pipers were chiefly employed as messengers and ammunition carriers. In the latter capacity they did excellent work in the fighting on 12th July, 1915. The acting pipers were employed as stretcher bearers. On the occasion of the 12th July attack a piper mounted the parapet and played the battalion over. The pipers have been kept out of action as far as possible.

REG. NO.	RANK.	NAME.	RECORD.
201471	Pipe Major	C. Hay	Wounded, 24/11/17.
	,,	Jas. Smith	
	Piper	Robert Smith	
	,,	Thomas Macdonald	
	,,	Robert Maclachlan	
200129	,,	James Blair	
200043	Lance-Cpl.	Fred Branwhite	
	Piper	Robert Macleod	Wounded, 25/12/15.
200300	Lance-Cpl.	Angus Macarthur	
300620	Piper	John Macleod	
200359	,,	James Murray	
	,,	Malcolm Stewart	
	,,	George Stirrat	
325764	,,	W. Hendry	Wounded, 29/7/18.
200325	,,	William Lepick	
201062	,,	J. M'Callum	
200357	,,	Donald Matheson	
202708	,,	William Matheson	
43040	,,	John Myles	
200780	,,	A. Neilson	
200855	,,	J. Oliver	
201925	,,	W. Ponton	

6th Battalion

While in the trenches were employed as orderlies, messengers, etc.

REG. NO.	RANK.	NAME.	RECORD.
362	Pipe Major	John M'Connacher	Transferred as C.Q.M.S.
275321	,,	D. Finlayson	
35	Corpl.	Andrew Ferguson	

REG. NO.	RANK.	NAME.	RECORD.
538	Lance-Cpl.	Thomas Dournie	Wounded, Richebourg, May 1915.
1704	Piper	William Henderson	
1365	,,	Robert M'Aulay	Gassed, 25/4/18.
1560	,,	David Gault	
1507	,,	Henry Murray	
1506	,,	William Park	Wounded, Festubert, 18/6/15.
1890	,,	John Craig	Killed, Longueval, 27/7/16.
3037	,,	James Pringle	Killed while trying to bring in wounded man, 18/6/15.
3042	,,	John M'Allister	Killed, Festubert, 18/6/15.
1653	,,	James Gillan	Invalided.
3256	,,	John M'Farlane	
3162	,,	William Carlyle	Killed, Festubert, 16/6/15; despatches.
3166	,,	William Ganson	
	,,	Thomas Myron	
250989	,,	A. M'Lintock	Wounded, 23/11/18.
250962	,,	H. Armstrong	
8016	Lance-Cpl.	J. Stewart	
251957	Piper	A. M'Askill	
202120	,,	N. Campbell	
252567	,,	F. M'Pherson	
250018	,,	W. Corsan	
252028	,,	J. Lang	
300099	,,	N. Crawford	
250919	,,	A. Gray	
325262	,,	M. Thomson	

7th Battalion

Pipers were employed as runners and orderlies.

REG. NO.	RANK.	NAME.	RECORD.
	Piper	John Walls, M.M.	Military Medal, 24/7/16.
277167	,,	Hugh M'Donald	Killed, Aug. 1917, Ypres.

8th Battalion

Until the Somme fighting the pipers went into the trenches but did not play. The battalion had a pipe band composed of officers, Capt. Alastair M'Laren, Lieuts. Graham Campbell, Yr. of Shirvan, and Leslie Smith. The drummers were the Adjutant, Major Lockie, the Quartermaster Lieut. Disselduff and Lieut. Clark.

As far as possible pipers were kept out of the trenches.

REG. NO.	RANK.	NAME.	RECORD.
	Pipe Major	W. Lawrie	Invalided home, and died of illness contracted on service.
	,,	J. Wilson	Received Certificate from Div. Comdr. for gallant conduct, May 1916.
	Lance-Cpl.	C. Jeffrey	Wounded at Richebourg, May 1915.
	Piper	J. M'Lellan, D.C.M.	Awarded D.C. Medal for gallantry at Magersfontein, Dec. 1899; wounded at Laventie, 1915.
	,,	N. Crawford	Invalided, August 1916.
	,,	A. Currie	
	,,	R. Ferguson	Time expired.
	,,	F. Fraser	Wounded.
	,,	D. Ferguson	Invalided, 1917.
	,,	D. Johnstone	Invalided, 1915.
	,,	A. Lauder	
	,,	J. M'Callum	Wounded, Somme, July 1916.
	,,	J. M'Dougall	
	,,	J. M'Donald	
	,,	J. M'Farlane	Invalided, 1915.
	,,	J. M'Intyre	
	,,	R. M'Lellan, M.M.	Wounded, Somme, July 1916; awarded Military Medal.
	,,	J. Orr	Wounded, La Boiselle, August 1915.
	,,	J. Risk	Time expired.
	,,	J. Shirlaw	Gassed.
	,,	J. Woodrow	
	,,	N. Fletcher	
	,,	T. Strathearn	
	,,	R. Morrison	Wounded Ypres.
	,,	J. MacLeod	
	,,	D. Robertson	Invalided.
	,,	D. Woods	Wounded twice.
	,,	T. Shearer	Wounded.
	,,	D. MacInnes	Invalided.
	,,	J. MacWilliams	
	,,	T. Moffat	
	,,	J. Hannon	

9th Battalion

Pipers were principally utilised, when in action, as stretcher-bearers, orderlies, etc.

Great bravery was shown by pipers when acting as bearers.

REG. NO.	RANK.	NAME.	RECORD.
	Pipe Major	J. R. GARSEWELL	
324	Corpl.	ALEXANDER M'ALLISTER	Missing since 10/5/15; 2nd Battle Ypres.
1790	Piper	DAVID PANTON	Wounded, 10/5/15, Ypres.
266	,,	GEORGE SHEARER, D.C.M.	Awarded D.C.M.
1711	,,	ALEXANDER RUSSELL	Killed, 8/4/15.

10TH BATTALION

During the trench fighting the pipers were kept in the reserve lines in order to avoid casualties. At Loos and on the Somme, however, they were employed with their companies, and at the taking of Longueval they behaved with quite remarkable gallantry. On this occasion Pipe Major Aitken, a man of sixty years of age, was awarded the D.C.M., and Pipers Wilson and Dall were commended for playing through heavy machine gun fire. At the same time Piper Donnachie greatly distinguished himself carrying despatches.

The commanding officer says the casualties on the Somme have led him to keep them out of action as far as possible, as he regards them as invaluable to a regiment. It was, in the later stages, only under dire necessity, that pipers were occasionally used as bearers.

REG. NO.	RANK.	NAME.	RECORD.
	Pipe Major	T. AITKEN, D.C.M.	Superannuated; D.C.M.
	,,	J. WRIGHT	
9263	Lance-Sgt.	J. MACKENZIE	
1720	Corpl.	J. DONNACHIE	
	Piper	MACNEILL	Killed, Longueval, Oct. 1916.
	Corpl.	W. LAURIE	Wounded, Dickebusch; invalided.
8860	Lance-Cpl.	D. CAMPBELL	
569	,,	J. GAMACK, M.M.	Military Medal.
4512	Piper	W. ANDERSON	Invalided.
3205	,,	J. CULLEN	
9835	,,	J. HEATHERINGTON	Wounded, Loos, 25/9/15.
3014	,,	J. KENNEDY	
1375	,,	J. M'DONALD	Wounded, Longueval; invalided.
2011	,,	W. M'GILLIVRAY	
8656	,,	D. M'RAE	
6153	Lance-Sgt.	D. D. M'SPORRAN	Wounded, Longueval.
10390	Piper	J. SMITH	Wounded, Ypres, Nov. 1915.
9339	,,	W. PIRRIE	
2616	,,	D. WILSON	Despatches.
570	,,	R. KENNEDY	Died of wounds, Longueval.

REG. NO.	RANK.	NAME.	RECORD.
9256	Piper	A. M'Lean	Invalided.
6191	,,	J. Dall	Wounded, Longueval.
5091	,,	J. Paterson	Wounded, Loos, 25/9/15.
	Sergt.	J. F. Sword	
8051	,,	Alex. MacLeay	Killed, 12/10/17, Ypres.
300583	,,	John Sinclair	Severely wounded, Oct. 1917.
302955	Piper	Walter Napier	Killed, 12/10/17, Ypres.
	,,	William Sinclair	
	,,	John Clark	
	,,	Andrew Thomson	

11th Battalion

When the battalion was in support of the 44th Brigade at Loos the pipers took a very prominent share in the glory and the losses of the day. One, Charles Cameron, stood out in the open and played as a rallying point, and the battalion called him " The Piper of Loos." Other pipers were employed as runners, or in the ranks.

The casualties during this part of the campaign were so heavy that the pipe band was kept, as far as possible, out of the front line.

REG. NO.	RANK.	NAME.	RECORD.
	Pipe Major	Donald Macfarlane	Wounded, Loos, 25-27/9/15.
	Sergt.	James Ritchie	Killed, Loos, 26/9/15.
	,,	John M'Millan, D.C.M.	D.C.M., 25/9/15, Loos.
	Piper	Chas. Cameron	
	,,	Chas. Hoey	
	,,	J. Barnett	Killed on Hill 70.
	,,	T. Wallace	
	,,	A. Gillespie	
	,,	F. M'Diarmid	Wounded, July 1915 ; killed, July 1916.
	Corpl.	M. W. M'Callum	
	Piper	D. Wood	Wounded, May 1916.
	,,	D. Macpherson	Wounded.
	,,	F. Harper	Wounded, Somme.
	,,	J. Bennet	
	,,	A. M'Diarmid	
	,,	Hamilton	
	,,	Campbell	
	,,	Ferguson	Died Dec. 1916.
	,,	M'Kellar	
	Corpl.	J. Gray	

12TH BATTALION

Were often employed as runners. When the battalion was due to go into support the pipers were sent on to meet the companies and bring them in. The officers value the band so highly that they consider they should not be sent into the front line if it can possibly be avoided.

During actual offensive operations pipers were also employed as runners or on forward trench dumps, etc., and sometimes in the ranks.

Marches in Macedonia were often very arduous "and the pipers made an amazing difference on the men's spirits."

REG. NO.	RANK.	NAME.	RECORD.
4492	Pipe Major	J. DOUGLAS	
275286	,,	J. M'EWAN	Wounded.
598	Sergt.	R. STEVENSON, M.M.	Twice wounded ; Military Medal.
6829	Piper	JOHN M'COLL	Died of disease, Salonika, 16/2/17.
284	Corpl.	J. BEATTIE	Wounded.
	,,	W. STIRLING	Killed, Oct. 1916.
5660	,,	D. ROBERTSON	Killed, 8/5/17.
409	,,	W. M'KAY	
10138	Piper	D. WILSON, D.C.M.	D.C.M.
20022	,,	W. NORRIE	
203267	,,	W. PIRRIE	
4564	,,	M. CONNELLY	
5808	,,	A. DONNELLY	
4738	,,	F. HINTON	
6468	,,	J. TRAILL	
5388	,,	A. DAVIDSON	
5896	,,	J. LINTON	
14389	,,	D. KELLY	
5705	,,	M. HARPER	
279048	,,	T. PHILLIBAN	
	,,	T. HILL	
4927	,,	L. M'CON	Killed in action, 8/5/17.
5813	,,	A. STRATHEARN	
5706	,,	J. M'KERROW	

14TH BATTALION

Owing to their value to the battalion the pipers were not employed in the front line.

REG. NO.	RANK.	NAME.	RECORD.
	Pipe Major	Henry Forsyth	
	,,	Donald Cameron	
	Piper	Philip Melville	
	,,	William Adams	
	,,	David Dean	
	,,	William M'Donald	
	,,	John M'Donald	
	,,	David Gibson	
	,,	Joseph Thomson	
	,,	John Kennedy	
	,,	James M'Isaac	
	,,	Charles Burness	
	,,	Alex. M'Kenzie	
	,,	James M'Arthur	
	,,	David Blyth	
	,,	Alexander Yule	
	,,	William Corson	
	,,	William Campbell	
	,,	William Maxwell	
	,,	Duncan Grant	

THE LONDON SCOTTISH

1st Battalion

During the earlier part of the war the pipers served in the ranks and suffered heavy casualties. In the fighting at Messines on 31st October, 1914, and the subsequent operations at Zillebeke, 4 were killed and 2 were wounded, and of the original pipe band only one remained after six months. All these casualties occurred while the men were acting as observers. Several pipers were subsequently given commissions in other regiments.

Owing to the great difficulty of replacement every effort has been made, during the last two years of the war, to keep pipers out of the front line.

REG. NO.	RANK.	NAME.	RECORD.
	Pipe Major	K. Greig	Lt. Army Ordnance Dept.
142	Corpl.	J. Carey	Killed at Messines, 1/11/14, when acting as observer.
139	Lance-Cpl.	M. G. Latham	Despatches; killed at Zillebeke, while sniping, 16/11/14.
	Piper	Nicol	

REG. NO.	RANK.	NAME.	RECORD.
	Piper	R. PORTEOUS	Wounded at Messines, 31/10/14-1/11/14.
1145	,,	W. PORTEOUS	Wounded at Messines, 31/10/14-1/11/14.
1341	,,	D. PARKYN	Missing since Messines, 31/10/14-1/11/14.
	,,	C. W. D. MACKAY	Lieut. 5th Camerons; wounded and missing, 17/8/16.
1870	,,	J. F. BENNIE	Killed at Zillebeke, 9/11/14.
	,,	R. F. GORDON FORBES	Lieut. Army Ordnance Dept.
	,,	G. ORAM	
	,,	A. JOSS	
4167	,,	D. S. PINNINGTON	Wounded, Loos, 25/9/15.
	,,	J. HENDERSON	
	,,	A. SUTHERLAND-GRAEME	
	,,	W. GORDON	
3599	,,	A. A. CORNELL	Died of wounds, Somme, 2/10/16.
	,,	ROBERT MORRISON	Transferred to R.E.; got D.C.M. and Military Medal.
	,,	A. CAIRNS WILSON	Formerly piper; 2nd Lieut.; killed; Military Cross.
	,,	SIMON CAMPBELL	Killed, 13/5/17, Arras.
510531	,,	A. B. PATON	Killed, 13/5/17, Arras.
511874	,,	M. W. DAVIDSON	Wounded.
	,,	R. S. D. GRANT CRAWFORD	Transferred to A.O.D., Lieut.

2ND BATTALION

The pipers of this battalion have served in three theatres of war. They have played through Flanders and France, across the desert and in Palestine. They led the battalion into Jerusalem on 9th Dec., 1917, and thereafter on across the Jordan, through the hills of Gilead, and in Jericho, and Bethlehem. Again in Salonika and among the Macedonian hills they carried the music of the Highlands. In the desert difficulties were experienced with the reeds and with the drought; and the men often had to keep the bags going out of their own scanty ration of water.

From the nature of the operations against the Turks, in which surprise played so important a part, pipers had no opportunity of playing their companies into action. So invaluable were they in keeping the men up in the long desert marches that they were, as far as possible, reserved for that duty.

REG. NO.	RANK.	NAME.	RECORD.
	Pipe Major	D. C. Wills	Invalided.
510021	,,	J. A. M'Gilvray	
510013	Corpl.	C. Oram	
	Piper	C. W. Cummins	Invalided.
513953	,,	D. K. Pullar	
510759	,,	E. J. Horniblow	
	,,	M. Mills	
511170	,,	D. A. Matheson	
511450	,,	C. A. Stewart	
510264	,,	O. Machell-Varise	
513865	,,	J. W. Macmillan	
513650	,,	D. Hay	Invalided.
S/18941	,,	F. A. W. Gillies	
S/41114	,,	A. MacFadyen	
290381	,,	A. Ewen	

THE TYNESIDE SCOTTISH

1st Battalion

In the Somme fighting on 1st July, 1916, the battalion was played into action by its pipers and had 5 killed and 2 wounded; the survivors, Pipe Major John Wilson and Piper George Taylor, were awarded the Military Medal.

REG. NO.	RANK.	NAME.	RECORD.
290	Pipe Major	John Wilson, M.M.	Military Medal.
237	Lance-Cpl.	Garnet W. Fyfe	Killed, 1/7/16.
	Piper	Alex. Boyd	Wounded, 1/7/16.
223	,,	E. Boyce	Killed, ? 1/7/16.
	,,	E. Scott	Wounded, 1/7/16.
	,,	Stephens	Wounded, 1/7/16.
1585	,,	William Fellows	Missing.
154	,,	James Downie	Missing.
840	,,	Charles M'Lean	Wounded, 1/7/16.
1594	,,	Robert Davidson	Missing.
1485	,,	William Inglis	Wounded, 1/7/16.
1525	,,	George Taylor, M.M.	Military Medal.

2nd Battalion

On the same occasion this battalion was played into action by its pipers. 1525 Piper James Phillips was mentioned in despatches.

REG. NO.	RANK.	NAME.	RECORD.
1147	Pipe Major	MUNRO STRACHAN	
1149	Piper	JOHN STRACHAN	Wounded, 1/7/16.
1150	,,	ALEX. SCOTT	
1230	,,	WILLIE SCOTT	Killed, 1/7/16.
1188	Lance-Cpl.	W. CLARK	
558	Piper	G. C. GRIFFITHS	
1151	,,	JAMES PHILLIPS	Killed, 1/7/16.
1225	,,	J. M. PHILLIPS, M.M.	Military Medal.
1228	,,	JAMES CARNEGIE	Wounded, 28/6/16.

3RD BATTALION

On the same occasion this battalion was played into action, but the whole of the pipers were killed or wounded.

REG. NO.	RANK.	NAME.	RECORD.
	Piper	A. BOYD	Wounded, 1/7/16.
	,,	J. STEPHENS	Wounded, 1/7/16.
	,,	D. STEELE	Missing, 1/7/16.
	,,	E. FINLEY	Killed, 1/7/16.
	,,	R. GREAVES	Died of wounds, 1/7/16.
	,,	T. WILSON	Wounded and missing, 1/7/16.

THE MIDDLESEX REGIMENT

16TH BATTALION

This was the first English regiment to have a pipe band, the men being recruited for the purpose from Glasgow.

REG. NO.	RANK.	NAME.	RECORD.
1152	Pipe Major	CHARLES STEWART	
1149	Corpl.	THOMAS GIBSON	
1144	Piper	JOHN GRANT	
2530	,,	WILLIAM SLOAN	Wounded, Oct. 1916, Somme.
1145	,,	FRED CARRUTHERS	
1148	,,	NORMAN M'DONALD	
1350	,,	DUGALD M'FARLANE	
1154	,,	HENRY MITCHELSON	
1151	,,	THOMAS LATHAM	Killed, 1/7/16, Somme.
1930	,,	JAMES GILCHRIST	
1153	,,	JOHN KERR	

THE LIVERPOOL SCOTTISH

At Bois Grenier, Piper Thomas Wilson played his company over the top. Mostly employed as stretcher-bearers, but in 1914 the pipers of 1st Batt. also served in ranks. Piper Sydney Wilson was three times awarded certificate of gallantry.

1st Battalion

REG. NO.	RANK.	NAME.	RECORD.
	Pipe Major	John Stoddart	Killed, Poperinghe, July 1917.
	,,	John Stoddart (Junior)	
	Lance-Cpl.	John White	Invalided.
	Sergt.	E. J. Ogilvie	
	Piper	James Rogers	
	,,	John Graham	
	,,	Thomas Wilson	
	,,	Sydney Wilson	Twice wounded.
	,,	William Barclay	
	,,	Charles Copland	

2nd Battalion

REG. NO.	RANK.	NAME.	RECORD.
358269	Piper	Thomas Wilson	Wounded (gas).
	,,	James Gilfillan	Twice wounded.
	,,	Henry Forrester	
	,,	Robert Johnson	Twice gassed.
	,,	Thomas Carlyle	Wounded.
	,,	Stanley Rae	
	,,	Archibald Service	
	,,	Don. Fowler	Twice wounded.
	,,	James Martin	
	,,	Sydney Rogers	Wounded.

THE ROYAL FUSILIERS

23rd Battalion

(1st Sportsman's Batt.)

The pipers, during the period of trench warfare, were employed behind the lines. The C.O. considers they were of the greatest value in keeping up the men's morale, on marches and in bringing companies out of the trenches.

REG. NO.	RANK.	NAME.	RECORD.
1339	Pipe Major	D. F. Robertson	
	Lance-Cpl.	T. M'Clunie	Wounded.
	Piper	W. Johnstone	
	,,	W. Foreman	
1345	,,	W. F. Suttie	Killed, 16/3/16.
	,,	Alex. M'Lennan	
	,,	David Seath	
	,,	John Adamson	
1827-	,,	William Mackenzie	Killed, 16/3/16.
	,,	D. Leath	

THE ARGYLLSHIRE MOUNTAIN BATTERY

The pipers in this Battery all served as gunners.

REG. NO.	RANK.	NAME.	RECORD.
	Pipe Major	William MacNeill	Died, pneumonia, 18/8/15.
	Corpl.	Neil Smith	Accidentally killed, 1/3/16.
	,,	James MacPhee	

THE ROSS AND CROMARTY BATTERY

REG. NO.	RANK.	NAME.	RECORD.
4403	Piper	John Macdonald	Wounded, 14/5/15; died of wounds.
5035	,,	Jas. Mackay	Wounded, 14/5/15.
4323	,,	Angus Macdonald	Wounded, 23/6/15.

MISCELLANEOUS

REG. NO.	RANK.	NAME.	RECORD.
318411	Pte.	William Scott	11th F.A., R.A.M.C.; Military Medal.
93110	Piper	Andrew M'Intosh	2/2nd Lothian Field Ambulance; severely wounded.

THE PIPE BAND OF THE 52ND (LOWLAND) DIVISION

This band was formed in Gallipoli in October, 1915.

It was understood then that a dull and dreary winter campaign was in front of the troops. A committee of officers was formed to find some sort of entertainment to keep the men as cheery as possible. It was decided that both a Military and a Pipe Band should be raised. This job was left entirely in the hands of Colonel C. A. H. MACLEAN of Pennycross, a critical and enthusiastic lover of music, who, being a Highlander and an accomplished piper, naturally insisted on the Pipe Band being a good one.

Practically all that was left of the pipers in the different regiments of the Division were used to form the band, which consisted of twelve pipers and six drummers, all having taken part in the severe fighting prior to this duty. Good players and members of some of the finest bands in Scotland, under the leadership of Pipe-Major Wm. Fergusson, 1/7th Battn. Highland Light Infantry, a well-known piper and exponent of "Ceol Mhor," the band made steady progress, and soon was in grand fettle. The way both bands were appreciated testifies to the sound judgment of the committee and the able management of the Colonel.

The Division, being entirely composed of Scots, hailed with delight the skirl of the pipes, which had been heard but too seldom since the Division landed.

The band had exceptional luck while on Gallipoli, never having had a casualty after it was raised, although often playing under heavy shell fire. They played and warmed the hearts of all true Scots, and must have given the wily Turk quite a shock with "Hey Johnnie Cope," which could be heard quite distinctly on a quiet morning in the firing-line, right up till within a few days of the final evacuation of the peninsula.

After sojourning for a month on the Island of Mudros, they sailed with the rest of the Division for Egypt. From Abbassia (Cairo) they moved to the desert front, and have been with the Division in the trek across Sinai.

From El Arish the band accompanied the Division right into Palestine, and is believed to be the first pipe band to play in the " Holy Land."

PRISONERS OF WAR BAND

One of the most remarkable of military pipe bands was one organised in the British prisoners' internment camps in Holland. At one time this band consisted of 13 pipers of different units, including two pipe majors, under Pipe Major Duff, 2nd Royal Scots.

OVERSEAS BATTALIONS

PRINCESS PATRICIA'S CANADIAN LIGHT INFANTRY

The pipers were mainly employed as bearers.

In the attack on the Vimy Ridge on 9th April, 1917, the battalion was played over by the nine pipers.

Pipers were also employed as runners.

REG. NO.	RANK.	NAME.	RECORD.
667	Pipe Major	John Colville	Invalided ; despatches.
12942	,,	W. Campbell	
	Sergt.	John Macdonald, D.C.M.	Died of wounds, 17/9/16 ; D.C.M.
262	,,	H. Laing	Wounded, 8/5/15 ; despatches.
672	Corpl.	D. M'Intosh	Invalided.
1770	Lance-Cpl.	J. Hunter	Wounded, Oct. 1918.
264	Piper	J. Ritchie	Wounded, 22/3/15.
676	,,	J. M'Loy	Wounded, 28/2/15.
265	,,	W. Robertson	Died of wounds, 25/3/15.
1296	,,	J. M. Robertson, D.C.M.	Wounded, 8/5/15, D.C.M.
679	,,	J. Wood	Wounded, 17/5/15.
1772	,,	G. Miller	Invalided.
266	,,	C. M'Lean	
1771	,,	G. Harvey	

REG. NO.	RANK.	NAME.	RECORD.
1174	Piper	H. LOGAN	Wounded, 15/3/15.
21499	,,	A. G. M'DONALD	
432938	,,	J. LAING	
432013	,,	R. RITCHIE	
432966	,,	W. ADAMSON	Wounded, March, 1916.
432862	,,	L. SMITH	
432137	,,	J. WOOD	
432812	,,	G. DUNBAR	
433130	,,	G. THOMSON	
432312	,,	G. MURRAY	

THE ROYAL HIGHLANDERS OF CANADA

13TH BATTALION

In the Ypres fighting in April 1915 the pipers suffered heavily, 3 of them being killed and 5 wounded. Some of them were employed as runners, others in the ranks.

At the recapture of Hill 70 in August 1917 the companies were led to the attack by their pipers.

REG. NO.	RANK.	NAME.	RECORD.
24002	Pipe Major	D. MANSON	
24962	Piper	D. A. M'ARTHUR	
24010	,,	J. BURNS	Wounded, Ypres, 23/4/15.
24011	Lance-Cpl.	J. DYCE	Wounded, Ypres, 23/4/15.
24012	Piper	W. LAWSON	Died of wounds, Fleurbaix, 16/3/15.
24013	,,	A. J. MACDONALD	Killed, 24/4/15.
24014	,,	N. SINCLAIR	
24015	,,	A. SINGER	Wounded, 3/5/15, Ypres.
24392	,,	H. ROBERTSON	Killed, Ypres, 2/5/15.
24155	,,	N. MACDONALD	Killed, Ypres, 24/4/15.
24704	,,	D. CAMPBELL	Wounded, 22/4/15.
25045	,,	J. W. MACDONALD	
8004	,,	C. S. MACDONALD	
11095	,,	A. EDEN	
12942	,,	W. CAMPBELL	
46636	,,	J. CONNACHER	
14536	,,	G. B. MACPHERSON	

THE 48TH HIGHLANDERS OF CANADA

15TH BATTALION

The battalion took out 19 pipers. At the battle of Amiens, 5th-8th August, 1918, their pipers played in the front line. They were fortunate as regards casualties during the war, having lost only one man killed.

REG. NO.	RANK.	NAME.	RECORD.
27221	Pipe Major	A. R. Keith, M.M.	
27386	Lance-Sgt.	A. A. Newlands	
27548	Corpl.	J. Thompson	Died of disease.
27925	Lance-Cpl.	A. M'Donald	
27659	Piper	K. Crosbie	Obtained commission in R.A.
27058	,,	F. A. Cowen	Gassed, Ypres, 22/4/15; invalided.
27883	,,	A. Donaldson	
27023	,,	K. Miller	
2709	,,	W. H. Wick	
13611	,,	D. Braidwood	Obtained commission.
30207	,,	A. Gordon	
152	,,	J. A. Mackinnon, M.C.	Obtained commission
43212	,,	A. Sturrock	
37451	,,	W. Macdonald	
41587	,,	N. A. Ross	
58456	,,	G. C. Henderson	
135514	,,	A. M. MacDonald	
192071	,,	D. MacDonald	
193489	,,	J. Hinshelwood	
799915	,,	A. MacDonald	
1045162	,,	T. Hamilton	
1045069	,,	J. M'Neill	
1045923	,,	H. E. Mathews	
1045177	,,	R. B. MacWilliam	
192170	,,	T. Martin	
1045779	,,	W. Hynd	
192270	,,	W. Mair	
799627	,,	R. Smith	
799248	,,	R. Anderson	
799041	,,	W. G. Watson	
799255	,,	W. Lawrie	
799704	,,	A. MacLachlan	
799258	,,	D. MacPherson	
799256	,,	P. T. Lamb	
2393381	,,	F. M'Dowall	
2393526	,,	J. Cant	

THE CANADIAN SCOTTISH

16TH BATTALION

At Ypres (April 1915) two pipers, Jas. Thomson and W. M'Ivor, were killed while playing the charge; and at Festubert in May, G. Birnie and A. Morrison were killed in the same way. Some of the pipers were employed as bearers, runners, etc., but, the casualties continuing, it was found necessary for a time to withdraw them from the firing line. During the Somme fighting, however, they were again used as pipers. In the attack of 8th October, 1916, Pipers Richardson, Park, Paul and M'Kellar played through very heavy fire for over half a mile, and Richardson and Park were killed. Piper Richardson was awarded the V.C. posthumously. On another occasion, in the attack on the Quirique Rue position, Pipers Birnie and Morrison stood on a ruined farmhouse and played until they were both killed.

In the attack on the Vimy Ridge on 9th April, 1917, the battalion was again led to their objective by the Pipe Major, Groat and five pipers for a distance of over a mile; Pipe Major Groat got the Military Medal.

For bravery at Paschendaele, Aug. 1917, Lance-Cpl. M'Gillivray—who was killed—got the Military Medal, and Piper Paul received the same distinction.

The C.O. regards the pipes as invaluable in action. Of the pipers one got the V.C., one the D.C.M. and nine the Military Medal. No man was recommended for a distinction unless he had twice played his company to an attack.

REG. NO.	RANK.	NAME.	RECORD.
28556	Pipe Major	DONALD M'LEOD	Invalided, 1915.
28558	,,	RONALD M'DONALD	
29327	,,	JAMES GROAT, D.C.M., M.M.	Pipe Major, Nov. 1915; D.C.M.; Military Medal and Bar.
28812	Piper	C. WILSON	Wounded, Ypres, 22-28/4/15; invalided.
28694	,,	JAMES THOMSON	Died of wounds, Ypres, 23/4/15.
28779	,,	WILLIAM M'IVOR	Died of wounds, 10/5/15.
29236	,,	JAMES LOWE	Wounded, Ypres, 22-28/4/15; invalided.

REG. NO.	RANK.	NAME.	RECORD.
28595	,,	George Birnie	Killed, Festubert, 20/5/15.
29468	,,	Angus Morrison	Killed, Festubert, 20/5/15.
28557	,,	Alec M'Gillivray (?), M.M.	Killed, 15/8/17; Military Medal.
29048	,,	Alan M'Nab, M.M.	Military Medal.
28559	,,	Hugh M'Donald	
29336	,,	George Inglis	
29149	,,	Gordon Ross	
28930	,,	James Richardson, V.C.	Killed, 8/10/16; V.C.
28561	,,	John Parks	Killed, 8/10/16.
28560	,,	Hugh M'Kellar	Invalided, 1917.
859495	,,	J. Lightheart	
429603	,,	G. Paul, M.M.	Killed, Amiens, 8/8/18; Military Medal.
467573	,,	Alex. Robertson, M.M.	Military Medal.
466703	,,	John M'Allister, M.M.	Military Medal.
183188	,,	William Buchanan	
183192	,,	Hugh M'Beth	
736522	,,	David Horn	
737176	,,	John J. M'Lean	Wounded, Amiens, 8/8/18.
736406	,,	William Goldie	
160387	,,	Norman M'Iver	
859059	,,	Arthur Duncan	
603174	,,	Gordon Cruickshank, M.M.	Military Medal.
633237	,,	Duncan M'Kinnon	Wounded, Oct. 1918.
633179	,,	Archibald M'Donell, M.M.	Military Medal.
633524	,,	Lawrence M'Gillivray	
189348	,,	Harry M'Lean	
603269	,,	Willie Darlow	
859498	,,	John Lightheart	
860095	,,	John Reid	
85959	,,	John M'Donald	Wounded, Sept. 1918.
959196	,,	David Hunter	
859941	,,	William M'Gregor	
693164	,,	Arthur Robertson	Wounded, Oct. 1918.
859100	,,	Robert M'Donald	
779259	,,	George M'Leod	
859454	,,	Donald M'Kenzie	

THE CAMERON HIGHLANDERS OF CANADA

REG. NO.	RANK.	NAME.	RECORD.
	Pipe Major	John Duke	
	Piper	James G. Munro	Taken prisoner, Somme, ? Sept. 1916.

THE 21ST CANADIANS

(Eastern Ontario Regiment)

It is considered in this battalion that pipers are quite indispensable, and should be spared as far as possible.

REG. NO.	RANK.	NAME.	RECORD.
	Pipe Major	IAN MACKENZIE	Killed, Cambrai, 11/10/18.
59224	Corpl.	WILLIAM CURRIE, M.M., M.C.	Wounded, 23/4/16; Military Medal; promoted Lieut.; got Military Cross.
59937	Sergt.	WILLIAM SUTHERLAND	Wounded, 27/11/15.
60115	Piper	HUGH MACKENZIE, M.M.	Military Medal.
59320	,,	C. FYFE	Wounded, 28/10/15.
59311	,,	J. EWART	Invalided.
59620	,,	H. M'KEACHEN	Invalided.
633985	,,	W. GRANT	Invalided.
401191	,,	MACDOUGALL	Wounded, 19/6/16.
59618	Pipe Major	J. M'DOUGALL	
59181	Corpl.	J. R. COGHILL, M.M.	Military Medal.
675268	Piper	W. H. COLLINS	
633879	,,	W. ALEXANDER	
675274	,,	J. LITTLE	
633643	,,	D. M'DONALD	

THE 25TH CANADIANS

Piper Telfer played his company into action at Vimy Ridge until wounded. He was awarded the Military Medal; Piper W. Brand also got the same distinction. Again, at Amiens, August 1918, the battalion was played over. There was great competition among the men to be allowed to perform this duty. Frequently they were employed as bearers.

REG. NO.	RANK.	NAME.	RECORD.
	Pipe Major	CARSON	Meritorious Service Medal; wounded, 13/8/18; Mons Medal.
	Corpl.	CANT	Invalided.
	,,	MORRISON	
	Piper	W. TELFER	Military Medal; wounded, 9/4/18.
	,,	W. BRAND	Military Medal.

REG. NO.	RANK.	NAME.	RECORD
	Piper	D. Brand	Invalided.
	,,	A. Campbell	Invalided.
	,,	M. M'Dougall	
	,,	G. Hooper	
	,,	P. Kitchenham	Wounded, 9/4/18.
	,,	G. Thomas	Wounded, 9/4/18.
	,,	H. O'Connell	
	,,	E. Stewart	Killed, 9/4/18.
	,,	T. H. M'Kinnon	
	,,	J. H. Shirley	
	,,	E. B. Thurlow	
	,,	W. Fyffe	Wounded.
	,,	A. Ritchie	Wounded.
	,,	H. M'Culloch	
	,,	N. M'Leod	
	,,	J. Macintosh	
	,,	A. Lavrey	
	,,	W. Buchanan	
	,,	F. MacBean	
	,,	Hector Maclean Angus	Invalided.

THE 29TH CANADIANS

(Vancouver Regiment)

Pipers were employed as bearers.

REG. NO.	RANK.	NAME.	RECORD.
75582	Pipe Major	W. Montgomery	Invalided.
75132	,,	D. M'Culloch	
75297	Corpl.	D. May	Wounded, 13/11/17 ; invalided.
75599	Piper	W. S. Grant	Killed, 6/11/17.
76216	,,	W. Burnside	Killed, 6/11/17.
76484	,,	J. R. Davidson	
76186	,,	A. Robertson	Invalided.
73583	,,	A. M. Bayne	Wounded, 20/4/16.
76482	,,	J. Clark	
75848	,,	R. M'Donald	
75673	,,	A. M'Lachlan	
76180	,,	A. M'Rae	
75298	,,	W. A. Robertson	
76481	,,	A. Dunsmuir	
30173	,,	A. Wilson	

THE 236TH CANADIANS

(The MacLean Regiment)

REG. NO.	RANK.	NAME.	RECORD.
1030319	Piper	E. BARTON.	
1030099	,,	W. H. BLAIR	
1030239	,,	W. W. BRADFORD	
1030098	,,	CECIL BREWER	
1030225	,,	DOUGLAS BURBRIDGE	
1030152	,,	JOHN CAMPBELL.	
1030076	,,	GEORGE CLARKE	
1030020	,,	W. H. COLLINS.	
1030328	Lance-Cpl.	CHARLES CROMWELL.	
1030253	Piper	ANDREW DODDS	
1030008	Corpl.	RICHARD FERRIE	
1030312	Piper	DONALD GRANT	
1030513	,,	KENNETH GREGORY	
1030010	Sergt.	FRED HAYTER	
1030043	Piper	FRED HARRIS	
1030012	,,	JOHN M'FADGEN	
1030511	,,	WILLIAM M'EWAN	
1030326	,,	JOHN M'NAMEE	
1030581	,,	JAMES MACK	
742630	,,	WALTER MORRELL	
1030196	,,	HAROLD MILES	
1030045	,,	EDWARD RALSTEN	
1030030	,,	A. REGAN	
743040	,,	CHARLES ROSS	
1030016	Pipe Sgt.	W. H. ROSS	
1030323	Piper	J. BENSON ROBINSON	
1030052	,,	GORDON SCOTT	
1030142	,,	E. J. SLOANE	
1030066	,,	JAMES SMITH	
1030014	Corpl.	ALEX. STEWART	
1030184	Piper	DOUGLAS STEWART	
291928	,,	J. SIMPSON	
1030545	,,	WILLIAM STEWART	
1030217	,,	GEORGE TANDY	
1030026	,,	A. E. WALKER	
1030093	,,	GEORGE WHITE	
1030110	,,	E. WILLIS	
1030061	,,	JAMES WILSON	
467264	,,	GEORGE WALKER	
1030143	,,	ROBERT JAMERISON	

THE CANADIAN PIONEERS

1st Battalion

Owing to the nature of the employment of this battalion on railway construction the pipers were principally in the ranks as sappers.

REG. NO.	RANK.	NAME.	RECORD.
154580	Pipe Major	H. M'Kenzie	
154492	Piper (Sapper)	William Henry	
154589	"	F. Macdonald	Wounded, 7/5/16.
154184	"	J. Grant	Killed, 13/6/16.
155016	"	William Gray	Wounded, 4/6/16.
154121	"	R. Kell	
154027	"	G. Mars	Wounded, 17/8/18.
491353	"	W. G. Richardson	
154231	"	P. Hyndman	Wounded, 17/9/17.

THE 2nd AUCKLAND REGIMENT

The band was started in Egypt in 1915 with 4 pipers, and gradually a few more were added. The pipers were not allowed to go into action as such. Pipe Major J. F. Robertson was given the Military Medal for gallantry during the operations round Bapaume in 1918.

REG. NO.	RANK.	NAME.	RECORD.
	Piper	H. Cameron	
	"	J. F. Robertson	Awarded Military Medal, Bapaume, 1918.
	"	H. M. Kennedy	
	"	J. Stevenson	
	"	J. Brown	
	"	D. M'Kinley	
	"	A. Lambie	
	"	F. Barry	
	"	F. M'Lean	
	"	J. Clothier	
	"	B. Johns	

THE 42ND AUSTRALIANS

This battalion raised a band of 8 pipers when they left Australia in 1916. They were largely employed as scouts, runners, etc.

The battalion was subsequently merged into the 41st.

Pipers A. Aitken and R. Gillespie were awarded Military Medals for valuable scouting work carried out prior to the action at Messines in June 1917.

REG. NO.	RANK.	NAME.	RECORD.
	Pipe Major	A. R. M'Coll	
	Corpl.	A. S. MacNaught	
	Piper	A. Aitken, M.M.	Wounded; Military Medal.
	"	R. Gillespie, M.M.	Military Medal.
	"	J. A. Murray	
	"	A. M'Pherson	Wounded.
	"	J. M'Coll	Wounded.
	"	J. Robertson	Wounded.
	"	A. Murray	Wounded.
	"	M. H. Fraser	Killed.
	"	D. Lathangie	
	"	T. A. Fraser	Wounded.
	"	A. S. Chaplin	
	"	W. Reid	
	"	W. Milne	
	"	A. M'Pherson	
	"	J. Clarke	
	"	A. Howie	Wounded.

THE SOUTH AFRICAN SCOTTISH

The pipers proved quite invaluable on the long marches in the operations against the Senussi, in keeping the men going, under the most trying climatic conditions.

The pipers were sometimes employed as bearers, or as carriers of stores, ammunition, etc., and as runners.

In the Cambrai advance by the Germans they had to serve in the ranks. At Houdincourt, having piled their pipes and taken up rifles, nearly all their instruments were destroyed by a shell.

REG. NO.	RANK.	NAME.	RECORD.
	Pipe Major	D. Cameron, D.C.M.	Became C. Sergt.-Major ; wounded.
	,,	Alexander Grieve	Gassed, March 1918.
	Lance-Cpl.	R. Hay	
	Piper	T. Scott	Killed, Arras, 9/4/17.
	,,	A. Gray, M.M.	Military Medal.
	,,	J. Waterhouse, M.M.	Military Medal.
	,,	J. Matheson	
	,,	D. A. Cummings	
	,,	F. Fraser	
	,,	C. Gordon	Invalided.
	,,	R. Lindsay	
	,,	M. M'Neil	
	,,	J. M'Calman	
	,,	J. Munro	Wounded, Oct. 1916 ; invalided.
	,,	M. Strang	
	,,	G. Collier	
	,,	W. Irons	
	,,	M'Gregor	
	,,	M'Coll	
	,,	W. Strang	

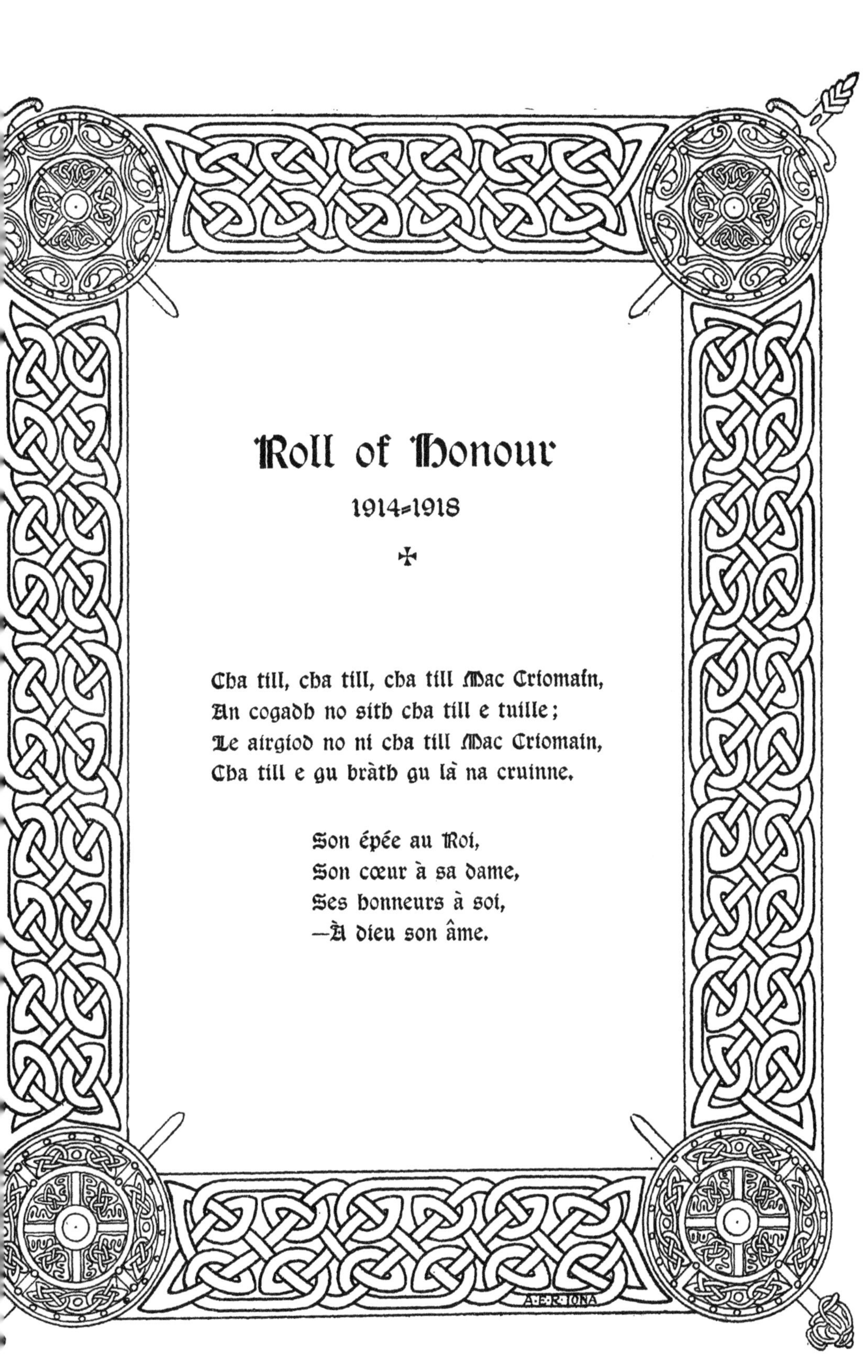

Roll of Honour

1914-1918

✠

Cha till, cha till, cha till Mac Criomain,
An cogadh no sith cha till e tuille;
Le airgiod no ni cha till Mac Criomain,
Cha till e gu bràth gu là na cruinne.

Son épée au Roi,
Son cœur à sa dame,
Ses honneurs à soi,
—À dieu son âme.

ROLL OF HONOUR. 1914-1918

1st SCOTS GUARDS.

3707	Sergt.	Samuel Richardson	Died of wounds, Aisne, 14/9/14.
8543	Piper	James Mackenzie	Killed, Ypres, 31/10/14.
991	,,	Alexander Martin, D.C.M.	Killed, 19/2/16.
	,,	Malcolm Mackenzie	Killed, 1914.
	,,	A. Carmichael	Killed, 1915.

2nd SCOTS GUARDS.

	Lance-Cpl.	Hector M'Kimm	Killed, Zonnebeke, 26/10/14.
8081	Piper	Charles M'Guire	Died of wounds, Ypres, 29/10/14.

1st ROYAL SCOTS.

48594	Piper	D. M'Donald	Died, Bulgaria, Oct. 1918.

2nd ROYAL SCOTS.

13459	Piper	William Fisher	Killed, 15/4/16.
8516	,,	J. Robertson	Killed, Croix Barbes, 13/10/14.
8450	,,	James Drummond	Killed, The Bluff, 23/1/16.
11484	,,	D. Lindsay	Killed, 4/5/17.
	,,	A. M'Kinlay	Killed, 9/4/18.
44118	,,	A. Cruickshanks	Killed, 27/9/18.
3190	,,	J. Thompson	Died, 30/9/15.
10536	,,	E. Duguid	Died of gas, 10/5/18.

4th ROYAL SCOTS.

Pipe Major	Andrew Buchan	Killed, Gallipoli, 28/6/15.
Piper	Charles Rutherford	Died, dysentery, Gallipoli.

5th ROYAL SCOTS.

1303	Piper	George Hardie	Killed, Gallipoli, 2/5/15.
766	,,	Alexander Lawson	Killed, Gallipoli, 28/4/15.
1824	,,	George W. Downie	Killed, Gallipoli, 7/5/15.

1235	Piper	WILLIAM SINCLAIR	Died of wounds, Gallipoli, 8/5/15.
8109	,,	DAVID ROSS	Killed, July 1916.

Lieut. TOM BARTLEMAN (formerly Piper), Seaforth Highlanders, killed, Sept. 1917.

6TH ROYAL SCOTS.

Piper	MURDOCH BETHUNE	Died of wounds, Somme, 2/7/16.
,,	THOMAS LEAKE	Died of disease.

7TH ROYAL SCOTS.

	Pipe Major	JAMES GEAR	Killed in railway accident.
	Piper	GEORGE SMEATON	Killed in railway accident.
	Piper	ALEXANDER NICOL	Killed in railway accident.
	,,	FRED TURNER	Killed, 12/7/15, Gallipoli.
251141	,,	PETER M'NEILL	Killed, 6/11/17, Palestine.

9TH ROYAL SCOTS.

Lance-Cpl.	A. L. FORSYTH, M.M.	Killed, 23/4/17.
Corpl.	G. LAUDER	Killed, 23/5/17.

11TH ROYAL SCOTS.

Piper	JOHN KANE	Killed, 14/7/16.

12TH ROYAL SCOTS.

12991	Piper	THOMAS HISLOP	Killed, Loos, 25/9/15.
200737	Lance-Cpl.	PETER WEST	Died of wounds.
13459	Piper	WILLIAM FISHER	Killed, 15/4/16.

13TH ROYAL SCOTS.

Pipe Major	MURDOCH MACDONALD	Died of disease, 9/2/16.
Piper	THOMAS FLOOD	Killed, 26/8/18.
,,	ROBERT CAMPBELL	Died as prisoner of war, Sept. 1915.
,,	ROBERT MITCHELL	Died of wounds, 26/8/18.

16TH ROYAL SCOTS.

Piper	M. BETHUNE	Killed, Somme, July 1916.
,,	H. GREY	Killed, Arras, April 1917.
,,	A. NOON	Killed, Arras, April 1917.

17TH ROYAL SCOTS.

Pipe Major	DONALD M'LEAN	Killed, 14/7/18 (Lieut. 1st Gordons).

2ND ROYAL SCOTS FUSILIERS.

	Corpl.	A. W. Richardson	Killed.
	Piper	W. Butterworth	Killed.
	,,	W. M'Lean	Killed, Messines, 1917.
	,,	W. Moore	Died after discharge.

4TH ROYAL SCOTS FUSILIERS.

	Pipe Major	N. Shaw	Died of wounds, Palestine, 21/4/17.
	Lance-Cpl.	J. M'Allister	Killed, Gallipoli, 12/7/15.
	Piper	P. Greig	Killed, Gallipoli, 12/7/15.
	,,	J. Milner	Killed, Gallipoli, 12/7/15.

5TH ROYAL SCOTS FUSILIERS.

7797	Lance-Cpl.	John Murdoch	Killed, 13/7/15.

1ST KING'S OWN SCOTTISH BORDERERS.

9884	Piper	Higginson	Died of wounds, Gallipoli, 26/4/15.
11315	,,	Maitland	Killed, Paschendaele, 27/4/17.

4TH KING'S OWN SCOTTISH BORDERERS.

778	Piper	Thomas Lunham	Died of wounds.
779	,,	J. Kerr	Died of wounds.
306	,,	C. Street	
822	,,	Alex. Hendry	

5TH KING'S OWN SCOTTISH BORDERERS.

308	Piper	R. Brown	Killed, 12/7/15.
1760	,,	Thomas Martin	Killed, 12/7/15.
	,,	James Gorman	Killed.

6TH KING'S OWN SCOTTISH BORDERERS.

14851	Pipe Major	Robert Mackenzie	Died of wounds, Loos, 25/9/15.
	Lance-Cpl.	J. Lomas	Killed, Loos, 25/9/15.
	Piper	J. Simes	Killed, Loos, 25/9/15.
	,,	P. Moffat	Killed, Loos, 25/9/15.
	,,	J. Pringle	Killed, Somme, Oct. 1916.

7TH KING'S OWN SCOTTISH BORDERERS.

	Piper	J. Taylor	Killed, Arras.

8TH KING'S OWN SCOTTISH BORDERERS.

14277	Lance-Cpl.	A. M'Vittie	Killed, Arras.
	Piper	C. Reid	Killed, Somme, July 1916.
	,,	G. Surriton	Killed, Arras.

1ST SCOTTISH RIFLES.

9429	Piper	T. Best
9441	,,	R. Black
10924	,,	P. Robertson

2ND SCOTTISH RIFLES.

Pipe Major	Alex. Cameron	Killed, 10/2/15, Laventie.
Corpl.	A. Horne	Killed, 31/7/17.
Corpl.	James Campbell	Killed, 16/5/15, La Bassée.
Piper	A. Macdonald	Killed, 10/2/15, Laventie.
,,	Forsyth	Killed, July 15, Bois Grenier.
,,	Clark	Killed, 10/3/15, Neuve Chapelle.
,,	Lauder	Died of wounds, March 1918.

5TH SCOTTISH RIFLES.

Pipe Major	Paterson	Accidentally killed.

5/6TH SCOTTISH RIFLES.

201124	Pipe Major	J. C. Purdie	Killed.

7TH SCOTTISH RIFLES.

1106	Piper	Archibald Ramage	Killed, 28/6/15, Dardanelles.
868	,,	Archibald Shearer	Killed, 23/7/15, Dardanelles.
1178	,,	William Deans	Killed, June, 1615, Dardanelles.
265958	,,	J. M'Iver	Killed, 12/11/17, Palestine.
1817	,,	J. Strachan	Killed, 4/11/17, Palestine.

8TH SCOTTISH RIFLES.

Pipe Major	Neil Macleod	Killed, 12/7/15, Dardanelles.
Piper	John MacIntyre	Killed, 28/6/15, Dardanelles.
,,	James Ferguson	Killed, 28/6/15, Dardanelles.
,,	James M'Indoe	Killed, 29/7/18, France.
,,	Robert Whitelaw	Killed, 28/6/15.

9TH SCOTTISH RIFLES.

30503	Piper	Hugh Macara	Killed, March 1917.

10TH SCOTTISH RIFLES.

	Piper	Robert Black	Killed, 28/1/16.
	,,	Duncan Mackenzie	Killed, 17/11/15.
	,,	Alex. Harris	Killed, 27/1/16.

11TH SCOTTISH RIFLES.

14631	Piper	Alexander Stevenson	Killed, 28/4/17.

1ST BLACK WATCH.

9617	Pipe Major	D. M'Leod	Killed, 21/8/16.
1956	Piper	T. M'Intyre	Missing, 14/8/14.

2ND BLACK WATCH.

1871	Piper	James Galloway	Killed, 8/10/15, Givenchy.
9908	Lance-Cpl.	James Wann	Died of wounds, 10/2/15, Neuve Chapelle.
1449	Piper	James Davis	Killed, 25/9/15, Mauquissart.
736	,,	David Simpson	Killed, 25/9/15, Mauquissart.
941	Lance-Cpl.	Peter M'Nee	Died of wounds, 25/9/15, Mesopotamia.
	Piper	Mackay	Died of wounds, 10/3/15, Neuve Chapelle.
	,,	William Mathieson	Killed, 25/9/15, Mauquissart.
1539	,,	Alex. Macdonald, D.C.M.	Discharged ; subsequently died, 26/3/17.

5TH BLACK WATCH.

1568	Piper	Alexander Howie	Killed, 10/3/15, Neuve Chapelle.
406	Lance-Cpl.	Fred Reid	Killed, 13/3/15, Neuve Chapelle.

6TH BLACK WATCH.

	Piper	L. Massie	Killed, Somme, Oct. 1916.
	,,	Donald Gillies	Died, July 1915.
	,,	P. Fallon	Killed, Festubert, May 1915.
	,,	J. Ferguson	Killed, La Boiselle, Aug. 1916.
	,,	J. Harper	Killed, Fremicourt, 23/12/17.
	,,	A. Tainsh	Killed, Fremicourt, 23/12/17.
	,,	A. Forbes	Killed, Fremicourt, 23/12/17.
	,,	A. Myles	Killed, Fremicourt, 23/12/17.
	,,	A. Paton	Killed, June 1915.

7TH BLACK WATCH.

4470	Piper	James Johnston	Killed, 7/1/17, Somme.
	Lance-Cpl.	G. Swan	Killed, Dec. 1916, Somme.
	Piper	James Ross	Killed, Dec. 1916, Somme.
	,,	Alexander Wilkie	Killed, Dec. 1916, Somme.

8th BLACK WATCH.

3014	Piper	Donald Wilson	Killed, Loos, 1915.
265912	"	R. Menzies	Killed, Meteren, July 1918.
3019	"	D. Simpson	Killed, Somme, 1916.
3375	"	W. Reilly	Killed, Loos, 1915.

9th BLACK WATCH.

	Piper	J. Johnstone	Killed, March, 1918.

1st HIGHLAND LIGHT INFANTRY.

6894	Sergt.	D. Buchan	Killed, 20/11/14, Festubert.
9615	Piper	C. Stewart	Killed, 1/5/15, Ypres.
10107	"	F. Burns	Killed, 20/11/14, Festubert.
9860	"	Thomas James	Killed, 20/11/14, Festubert.
9011	"	J. Morrison	Killed, 20/11/14, Festubert.
11499	"	J. M'Naught	Killed, 20/11/14, Festubert.
11470	"	J. Smith	Killed, 7/9/16, Somme.
	Lance-Cpl.	Mitchell	Killed, 18/9/14, Vermeuil.
11468	Corpl. (acting Pipe Major)	J. Smith	Died enteric, Mesopotamia.

2nd HIGHLAND LIGHT INFANTRY.

10264	Sergt.	T. Findlay	Killed, 14/3/15, Neuve Chapelle.
10976	Piper	J. Irving	Killed, 3/11/14.
9272	Corpl.	J. Mackenzie	Killed, 21/10/14.

4th HIGHLAND LIGHT INFANTRY.

	Piper	Charles Stewart	Killed.

5th HIGHLAND LIGHT INFANTRY.

	Pipe Major	John Thomson	Killed, 12/7/15, Dardanelles.

6th HIGHLAND LIGHT INFANTRY.

1237	Piper	Peter M'Niven	Killed, 12/7/15.

9th HIGHLAND LIGHT INFANTRY.

1666	Piper	John Drummond	Killed, 3/6/15, Vermelles.
333792	"	T. Crawford	Died of wounds.
333138	"	J. M'Creath	Died of wounds, Oct. 1918.

10TH HIGHLAND LIGHT INFANTRY.

12562 Piper ALEX. WHITEFIELD Killed, 25/9/15, Cambrin.
902 Lance-Cpl. DAVID DONALDSON Killed, 9/7/15, Festubert.
17505 Piper PETER M'INTYRE Gassed, Cambrai; died, 8/11/18.

12TH HIGHLAND LIGHT INFANTRY.

Piper WILLIAM THOMPSON Killed, Arras, 9/4/17.
,, JOHN M'KEAN Killed, Loos, 25/9/15.
Sergt. WILLIAM PIERCE Killed, Somme, Sept. 1916.

14TH HIGHLAND LIGHT INFANTRY.

Piper PETER THOMSON Killed, 24/4/17.

15TH HIGHLAND LIGHT INFANTRY.

353152 Piper D. M'KENZIE Killed, Ayette, 13/4/18.

16TH HIGHLAND LIGHT INFANTRY.

15032 Lance-Cpl. WALTER ORR Killed, 1/7/16, Somme.
14699 Piper ARCHIBALD RANKIN Killed, 1/7/16, Thiepval.

17TH HIGHLAND LIGHT INFANTRY.

Piper ARCHIBALD FORREST Died.

20TH HIGHLAND LIGHT INFANTRY.

26650 Lance-Cpl. DEVLIN Killed, Ypres, 25/9/17.
30503 Piper HUGH MACARA Killed, March 1917.

1ST SEAFORTH HIGHLANDERS.

Lance-Cpl. HEARNE Died of disease.
709 Piper J. WILKINSON Killed, France.
7900 ,, WILLIAM COWANS Killed, 7/11/14, "Port Arthur."
9291 ,, J. PRATT Died of wounds, 9/5/15, Neuve Chapelle.
479 ,, D. BLACK Killed, 3/11/14, "Port Arthur."
788 ,, T. URQUHART Killed, 20/12/14, Givenchy.
9158 Actg. Pipe Major J. MACLELLAN Killed, 21/4/17, Mesopotamia.
10457 Lance-Sgt. STEWART Killed, 1917.
311 Lance-Cpl. D. CAMPBELL Killed, Mesopotamia, Oct. 1917.
529 Sergt. C. M'KAY Died of wounds, Baghdad, 1916.
,, COOK Killed, Mesopotamia, 1916.
,, SMITH Killed, France.

2nd SEAFORTH HIGHLANDERS.

9106	Lance-Cpl.	William Ross	Killed, /6/15.
9223	Lance-Cpl.	John Grant	Killed, /10/14.
283	Lance-Cpl.	Dougal MacMillan	Died, /2/15.
	Piper	David Macrae	Killed, /2/15.
	"	Kenneth Mackenzie	Killed, /5/15.
	"	Robert Rennie	Killed, /5/15.
	"	Alex. Clark	Killed, /5/15.
9494	"	James Rennie	Killed, Loos, 3/10/15.
3	"	Robert Hall	Killed, 1/7/16.
9132	"	N. Johnstone	Wounded, 25/4/15; killed, 26/1/17.
10456	Lance-Sgt.	James Stewart	Killed, Somme, 1917.

4th SEAFORTH HIGHLANDERS.

24316	Piper	Donald M'Kenzie	Prisoner; died of wounds, May 1918.
	"	J. Kemp	Died of wounds, Neuve Chapelle, 1915.
	"	A. M'Aulay	Died of wounds, Valenciennes, 1918.
	"	J. M'Kenzie	Died of wounds, Neuve Chapelle, 1915.
	"	A. M'Lennan	Killed, Neuve Chapelle, 1915.

5th SEAFORTH HIGHLANDERS.

422	Lance-Cpl.	G. Ross	Killed, 21/7/15, Fauquissart.
251	Piper	R. Ross	Killed, 21/7/15, Fauquissart.
599	"	Donald M'Kay	Killed, 13/11/16, Beaumont Hamel.

6th SEAFORTH HIGHLANDERS.

Lieut. (formerly Piper)	J. Hector Ross	Killed, 23/4/17.
Piper	W. Sutherland	Roclincourt, 9/4/17.
Sergt.	William M'Leod	Killed, May 1916.
"	C. D. Macdonald	Killed, 13/11/16, Beaumont Hamel.
"	H. Mackie	Killed, 13/11/16, Beaumont Hamel.
"	J. Brown	Killed, May 1917, Arras.
Piper	J. Alexander	Killed, April 1918, La Bassée.
"	A. Mackay	Killed, 9/4/17, Roclincourt.
"	J. Robertson	Killed, July 1915.

7th SEAFORTH HIGHLANDERS.

40417	Lance-Cpl.	O'Kain M'Lennan	Died of wounds, 11/4/17.
1456	Piper	D. Fraser	Killed, Loos, 25/9/15.
4181	,,	R. Galbraith	Killed, Loos, 25/9/15.
9070	,,	G. Grant	Died of wounds, 30/6/16.
2177	,,	B. Halliday	Died of wounds, at Loos.
3843	,,	K. Thyne	Killed, Somme, 14/7/16.
4661	,,	B. Hamilton	Killed, Loos, 25/9/15.

8th SEAFORTH HIGHLANDERS.

5721	Piper	Charles Anderson	Killed, 25/9/15, Loos.
6567	,,	George Spence	Killed, 25/9/15, Loos.
6400	,,	William Mackay	Killed, 25/9/15, Loos.
6546	Lance-Cpl.	Duncan MacGregor	Killed, 25/9/15, Loos.
	Piper	Hugh Sutherland	Died of disease, France.
	,,	Andrew Clark	Killed, 25/9/15, Loos.

9th SEAFORTH HIGHLANDERS.

267336	Piper	James Sutherland	Killed, 19/4/17.
240018	,,	Robert Ross	Killed, 11/4/18.
3964	,,	William M'Mahon	Killed.
23879	,,	William Duncan	Killed.

1st GORDON HIGHLANDERS.

Piper	Frederick Paterson	Killed, 26/8/14, Mons.
Lance-Cpl.	W. M'Fall	Killed, 24/10/14.
Piper	W. Howie	Killed, 24/10/14.
,,	A. M'Kay	Died of wounds, /1/15.
,,	W. Allan	Killed, 14/12/14.
,,	Hector Ross	Killed, /3/16.

2nd GORDON HIGHLANDERS.

430	Piper	J. Robertson	Killed, Ypres, 30/10/14.
10655	,,	R. Grant	Killed, Loos, 25/9/15.
10639	,,	J. Grant	Killed, Loos, 25/9/15.
110	,,	R. Wilson	Killed, Loos, 25/9/15.
219	,,	W. Bruce	Killed, Loos, 25/9/15.
10653	Corpl.	J. M'Kenzie	Killed, Loos, 25/9/15.
205	Piper	J. Ledingham	Killed, Loos, 25/9/15.
10139	,,	J. Ramage	Killed, Loos, 25/9/15.
	,,	D. White	Killed, Loos, 1915.
7383	,,	A. Cassie	Killed, Loos, 25/9/15.
	,,	P. Brown	Killed, Ypres, 5/10/17.

	Piper	J. Bissett	Killed, Loos, 25/9/15.
10296	,,	W. Sinclair	Died of wounds, Loos, 25/9/15.
7375	Corpl.	A. Smith	Killed, Loos, 25/9/15.
6853	Sergt.	R. Stewart, D.C.M.	Killed, Loos, 25/9/15.
8390	Piper	J. Scott	Killed, Somme, 1916.
335	,,	J. M'Crimmon	Killed, Loos, 25/9/15.

4th GORDON HIGHLANDERS.

	Piper	A. Thomson	Killed while serving with R.F.C.

5th GORDON HIGHLANDERS.

1156	Piper	William Graham	Killed, 3/6/15, Festubert.
11586	,,	Alexander Willox	Killed, 31/7/16, High Wood.
	,,	Andrew Brown, M.M.	Killed, 31/7/16, High Wood.

6th GORDON HIGHLANDERS.

62	Piper	George Milton	Killed, 10/3/15, Neuve Chapelle.

9th GORDON HIGHLANDERS.

9023	Piper	C. Campbell	Killed, Somme, 1916.

1st CAMERON HIGHLANDERS.

6720	Sergt.	G. Selby	Killed, 22/10/14.
5173	Piper	H. Barrie	Killed, 5/11/14, Ypres.
8535	,,	Gilbert M'Calman	Died of wounds, Feb. 1918.
9345	,,	L. M'Bean	Died of wounds, Arras, Aug. 1918.

2nd CAMERON HIGHLANDERS.

	Piper	John MacAskil	Killed, Hill 60, April 1916.
	,,	Donnachie	Killed, 1915.
	,,	John M'Cabe	Died.
	,,	Thompson	Died, 1918.
	,,	Archibald M'Kenzie	Killed, Hill 60, April 1916.
	,,	Lachlan M'Bean	Died of wounds, St. Eloi, 10/5/15.
	,,	William Stewart	Died, Salonika, 18/10/17.

4th CAMERON HIGHLANDERS.

1120	Piper	J. Cheyne	Killed, Festubert, 17/5/15.
645	Lance-Cpl.	D. Paterson	Killed, Festubert, 17/5/15.
200120	Piper	William Macdonald	Died of wounds, 14/10/17.

5TH CAMERON HIGHLANDERS.

5497	Piper	ALEX. MACEACHERN	Died of wounds, Loos, 25/9/15.
5113	Lance-Cpl.	A. J. M'DONALD	Killed, Loos, 25/9/15.
3931	Piper	NEIL WILSON	Killed, Loos, 27/9/15.
	,,	JOHN MACLELLAN	Killed, Sorel, 21/3/18.
	,,	ALEXANDER CLUNIE	Killed, Arras, 3/5/17.
	,,	ARCHIBALD CRAWFORD	Killed, Sorel, 21/3/18.
	,,	JAMES PORTEOUS	Killed, Oct. 1918.

6TH CAMERON HIGHLANDERS.

22461	Piper	JAMES WALKER	Killed, 26/4/17.

7TH CAMERON HIGHLANDERS.

Piper	G. ALVES	Killed, Loos, 25/9/15.
,,	A. SMART	Killed, Loos, 25/9/15.
Pipe Major	KENNETH MACLEOD	Died.

1ST ARGYLL AND SUTHERLAND HIGHLANDERS.

	Piper	WOODSIDE	Killed, 16/2/15, St. Eloi.
570	,,	ROBERT KENNEDY	Killed, 30/7/16, Somme.

2ND ARGYLL AND SUTHERLAND HIGHLANDERS.

567	Piper	PETER M'LINTOCK	Killed, Armentiéres, 27/11/15.
	Lance-Cpl.	MILNE	Killed, Armentiéres, 27/11/15.
90	Piper	M'KAY	Killed, Armentiéres, 27/11/15.
8157	,,	L. PLANNER	Killed, October 1918.

6TH ARGYLL AND SUTHERLAND HIGHLANDERS.

3037	Piper	JAMES PRINGLE	Killed, 18/6/15, Festubert.
3042	,,	JOHN M'ALLISTER	Killed, 18/6/15, Festubert.
3162	,,	WILLIAM CARLYLE	Killed, 16/6/15, Festubert.
1890	,,	JOHN CRAIG	Killed, 27/7/16, Longueval.

7TH ARGYLL AND SUTHERLAND HIGHLANDERS.

277167	Piper	HUGH M'DONALD	Killed, Aug. 1917, Ypres.

8TH ARGYLL AND SUTHERLAND HIGHLANDERS.

Pipe Major	WILLIAM LAWRIE	Died, Nov. 1916.

9TH ARGYLL AND SUTHERLAND HIGHLANDERS.

324	Corpl.	ALEX. M'ALLISTER	Killed, 10/5/15, Ypres.
1711	Piper	ALEX. RUSSELL	Killed, 8/4/15.

10TH ARGYLL AND SUTHERLAND HIGHLANDERS.

	Piper	MACNEILL	Killed, Oct. 1916, Longueval.
570	"	R. KENNEDY	Died of wounds, Longueval.
8051	"	ALEX. KENNEDY	Died of wounds, Ypres, 12/10/17.
302955	"	WALTER NAPIER	Killed, 12/10/17, Ypres.

11TH ARGYLL AND SUTHERLAND HIGHLANDERS.

	Sergt.	JAS. RITCHIE	Killed, 26/9/15, Loos.
	Piper	JAS. BARNETT	Killed, 26/9/15, Hill 70.
	"	F. M'DIARMAID	Killed, July 1916, Somme.
	"	FERGUSON	Died, Dec. 1916, Somme.

12TH ARGYLL AND SUTHERLAND HIGHLANDERS.

	Corpl.	W. STIRLING	Killed, Oct. 1916.
6829	Piper	JOHN M'COLL	Died of disease, Salonika, 16/2/17.
5660	"	D. ROBERTSON	Killed, 8/5/17.
4927	"	L. M'CON	Killed, 8/5/17.

LONDON SCOTTISH.

	Corpl.	T. CAREY	Killed, 1/11/14, Messines.
139	Lance-Cpl.	H. LEATHAM	Killed, 16/11/14, Zillebeke.
? 1341	Piper	D. PARKYN	Killed, 1/11/14, Messines.
	"	C. W. MACKAY	Killed, 17/8/16, Somme (Lieut. 5th Camerons).
1870	"	J. BINNIE	Killed, 9/11/14, Zillebeke.
3509	"	A. CORNELL	Died of wounds, 2/10/16, Somme.
	Lieut.	A. CAIRNS WILSON (formerly Piper)	Killed, 1917; Military Medal.
513657	Piper	SIMON CAMPBELL	Killed, 13/5/17, Arras.
510531	"	A. B. PATON	Killed, 13/5/17.
	"	WOODCOCK	Killed.

1ST TYNESIDE SCOTTISH.

237	Lance-Cpl.	GARNET FYFE	Killed, 1/7/16, Somme.
223	Piper	E. BOYCE	Killed, 1/7/16, Somme.
1585	"	WILLIAM FELLOWS	Killed, 1/7/16, Somme.
154	"	JAMES DOWNIE	Killed, 1/7/16, Somme.
1485	"	WILLIAM INGLIS	Killed, 1/7/16, Somme.

2nd TYNESIDE SCOTTISH.

1230	Piper	William Scott	Killed, 1/7/16, Somme.
1151	„	James Phillips	Killed, 1/7/16, Somme.

3rd TYNESIDE SCOTTISH.

Piper	J. Steele	Killed, 1/7/16, Somme.
„	E. Finlay	Killed, 1/7/16, Somme
„	T. Wilson	Killed, 1/7/16, Somme.
„	R. Greaves	Died of wounds, 1/7/16, Somme.

16th MIDDLESEX.

1151	Piper	Thomas Latham	Killed, 1/7/16, Somme.
	Sergt.	George Kirkland (formerly Piper, 11th Middlesex)	Killed, Ypres, 17/2/17.

1st LIVERPOOL SCOTTISH.

Pipe Major	John Stoddart	Killed, Poperinghe, July 1916.

23rd ROYAL FUSILIERS (1st SPORTSMAN'S BATT.).

Piper	W. Suttie	Killed, 16/3/16.
„	William Mackenzie	Killed, 16/3/16.

ARGYLL MOUNTAIN BATTERY.

Pipe Major	William MacNeill	Died, 18/8/15.
Corpl.	Neil Smith	Accidentally killed, 1/3/16.

ROSS AND CROMARTY BATTERY.

4403	Gunner	John Macdonald	Died of wounds, 14/5/15.

OVERSEAS BATTALIONS

PRINCESS PATRICIA'S CANADIAN LIGHT INFANTRY.

265	Piper	J. M. Robertson, D.C.M.	Died of wounds, 25/3/15.
	Sergt.	John M'Donald, D.C.M.	Died of wounds, 17/9/16.

ROYAL HIGHLANDERS OF CANADA, 13th BATTALION.

24013	Piper	A. J. Macdonald	Died of wounds, 16/3/15, Fleurbaix.
24012	„	W. Lawson	Died of wounds, 16/3/15, Fleurbaix.
24392	„	H. Robertson	Killed, 2/5/15, Ypres.
24704	„	N. Macdonald	Killed, 24/4/15, Ypres.

48TH HIGHLANDERS OF CANADA, 15TH BATTALION.

27548	Corpl.	J. Thompson	Died.

CANADIAN SCOTTISH, 16TH BATTALION.

28694	Piper	James Thomson	Died of wounds, 23/4/15, Ypres.
28779	,,	William M'Ivor	Died of wounds, 10/5/15, Ypres.
28595	,,	George Birnie	Killed, 20/5/15, Festubert.
29468	,,	Angus Morrison	Killed, 20/5/15, Festubert.
28930	,,	James Richardson, V.C.	Killed, 8/10/16, Somme.
28561	,,	John Parks	Killed, 8/10/16, Somme.
28557	,,	Alec M'Gillivray	Killed, 15/8/17, Paschendaele.
429803	,,	George Paul	Killed, 8/8/18, Amiens.

21ST CANADIANS (EASTERN ONTARIO REGIMENT).

Pipe Major	Ian Mackenzie	Killed, Cambrai, 11/10/18.

25TH CANADIANS.

Piper	E. Stewart	Killed, 9/4/18.

29TH CANADIANS (VANCOUVER REGIMENT).

75599	Piper	W. Grant	Killed, 6/11/17.
76126	,,	W. Burnside	Killed, 6/11/17.
76484	,,	J. R. Davidson	Killed, 6/11/17.

1ST CANADIAN PIONEERS.

154184	Piper	John Grant	Killed, 13/6/16.

42ND AUSTRALIANS.

Piper	M. H. Fraser	Killed.

5TH VICTORIAN INFANTRY.

32	Corpl.	Gordon Inglis	Died of wounds, 24/1/16, Gallipoli.

SOUTH AFRICAN SCOTTISH.

Lieut. (formerly Pipe Major)	Robert Thorburn	Killed, 20/7/16, Somme.
Piper	Thomas Scott	Killed, Arras, 9/4/17.

NEW ZEALANDERS (OTAGO REGIMENT).

8/2519	Corpl. Piper	Neil MacDonald	Killed, 15/7/16, Somme.

"So he passed over. And all the trumpets sounded for him on the other side."

CANNTAIREACHD

By Major J. P. Grant, M.C., Yr. of Rothiemurchus

It is related [1] by Sir John Graham Dalyell how in 1818, one John Campbell from Nether Lorn, brought "a folio in MS., said to contain numerous compositions," for the inspection of the judges at the annual piping competition held in Edinburgh under the auspices of the Highland Society: the story goes on, "but the contents merely resembling a written narrative in an unknown language, nor bearing any resemblance to Gaelic, they proved utterly unintelligible. Amidst many conjectures relative both to the subject and the language, nobody adventured so far as to guess at either airs or pibrochs." It is believed that this is the earliest authentic reference to the pipers notation known as Canntaireachd, and it is of interest to note that even as early as 1818, [2] among the class of Highland gentlemen who acted as judges at the biggest competition in the country, the very existence of the notation was unknown. Sir John mentions also that he made later attempts to acquire this MS. volume and to trace two others in the possession of John Campbell's father: his attempts were unsuccessful.

In 1828 Captain Macleod of Gesto published some pipe tunes in Canntaireachd as taught by the MacCrimmons in Skye. The merits of this publication have been made the subject of controversy among pipers and others; this controversy has no place in this paper. The late John Campbell (Iain Ileach) of *Tales of the West Highlands*, wrote a monograph on Canntaireachd in 1880, in which he reviewed Gesto's book: the monograph, interesting as it is and written in Iain Ileach's easy flowing style

[1] *Musical Memoirs of Scotland*, 1849, p. 9.

[2] Sir John was wrong in his date: this incident happened in 1816.

is extraordinarily disappointing. In spite of his comprehensive knowledge of folk-lore—more particularly of Gaelic folk-lore—he fails to indicate any probable source of this notation—probably no one in Europe was, or is better fitted to make conjectures on the point. However, he made two statements of interest in the late history of the notation, (1) that he had " often seen my nurse John Piper reading and practising music from an old paper manuscript, and silently fingering tunes. I have tried to recover this writing, but hitherto in vain," and (2) that there were three local varieties of the notation (*a*) MacCrimmon (*b*) MacArthur, and (*c*) Campbell of Nether Lorn. Now " John Piper " was this same John Campbell of the family of Nether Lorn, which possessed three MS. volumes of Canntaireachd.

Among the older-fashioned pipers in Scotland, even just before the war, one constantly heard syllables (hodroho, hiodro, etc., etc.) being used, generally at haphazard, seldom in their correct place. The astounding thing is that even fragments of a notation, the system of which had been out of use for so long, should have survived to this day.

About 1912 two of the Nether Lorn MS. books were rediscovered, and from them it has not been hard to reconstruct the system of notation. Those tunes with recognisably the same names as we know them by to-day, furnished the first step in the problem : after that it became easy to identify other tunes with different names, and finally to rediscover a number of tunes which have been lost for an undetermined period.

One word of caution will be necessary to certain pipers before going further into this subject. This notation, invented for and suitable only to piobaireachd, is not going to teach pipers how to *play* piobaireachd. There is and always has been, one way and only one way to do that—to get instruction from a master ; once that is accomplished, a pupil may be fit to learn more tunes by himself from books written in any intelligible notation. This I take to be true of any musicians and any music.

The piobaireachd pupil might well get his instruction through the medium of canntaireachd, for it has been made solely for this music, and is in point of fact very suitable for the purpose. To begin with, if the few master-instructors of piobaireachd will take the trouble (and assuredly it will not be great to them) to become familiar with canntaireachd, and to use it as a medium of instruction, it is a matter of certainty that they will realise its use for this end—for instead of a perplexing maze of notes and grace-notes in staff notation to correspond to any movement which they are trying to teach their pupil, they will have pronounceable vocables which will act as *memoria technica* to the pupil: the pupil will, at first, learn these parrot style, until he gets to a certain length, when, unaided, he will begin to see that these vocables he has learnt convey a definite meaning—a definite combination of note and grace note, in a form which can be crooned to the air. I have found that for the purposes of learning new tunes, staff notation compared with canntaireachd is cumbrous and misleading: and even when written in an abbreviated form (as in General Thomason's great book, *Ceol Mor*) it appeals mainly to the eye, while canntaireachd appeals to the ear.

For some years now I have found it invaluable as a kind of musical shorthand, and with a certain amount of practice it becomes possible to write down a tune in canntaireachd while it is being played, and then to learn it at leisure. I had the triumph of converting a brother piper a few years ago. He was inclined to be sceptical about the whole system, so to test me and it he played me a tune which I had never heard and I wrote it down as he played it. After he had finished he said, "Now we shall see what is in it, for I made two mistakes: play what you have got and we shall see." I played on the practice chanter just what I had written, with the mistakes, of course, included.

Again, when one is judging piobaireachd competitions, it is valuable as shorthand to jot down notes of mistakes, etc.

Before coming to the notation itself, it should be explained that it is not maintained for a moment that this variety (the Nether Lorn) is superior in any way to the MacCrimmon or MacArthur varieties. It is merely given and suggested for use, because it is this variety which has become once more available to pipers at large. There are people who undoubtedly can do the same for the MacCrimmon variety also, and it is sincerely hoped that they will do so. That all three varieties are first cousins to each other is beyond doubt to any one who compares them ; perhaps at a later date, when more knowledge of canntaireachd becomes available, it may be possible to point to one as the original, or to find a common ancestor to all.

Coming now to the actual notation, the following paragraphs should be read, subject to this note that the pronunciation of the vocables must be largely a matter of conjecture, but it is reasonable to suppose that, as they were written in the manuscript and used by Gaelic-speaking pipers,[1] the pronunciation should have at least some reference to Gaelic pronunciation —thus the vowels, when occurring as the last letter of the syllable, would be pronounced

'a' as in English h*a*rd
'e' „ h*ay*
'i' „ h*ee*d
'o' „ h*o*me

and probably the consonants should be given their Gaelic equivalents also (all which can best be obtained verbally from a Gaelic speaker).

In addition to the simple vowels, combinations occur which require to be sounded as diphthongs :

'io' } as in English *yo*ke, *e.g.* hioeo
'eo' }
'ea' „ *ya*rd, *e.g.* haea.

[1] The names of the tunes are largely written in rather badly spelt Gaelic, including in some cases the letter 'v,' *e.g.*, Vuirlin instead of A Bhirlinn, and h is the commonest consonant in the vocables—neither 'v' nor 'h' alone being used in correct Gaelic.

KEY TO NETHER LORN CANNTAIREACHD.

	Scale with high G grace note.	Scale with D grace note.	Scale with E Grace note.	Scale with no grace notes.	Siubhal.	Siubhal Sleamhuinn.	Leumluath to E.	Taorluath to low A.	Tripling or Taorluath Breabach.	Crunluath.
w G	him	dam or bam	em	em	himen	himem	himbare	himdarid	himbabem	himbandrc
w A	hin	dan	en	en	hinen	hinen	hinbare	hindarid	hindaen	hinbandre
B	hio	to	eo	o	hioen	hioeo	hiobare	hiodarid	hiotoeo	hiobandre
C	ho	do	eo	o	hoen	hoeo	hobare	hodarid	hodoeo	hobandrc
D	ha	—	ea	a or da	haen	haea	habare or harodde	hadarid	—	habandre or haroddre
E	che	—	—	e or de	che-hin	cheche	chebare	chedarid	—	chebandre
F	he	—	—	ve or dhe	hehin	hehe	hebare	hedarid	—	hebandre
G	hi or chi (high Ag-n.)	—	—	di	hihin	hihi	hibare	hidarid	—	hibandre
A	—	—	—	I	Ien	no example	Ibare	I darid	—	Ibandre

The nomenclature of most of the different movements has for convenience been taken from the Piobaireachd exercises in Logan's Tutor, price 1s., and the examples here given refer to the staff notation examples given there and should be compared with them.

PIOBAIREACHD EXERCISES

(*Cf.* Logan's Tutor.)

1st Scale of Instructions, pp. 34 and 35. On the *Urlar.*

Chedari, hiriri, herere, cherede, hiharara, hihodro, hihorodo, hiharin. (See *Cadences*, p. 185.)

2nd Scale of Instructions.

Enbari (should be embari, *i.e.* from low G), endare, endre (note : if this shake on F or E is approached from a higher note the vocables become vedare and edre respectively ; thus one gets Ivedare, but hiodare, heedre but hiodre) tradarodo (tra being the usual throw on D, *e.g.* hiotra), p. 36, hihorodin, hodrodin, hiotrodin.

3rd Scale of Instructions. On *Crunluath.*

Hinban or hinbain, dre—together hinbandre, Ibandre.

4th Scale, p. 37. On *Crunluath Breabach.*

Hinbandreendi.

IbandreenI hibandreendi, hibandreendhe chebandreende, habandreenda hobandreendo, hiobandreemto hinbandreendan.

5th Scale. On *Crunluath Fosgailte.*

Hindodre.

No examples of open : closed, himdandre hintodre, hindodre hindadre, twice over.

6th Scale. On *Crunluath Mach.*

Hiotradre hodrodre, hiotrodre himbamdre, twice over.

7th Scale. The *Exercise on Accidentals.*

IbarI dibari (no example known), vebarhe edre, adeda odro, otro enban or enbain, twice over.

CHA TILL MACCRUIMEIN

1st. Dreve hiove, cheve cheento, dreve hiove, cheve cheemto, dreve hioe, trae haento,

2nd. Dreve hiove, cheve cheemto, dreve hioe, trae haemto, dreve hioe, trae haento,

3rd. Dreve hiove, cheve cheemto, dreve hioe, trae haento.

Var. 1st.

1st. DreI ove, cheI deento, dreI ove, cheI deemto, dreI oe, traI aento, etc.

Var. 2nd.

1st. Cheve hiove, cheve cheento, cheve hiove, cheve cheemto, cheve hioe, trae haento, etc.

Doubling of Var. 2nd.

1st. Chea cheo, cheve cheento, chea cheo, cheve cheemto, chea cheo, trae haento, etc.

Various Vocables not previously included.

Throw on high A	dili.
Taorluath to low G	hiodarem, chedarem, etc.
Low A with low G grace-note before	-din (*e.g.* hiodin).
D or C followed by B grace-note on low G grace-note followed by A with low G grace-note before	harodin or horodin.
Taorluath mach	hiotroeo, hodroeo, hiotraea.
Crunluath to low G.	hiobamdre, or hiobaemdre or (on D) haromdre.

Cadences

By cadences I mean those notes often printed as grace-notes, GED, followed by C, B, low A, or low G melody notes, and GE followed by D, low A, or low G melody notes. The prefix 'hi' is in general terms used for this, *e.g.* hiharin, hihorodin. Taking them in above order, examples of the vocables used are, of the former, hihodin, hihioem, hihinbain, and hiham-bam, and of the latter hiaen, hienem, hiemto. It is one of the remarkable points in the MS. that these cadences are indicated to a far less extent than is played by traditional players of modern times, and I am as yet unable to make any deductions from the manner in which they appear as to the style in which the MS. intends them to be played. To avoid confusion between ' hi ' as cadence and high G with A grace-note, it would be better to use the alternative ' chi ' for the latter.

General

A study of the key will reveal various noticeable points, some of which I will touch on here. It will be seen that some of the composite vocables can be pulled to pieces into their component parts, *e.g.*, hiotroeo, hinbandre, etc., while others can only be dissected to a lesser extent, *e.g.*, hindaen in the Tripling or Taorluath Breabach ; in this latter case the vocable must be read in its context, for hindaento might be ᴳ low A, D, low A, ᴰB, while standing by itself, but in conjunction with a string of others it is undoubtedly meant to be the Taorluath Breabach. Again there is liable to be confusion between 'en ' low A without any and with an E grace-note, and in some few cases it is impossible to say definitely which is meant : on the other hand it is used in the siubhal variation, and there can be no doubt in such a context : hinen by itself is unambiguous, and in various combinations, *e.g.*, hiaendre, it is highly probable that no E grace-note is intended. The question of the eo and o, B or C, is a little more difficult in theory, but in practice it will be found to narrow down to one or two instances; the most common instance of this ambiguity is odro, which may be either B grip C, or C grip C. It seems likely that this confusion is the origin of this difference in existing settings of various tunes, *e.g.*, An Daorach Mhor (The Big Spree) Var. 1st and doubling, The Battle of Auldearn, The Carles of Sligachin and many others. Campbell often writes ' ho ' for ' o,' obviously not intending a G grace-note, but to avoid this ambiguity.

Time signature and rhythm are, I think, sufficiently shown to enable a trained player to find no difficulty in playing; bar divisions are indicated by commas, and each part of each tune is divided into lines numbered 1st, 2nd, etc.: and a repeat is written at the end of the line to be repeated, thus: Two times or twice over. '3 times,' etc., is often used in the MS. to refer back only to the last comma, not to the beginning of the line. The smaller details of time, which I will call "pointing," is a matter of greater doubt. I have said above why I think Gaelic standards should be applied to the pronunciation of the vocables, and my opinion is that the same applies to this question in general terms: it can be said that as a rule the vocables are separated into distinct words, the accent or stress (and in this case the longer note) being represented as the first syllable of the word (an almost invariable rule in Gaelic). Thus one gets hodarid hiodarid—not daridho daridhio darid. Many exceptions can be pointed out no doubt, but the above will serve as a broad rule.

It should be made clear to any reader of this paper that it has been written in haste. Most of it is written from memory after four and three-quarter years separation from MSS., books and notes, and I have no doubt that mistakes will be discovered later. Further, it does not profess to be complete, for there are some vocables not included, the meaning of which is not yet clear to me.

The two volumes of the MS. contain 169 tunes of which I can trace in no other collection, printed or MS., 65 tunes: moreover, many tunes which exist already in printed collections are written in entirely different settings, and under different names from those known by present day players. To illustrate this I have included at the end of this paper the MS. style of An Ceapadh Eucorach (translated as the "Unjust Incarceration"). This setting, apart from smaller differences, contains one line in each part which, so far as my knowledge goes, is unknown to-day, and which in my opinion is an essential part of the theme, leading the 3rd line up to the musical climax of the ordinarily accepted 4th line.[1] The names of the tunes as written in the Index or as headings in the MS. present a very difficult problem. Some are in English; some are in recognisable Gaelic; some are

[1] Since this was written I have discovered this line in staff notation in an old MS. by Donald Macdonald, son of the man who published the Collection of Piobaireachd in the early nineteenth century.

in unrecognisable Gaelic, some give the first few notes of the tune, and some are ludicrous mistranslations of Gaelic into English. Only approximately 42 out of the total have anything like the names by which the tunes are known to-day.

It is to be hoped that some day soon the whole MS. will be printed, so that enthusiasts who have the time may really get to work and unravel some of the conundrums which still remain so. I have a feeling that the vocables used in so many Gaelic songs are distantly related to canntaireachd, and research into this might conceivably throw light on the larger question of the origin of canntaireachd. It would also be interesting to know of any examples of similar notations in foreign countries. But the main thing to be done by all pipers at the present day is to make real attempts to discover other canntaireachd manuscripts: and the ideal should be that all MSS. now known to exist or discovered at a later date should be made available for comparison and information of other players; this is best done by publication in as near the original form as possible, and failing that by loan or gift to some responsible piping society, such as the Scottish Pipers Society, The Piobaireachd Society, the Caledonian Pipers Society, London, The Inverness Pipers Society, The Highland Pipers Society, Edinburgh, or any other well-known society. This would ensure that the information would get into the hands of those who can most easily disseminate it.

AN CEAPADH EUCORACH

(From the Campbell MS. vol. i. p. 1.)

1st called *Kepper Eggarich.*

Hiharin hioen[1], hodrooen, himen hoen, hiotroenem, hihodrooen, hiotroenem hihodroen hioem hiharinen

2nd Hiharin hioen hodrooen, himotrao hoen, hiotroenem, hihodrooen hiotroenem, hihodroen, hioem hiharinen

3rd Hihodrotra, cheredea hoen, hadrea hoen, hihorodoenem, hihodrotra, cherededea[2] hihodroen hioem, hiharinen

[1] The commas are thrown about haphazard in this tune. [2] Something is omitted here—probably 'a.'

4th Hihararache, hiveda͡reve[1] cheho, haem, barivecheho, hiharara[2]hohic, hihodrotraem, bariveda͡revechea,[1] hihodroen, hioem, hiharinen

5th Chedari Ie, hiririeha diliedrehia, cheredeaho himbarihia, cheho, hadre himbaria, chedaria, hioem hiharinen.

The First Motion

1st Hinen hinen hioen, hoen, hoen, hinen, himen, hinen, hoen, hioen, hioen, himen, hoen hoen hinen hioen, hioen, himen hoen hoen hioem, hinen hinen hinen

2nd Hinen hinen hioen hihoen[3] hoen hinen himen haen hoen, hioen hioen, himen hoen hoen hinen hioen hioen himen hoen hoen hioem, hinen three times.

3rd Hoen hoen haem, chehin chehin, hoen haem, chehin hoen hioen hioen, himen hoen hoen haem, chehin chehin chehin hoen hoen hioem, hinen three times.

4th Haen haem, chehin hien hien chehin haem hien chehin haen haen hioem, hoen hoen haem hien hien chehin hoen hoen hioem, hinen three times.

5th Chehin hien, dilien hien hien, haen dilien, chehin hien, chehin chehin, hoen hien hien, chehin haem, chehin hien, chehin hien, hioem, hinen three times.

The 2nd Motion, called Tolive

1st Hindarid hindarid hiodarid hodarid hodarid hindarid himdarid hindarid hodarid hiodarid hiodarid himdarid hodarid hodarid hindarid hiodarid hiodarid himdarid hodarid hodarid hiodarem, hindarid three times.

2nd Hindarid hindarid hiodarid hodarid hodarid hindarid himdarid hadarid hodarid hiodarid hiodarid himdarid hodarid hodarid hindarid hiodarid hiodarid himdarid hodarid hodarid hiodarem hindarid three times.

[1] It is not easy to see what 'veda͡re' means here : comparing it with same point in First, Second and Third Motions, it should probably be 'dari' instead of veda͡re or 'vedari' perhaps. As written in D. Macdonald, Jr's. MS. it would be 'dari.'

[2] 'h' is probably inserted here to show that C and not B is meant.

[3] Perhaps this cadence is a clerical error.

3rd Hodarid hodarid hadarem, chedarid chedarid, hodarid hadarem, chedarid hodarid, hiodarid hiodarid, himdarid hodarid hodarid, hadarem, chedarid three times, hodarid hodarid, hiodarem hindarid three times.

4th Hadarid hadarem, chedarid hidarid hidarid chedarid hadarem hidarid, chedarid hadarid hadarid hiodarem, hodarid hodarid hadarem hidarid hidarid chedarid hodarid hodarid hiodarem, hindarid three times.

5th Chedarid hidarid Idarid hidarid hidarid hadarid Idarid chedarid hidarid chedarid chedarid hodarid hidarid hidarid chedarid hadrem,[1] chedarid hidarid chedarid hidarid hiodarem, hindarid three times.

Part 3rd, Crolive

1st Hinbandre hinbandre, hiobandre hobandre hobandre hinbandre himbandre hinbandre hobandre hiobandre hiobandre himbandre hobandre hobandre hinbandre hiobandre hiobandre himbandre hobandre hobandre hiobaemdre hinbandre hinbandre hinbandre hinbandre.

2nd Hinbandre hinbandre hiobandre hobandre hobandre hinbandre himbandre habandre hobandre hiobandre hiobandre himbandre hobandre hobandre hinbandre hiobandre hiobandre himbandre hobandre hobandre hiobaemdre, hinbandre hinbandre hinbandre.

3rd Hobandre hobandre habamdre chebandre chebandre hobandre habamdre chebandre hobandre hiobandre hiobandre himbandre hobandre hobandre habaemdre, chebandre three times, hobandre hobandre hiobamdre hinbandre hinbandre hinbandre.

4th Habandre habaemdre chebandre hibandre hibandre chebandre habaemdre hibandre chebandre habandre habandre hiobaemdrehobandre hobandre habaemdre hibandre hibandre chebandre hobandre hobandre hiobaemdre, hinbandre three times.

5th Chebandre hibandre Ibandre hibandre hibandre habandre Ibandre chebandre hibandre chebandre chebandre hobandre hibandre hibandre chebandre habaemdre chebandre hibandre chebandre hibandre hiobaemdre hinbandre three times.

[1] Probably a clerical error for hadarem.

THE IRISH PIPES:

THEIR HISTORY, DEVELOPMENT, AND DIVERGENCE FROM THE SIMPLE HIGHLAND TYPE

By W. H. Grattan Flood, Mus.D., K.S.G.

There is ample evidence that the bagpipe was used in pre-Christian Ireland, whence it was brought to Scotland. It is referred to in the Brehon Laws of the fifth century. Irish writers allude to it as *Cuisle* and as *Piob mor*—and this is the warlike instrument which was adopted by our Scottish brethren and became the national instrument of Scotland.

During the thirteenth and fourteenth centuries Irish pipers accompanied the Irish troops that fought in Gascony and Flanders under King Edward I. Strange, too, that Irish pipers were heard, in opposition to the Scots, at the battle of Falkirk (July 22, 1298), and it is surmised that the strident tones of the Irish *piob mor* suggested to the Scotch the employment of this warlike instrument in battle. At Crecy (August 26, 1346) the Irish pipes were also in evidence, and again at Harfleur (1418) and at Rouen (1419). Incidentally, it may be stated that there is no sound historical evidence for the Scotch bagpipes in battle at Harlaw (1411), but it would appear that they were employed at the battle of Inverlochy (1431). Irish pipers were heard to advantage in Henry VIII.'s Tournay campaign (1513) and also at the siege of Boulogne (1544). This association of Irish pipers leading the charge is strikingly pourtrayed in the *Mask of Irishmen* played before Queen Mary at the English Court, on April 25, 1557, in which there were six Irish *Kerne* and two *Bagpipers*.

Here is Stanihurst's description of the Irish *piob mor*, in 1575: "The Irish, likewise, instead of the trumpet, make use of a wooden pipe of the most ingenious structure, to which is joined a leather bag, very closely bound with bands. A pipe is inserted in the side of this skin,through which the piper, with his swollen neck and puffed-up cheeks, *blows in the same manner as we do through a tube.* The skin, being thus filled with air, begins to swell, and the player presses against it with his arm; thus a loud and shrill sound is produced through two wooden pipes of different lengths. In addition to these, there is yet a fourth pipe (the chanter), perforated in different places (having five or six holes), which the player so regulates by the dexterity of his fingers in the shutting and opening of the holes, that he can cause the upper pipes to send forth either a loud or a low sound at pleasure."

A few years after Stanihurst presented this description of the Irish *piob mor,* a new development of this instrument came into vogue, that is, about the year 1580, and almost immediately came into favour. This development was the Irish *Uilleann* (elbow) pipes, or domestic pipes, in which the wind was supplied by a bag blown by the elbow. Shakespearian commentators have been puzzled over the term "woollen" pipes in the *Merchant of Venice* (Act iv. Sc. 1); but the great bard of Avon, who derived much information regarding Ireland from Stanihurst and Dowland (if he did not actually visit Ireland at the close of the sixteenth century), used the Irish term *Uilleann,* equating it with "woollen"—a corruption which subsequently blossomed forth as "Union pipes." All during the seventeenth century the *Uilleann* pipes became immensely popular, and were used as an accompaniment for dancing, especially the *Rinnce Fada* (The Long Dance), the qualifying word *Fada* becoming Anglicised as "the Fading," also alluded to by Shakespeare (*Winter's Tale,* Act iv. Sc. 3). Subsequently keys or regulators were added, a feature that we also find in the *Surdelina,* or Neapolitan bagpipe, in 1625, as described by Père Mersenne. It is of interest to note that the great English composer, William Byrd, *circâ* 1590, wrote a piece of programme music called "Mr. Byrd's Battle," in which there are three movements; the *Irish March,* the *Bagpipe,* and the *Drone.* Thus the Irish bagpipe furnished the musical form known as "pedal point" or "drone bass."

When the Regiment of Irish Guards was formed in 1662, provision was made for a drum major, twenty-four drummers, and a piper to the King's Company. At the siege of Derry in 1689, the Jacobite regiments had each fourteen pipers and eighty-six drums.

Further improvements in the *Uilleann* pipes were effected between the years 1700 and 1720, and, in consequence, they were taken up by musical amateurs or "gentlemen pipers," of whom Larry Grogan, Parson Sterling, and Walter Jackson were famous.

The Irish *piob mor* was heard at the battle of Fontenoy (May 11, 1745), on which occasion the pipers played "St. Patrick's Day in the Morning," and "The White Cockade"—two characteristic Irish airs. Irish pipers were also heard during the American War of Independence, and, in 1778, Barney Thompson, from Hillsborough, Co. Down, was pipe major of Lord Rawdon's "Volunteers of Ireland," which corps merged into the 100th Regiment in 1780.

The revival of the Irish bagpipes in Irish regiments is due to Major Doyle, in September, 1793. A few months previously, on May 23, his brother, Colonel Doyle, in command of the 14th Regiment, found the fortunes of the day at the siege of Famara going against the British troops, when, by a happy inspiration, he ordered his band to play up the French revolutionary march of "Ça Ira," and shouted to his troops: "Come on, boys, and we'll beat 'em to their own damned tune." As a result, Doyle's regiment successfully routed the French, to the strains of "Ça Ira," which has ever since been the quick-step of the West Yorkshire Regiment (the old 14th). The Colonel wrote to his brother the Major, who was M.P. for Mullingar, telling him of the advantage of a good band, and, as at that very time (August) Major Doyle had been commissioned by King George III. to form a new Irish regiment, originally called "Major Doyle's Legion," the Major recruited a gallant body of his countrymen, known as "The Prince of Wales' Royal Irish Regiment"—with a band of Irish pipers.

Not long afterwards, in October 1793, Colonel de Burgh (brother of the Marquis of Clanrickarde) formed the "Royal Connaught Rangers," with a fine band of pipers and drummers. The Wexford Regiment (the 38th), commanded by Lord Loftus, had also a pipe band ere the close of the year 1794 or early in 1795. Several years later there were pipers attached to the Tyrones (4th Inniskilling Fusiliers).

However, after the year 1815, the vogue of a pipe band in Irish regiments waned, and it was not till 1903 that the Queen's County Militia—the 4th Battalion of the P.O.W. Leinster Regiment—again took up the war pipes, thanks to the enthusiasm and generosity of their commander, Lieut.-Col. Lord Castletown, K.P.

To the Tyrone Fusiliers, a link battalion of the 27th Royal Inniskilling Fusiliers, is due the revival of the Irish *Piob mor* in 1859. Some years later, Colonel Cox, commanding the 87th Royal Irish Fusiliers, supplied eight sets of war pipes, as well as two drums, to eight Irish pipers in his regiment. More recently, the 4th Battalion of the Leinster Regiment (late Queen's County Militia) formed a pipe band under the direction of their gallant Colonel, my dear friend, Lord Castletown of Upper Ossory, K.P., who presented the pipes, in 1903. Since then all five battalions of this regiment have pipe bands, mainly through the enthusiastic zeal of Captain Orpen Palmer who published an excellent little book for the war pipes in 1913. Other Irish regiments having pipe bands are the 2nd Battalion of the Dublin Fusiliers and the 3rd Battalion of the 18th Royal Irish.

In conclusion it may be briefly said that the Irish war pipe of to-day is the same as the Scottish or Highland war pipe. On the other hand, the Irish *Uilleann* pipes may be regarded as a miniature organ. The old war pipe is only capable of eight notes with certain limitations, whereas the *Uilleann* pipes are of two full octaves, including chromatic intervals, and are thus capable of performing most classes of music, added to which the four keys of the regulator on the chanter make for a wonderful effect.

THE TUITION OF YOUNG REGIMENTAL PIPERS

By JOHN GRANT, Pipe Major

THERE is an establishment for the training of bandsmen at Kneller Hall, Twickenham, known as "The Royal Military School of Music," where regular soldiers are trained in a very efficient manner both in theory and practice, for brass bands. Each pupil remains for a considerable period, extending from one to three years, and not only do they become good performers on the various instruments, but they qualify for the rank of bandmaster in any regiment. A bandmaster holds the rank of a warrant officer, and, in some cases, a commissioned officer.

Some months ago a colonial soldier asked the question in a Highland newspaper why the pipe major in a Highland regiment did not also hold the rank of a warrant officer. In fact pipe major is only an honorary rank. In reality he is only "sergeant piper." It would be very interesting to know the difference between the person in charge of the one band and the other. When the regiment is on the march the one band leads the men as well as the other. In fact many prefer a pipe band to a brass band on a long route march. In a pipe band the pipe major has to train his pipers efficiently in the performance of their music just the same as the bandmaster of a brass band, and why should a pipe major not be raised to the rank of a warrant officer along with his brother bandmaster? True it is that in a brass band there are many instruments for the bandmaster to teach and bring in in their proper places, in order to have a perfect band. But then the pipe major has the same task in front of him in training a perfect pipe band. In fact—if I may be allowed the analogy—in the case of a brass band a bandmaster might have many glaring errors and flaws in instrumentation and harmony in his band, and this is passed over by the average listener but detected by the expert conductor. The brass band, from its construction, has more scope for covering errors than the pipe band.

The regimental pipe band is so constructed that each performer must play in perfect unison, with pipes all timed in unison, and every finger should be lifted and laid down together, a thing which is much more difficult to do than is the case with a brass band. The errors in a badly trained pipe band are much more easily detected where every performer has to play in perfect unison, than the errors in a brass band, where different instruments take different parts.

The next important point is the bandmaster has been properly trained in his profession at the "Royal Military School of Music," Kneller Hall, but the pipe major in a pipe band has not had this coveted opportunity. There is no school where pipe music is taught in theory and practice, and that may be one of the chief reasons why the pipe major falls short of the trained bandmaster. If a military school of piping were instituted by the War Office, such an institution would supply a long felt want. The piper could then be educated in piping, to understand music in theory, and be instructed in practice on a sound basis and fixed system.

Few pipers in pipe bands, if any, are trained at the proper age, *i.e.*, 12–14–16 years, except in industrial schools, where they are in many cases improperly taught. When the boy is young his fingers will do anything because they are very supple, but at the age of twenty they become stiff and set against perfect manipulation. At this age theory is picked up in a masterly fashion, and the pupil is unconscious of difficulties in fingering, which simplifies everything in the process of his training.

At no period in the history of our nation was there greater need for a military school of piping than at the present moment. There are hundreds of young pipers required to fill the places of those who have fallen in action. As can be seen from the record contained in this volume many pipe bands have suffered most heavily. In fact some have been entirely wiped out.

From experience of class-work in piping it has been proved that the training of young pipers at the age of fourteen to sixteen years under a fixed system is an ideal method of creating good performers. Boys who have never had a finger on the chanter before, are started in classes of from eight to ten in number. This prevents them from making an improper use of the chanter or creating bad fingering which, if allowed to go too far, can never be got out of. Each pupil should be provided with a properly made chanter, and all the chanters in the class should be of the same make and correctly tuned, so that, while at practice in class-work, they are all in perfect unison. If one or two improperly made and badly tuned chanters are used in a class, this is the cause of two great evils. The performer's ear becomes less sensitive to the notes in proper pitch ; and it discourages the training of a pupil to detect improper sounds and slovenly fingering. If there are two or three chanters out of tune in a class of ten they prevent the instructor from detecting errors in fingering.

The use of a properly tuned chanter tends to cultivate a good ear, whereas if the ear is used to improper sounds it loses its power of detecting the difference between what is real and that which is false.

In class-work it is hardly possible to get ten pupils with equal powers of picking up tunes and correct fingering. The ear may be compared to a machine which records musical compositions and sounds. In this respect the perfect machine has already been found. The phonograph will record and reproduce a tune in perfect form, but then it is only a reproduction, whereas the musician has life and power to create new and original tunes.

Take the human ear. Where it is perfect it will record a tune with the same accuracy as the machine ; but, where the ear is defective, it will only take in what it is capable of. In cases where there is only a slight defect in ear, and where a pupil is somewhat slow at fingering, care must be taken that the slow pupil is brought up in line with the smart pupil. This makes the results in class-work equal. Many instructors of piping fail because they overlook slovenly fingering. Each pupil must be made to finger exactly. The slovenly player spoils the class and every band into which he may go, so that, if a class is to be properly taught, each pupil must come to know his class mate as a musician as well as a companion. Each performer in a pipe band must form part of a machine, as it were, which acts systematically as a clock, in order to give good results and render a tune like one man. A properly trained class with a sufficiently long period of training will, in time, finger together in a manner which is most surprising as regards regularity.

As an example of irregularity in fingering, take for instance—one pupil is playing in perfect time, one graces his note a little too soon and another a little too late. This gives three different renderings as regards time, and how could they become pleasing to the ear or ever attain regularity in time or fingering ?

"Patience is a virtue," and an instructor of piping must be imbued with that qualification. Without patience there can be no climax, no perfection, and no goal to aim at. One may compel a person to do work even by punishment, but to compel a pupil to play the pipes would be hopeless. If a pupil has to be forced to play an instrument against his will, the music will be anything but pleasing to the listener's ear. Then it will lack expression, the most important and wonderful thing in all musical performances. To be successful as an instructor of piping one must first win the hearts of his pupils, so that they will like and respect him ; speak firmly but kindly to them ; enforce strict discipline and good behaviour ; and conduct his school just the same as all well-governed establishments of education. One hour's instruction should be given at a time, and this should be given by the instructor of the school himself. Although boys are boys, they are sensitive to insult and degradation, and they will not accept tuition from another boy, even although he is a good performer. It has been found to be the case that intelligent pupils must have instruction from the proper source, and, when one boy teaches another, their time is wasted and they drift into slovenly and careless fingering. This constitutes a reason for strict supervision on the part of an instructor himself in a school of piping, so that the best results may be attained and good order and obedience maintained.

In bagpipe music, theory is entirely neglected. The average piper is able to read the names of the notes : G A B C D E F G and A, and he plays from them and pays little attention to their value. They may be all crotchets, quavers or semi-quavers, for all he cares. In almost every case the piper has already heard the tune played on the chanter, and the relative value of the notes mean nothing to him. Then, one hears illegal syncopation, *e.g.*, the taking of the value from the lengthened note and giving it to the next one, which should be the shortest note in the beat, especially in six-eight time. Then, in writing down an original tune without a knowledge of the theory of music, the average piper is of no use.

Boys should be started on the chanter at fourteen to sixteen years of age, and given a period of chanter practice of from six to nine months; at the same time it is necessary to see that, from the very start, they are able to read music at sight. Then, towards the end of nine months tuition in practice, theory should be taught; then they make more progress than they would at the very beginning of their training. Theory enables the piper to put expression into his playing, and, in his turn, he can in time take his place as a qualified instructor of piping.

One thing of great importance in piping and the training of young pipers is the rate of speed at which they play. The regimental regulation pace is 120 paces to the minute. This may be all very well with a brass band, where the performer with his 120 paces to the minute has a curtailed, nipped, or broken step, but in pipe music it is far different. Any one who has a knowledge of the Highland bagpipe and its music knows that piping at the rate of 120 paces to the minute is not pipe music at all. The great majority of marches for the pipes are written in two-four and six-eight time. Two-four time has a crotchet beat and six-eight has a dotted crotchet beat. The beat in six-eight being a dotted crotchet is of longer duration than the two-four or crochet beat. When both are played at 120 paces to the minute they are more or less equalized and spoiled. Time must be given to the beat note in six-eight to distinguish it from the two-four beat; hence, 100 to 105 paces to the minute in two-four time is good marching, and 90 to 95 paces to the minute in six-eight time gives the proper swinging pace which the men in a Highland regiment like. To adopt such a suggestion would give time and expression to pipe music, differentiate the pace in one time signature from another, and, above all, would tend to give more time for correct fingering and clear, distinct playing. A young piper who has only been playing the bagpipes for about six months is very often spoiled for life as a performer when he begins, at that stage, to play at 120 paces to the minute. He is unable to get the fingering in in time. What he cannot find time to finger is left out altogether, and then, worst of all, he becomes a slovenly and incorrect performer.

The teaching of piping has always been placed on an unequal footing as compared with brass bands in His Majesty's forces, and one wonders how long it is to be allowed to remain so. It is absolutely certain that a Military School of Piping would be a blessing to regimental pipe bands, and the standard of performance could be raised to the highest point of perfection. In times of peace many people single out the brass band as the apple of their eye in the garden of music, so to speak, but let us Higlanders mark time and see what the great Highland bagpipe has done in war.

Many pipers have gone over the parapet playing the bagpipes and have won laurels which can never be forgotten. Hundreds of pipers have fallen in the great war to sleep their last sleep in the graves of heroes, after sounding the triumphant charge. The bagpipe has lived in war in its majestic power and splendour, and in peace it should not be allowed to die.

In war there is, to our Highland regiments, no music like that of the great Highland bagpipe. Its notes inspire the men to victory, and the glory of the results of the music of the *Piob Mhor* with its fluttering pennons has left a landmark in the history of the world's war.

The great Highland bagpipe is the hallmark of a race whose achievements are second to none in the world. It has been played in every great battlefield in the history of our nation, and the heroic deeds done by Highland regiments inspired by its music deserve to be perpetuated in a lasting memorial.

THE SPIRIT OF THE MACCRIMMONS

By Fred T. MacLeod, F.S.A. (Scot.)

It was the year 1626, a memorable year in the history of the Western Isles of Scotland, and singularly eventful in the history of Skye and of the Dunvegan family. Sir Rory Mor MacLeod, warrior and statesman, patron of Art, of Music and of Letters, and dispenser of lavish hospitality to rich and poor alike, had died in the Chanonry of Ross an event " greatly deplored among the Gael at that time." The ancient sea-gate of Dunvegan Castle was opened, and into a waiting boat stepped Patrick Mor MacCrimmon, the dead chief's hereditary piper, the representative of a line of pipers almost as long as the line of MacLeod chiefs. Swiftly, yet silently, the piper was rowed across Loch Dunvegan to Boreraig. MacCrimmon stepped ashore and took from his servant the instrument which had on many occasions cheered his beloved master. His heart could no longer contain its pent-up emotion, and his frame shook with a violent outburst of grief. Then, with head erect and firm step, he walked the remaining distance to the renowned College of Pipers, the home of his family for many generations. The fingers of a master player lingered for a moment lovingly on the chanter. In swift succession there fell upon the ears of his pupils, themselves no mean players of ancient piobaireachd, the arresting, appealing, plaintive notes of " Cumha Ruaridh Mhoir," " Lament to Rory Mor."

To-day, cattle browse upon the site of the MacCrimmon College, within whose walls instruction on the *Piob mhor* had been given by members of the MacCrimmon family to countless students from all parts. Thither too had come the best pipers of Scotland to receive the finishing touches to a piping education well-nigh perfect in itself, including representatives of the three well-known piping families, MacArthur, Mackay and Campbell. The musi of the pipes is now seldom, if ever, heard on the plateau upon which in former days many pipers were wont to assemble. Sassenach inhibitory legislation followed by the unsympathetic action of the Highland clergy combined in an attempt to stifle for ever the majestic notes of ancient piobaireachd, and the free, independent, social temperament of the Children of the Island. But, while the grass grows green on the spot where the college stood, the memory of these master musicians is enshrined in the ancient traditions of the island, in the MacCrimmon compositions preserved and played to-day, and in the names of places in the vicinity of the MacCrimmon homeland. The ancient castle, dating from the ninth century, is occupied to-day by Norman Magnus MacLeod, the 23rd chief of his line, as it has been continuously occupied by his forefathers, and among the relics carefully preserved is an ancient set of MacCrimmon pipes. One can still enjoy the shelter of "Slochd nam Piobairean"[1] and he who desires to do so can honour the dust of several members of the MacCrimmon family in the little burying-ground at Kilmuir, overlooking Dunvegan Loch. Nay more, one may converse with living descendants of the family within a stone's throw of the home of their forefathers. The fame of the MacCrimmons will never die so long as these features or the memory of them remains, and, when these are no longer remembered, the honour due to these Kings of Pipers will be enshrined in the music they have left behind them.

It is impossible in this article to do more than touch the fringe of an almost illimitable subject. There are many controversial points into which it is not desirable to enter, *e.g.*, the origin of the family name, the exact period during which the MacCrimmons held their hereditary office, and the "Cainntaireachd" invented and used by them. The old papers in the castle are singularly silent in regard to the history of men so closely allied with the fortunes of the Dunvegan family. The only two documents among these papers, so far as I am aware, which bear upon the subject, are a lease of the lands of Galtrigal in Skye to the MacCrimmons in virtue of their hereditary office, and a rent-roll of the latter years of the eighteenth century,

[1] "The pipers' hollow."

which contains entries of payments made by MacLeod tenants, in the form of a tax to assist a member of the MacCrimmon family in his declining years. But while contemporary documentary evidence is practically unavailable, tradition has preserved a great deal of interesting information. While it may not be advisable to accept as accurate many oral traditions of a country, we are entitled to rely to a considerable extent upon, and to accept as generally trustworthy, Highland oral tradition, which every student of Highland history knows was the common mode of preserving what otherwise would have been long ago irretrievably lost. The office of "Seanachaidh"[1] was recognized and honoured in leading Highland families and, subject to the legitimate criticism that a Seanachaidh was apt unduly to extol the virtues of those whose praises he sang and to decry the virtues of rival families, we are entitled to draw upon this source of information.

The first published account of the family known to me is Angus MacKay's collection of *Ancient Piobaireachd*, or Highland Pipe Music, published in 1838, which forms the basis of most, if not all, the subsequent published references to the family. Dr. Norman MacLeod's account (in Gaelic) of the MacCrimmons must also be mentioned, and of more modern date Dr. Fraser's interesting book on the *Highland Bagpipe*. The Rev. Archibald Clerk contributed an article worthy of notice in the *New Statistical Account of Scotland*, and Fionn's *Martial Music of the Gael* contains some interesting notes.

I regard, however, as the most authoritative contribution a series of Gaelic articles contributed to the *Celtic Monthly* by the Rev. Neil Ross of Buccleuch Parish Church, Edinburgh. Mr. Ross is one of our ablest Gaelic scholars, and, having been born and brought up in the heart of the MacCrimmon country, he has had the peculiar advantage of obtaining the local traditions of the family at first hand, from old people practically all of whom have passed away.

I am inclined to place the commencement of the MacCrimmon era so far as their relationship with the Macleods of Dunvegan is concerned,

[1] Keeper of family records, genealogist.

approximately as 1500, and the termination thereof as 1822. My reasons for doing so are first that we find that in 1651 one of the family was publicly acknowledged as the King of Pipers. In the old chronicle detailing this incident the name of the piper upon whom this honour was bestowed is given as John Macgurmen (MacCrimmon) which I believe to be a mistake for Patrick MacCrimmon, he who composed the well-known port, "I gave a kiss to the hand of the King." If the old adage is true that it took seven years of a man's life and seven generations of pipers before him to make a perfect piper, the date 1500 is by no means too remote. Further, the traditional list of MacCrimmon pipers who held their hereditary office is sufficiently long to bridge that period. Dr. MacLeod enumerates seven successive members of the family, whereas Mr. Ross furnishes us with twelve names inclusive of those mentioned by Dr. MacLeod. The following is Mr. Ross' list :

Finlay of the Breacan.	Patrick Òg.
Iain Odhar.	Donald Bàn.
Patrick Caogach.	Angus Òg.
Patrick Donn.	Malcolm.
Donald Mór.	Iain Dubh.
Patrick Mór.	Patrick Mór.

It is outwith the scope of this article to deal with the MacCrimmon genealogy, or to discuss in detail the different members of the family. Interesting notes might be furnished concerning most of the men whose names are enumerated above, and it might not be difficult for a skilled player of pibroch, by a careful analysis of the MacCrimmon compositions, to assign many of the extant compositions to the appropriate composers. I prefer to gather together from the available sources known to me a few incidents in the lives of three outstanding members of the family, Donald Mór, Patrick Mór and Donald Bàn.

DONALD MÓR MACCRIMMON

We shall probably not be very far wrong if we regard the period during which this piper lived as that embracing the concluding years of the sixteenth century and the early years of the seventeenth. I realise that, in so placing him, I lay myself open to the criticism that I post-date the period of Patrick Mór's activities. Patrick Mór is regarded as the son of Donald Mór, and it is probable that both father and son were in the service of Sir Rory Mór. It is stated that, being a special favourite of his chief, Donald was sent to Ireland to complete his musical education. There can be little doubt that as Ireland was the early home of Celtic letters so she was the early home of musical culture, and that the high degree of efficiency attained by the MacCrimmons was, at least in part, due to the finishing touches obtained by them in the sister island. We learn that Donald Mór played before many of the nobility and gentry of the country and greatly distinguished himself. Mr. Ross has an interesting note that Donald accompanied his chief to Ireland in the reign of James VI., on the occasions when MacLeod led his clan in battle, and that about that time Donald composed "The Lament to the Earl of Antrim." Among the compositions attributed to him are "The Macdonald Salute," "Welcome to Rory Mór," and "The Salute of the Earl of Ross." Mr. Ross, whose knowledge of pibroch entitles him to speak with authority, states that close analysis of Donald Mór's compositions reveals the fact that he frequently used the lower notes of the chanter, and that there is internal evidence that he possessed great skill in changing from the low to the high notes.

PATRICK MÓR MACCRIMMON

It is generally agreed that Patrick succeeded Donald as hereditary piper to the MacLeods of Dunvegan. He is generally admitted to have been the most distinguished member of his race. His life was spent in the service of Sir Rory Mór MacLeod, who succeeded to the chiefship in 1596, and who died as stated in 1626. Under the protection of this powerful chief the practice of Piobaireachd received an impetus which is bearing fruit to-day. The Scottish Privy Council, at a comparatively early date, struck a severe blow at what was regarded as the despotic power of the chiefs by limiting the number of the retinue each chief was entitled to gather round him. An important member of that retinue was the person who held the office of hereditary piper. In addition to the honour such an office carried, there were certain material advantages *e.g.*, the freeholding of land and the right to certain dues and liberties which were not lightly esteemed. As indicating the dignified nature of the office, it may be mentioned that, included in the chief's retinue, was the piper's man, whose duty it was to act as servant to the piper and to carry his instrument for him when not in use.

To Patrick Mór MacCrimmon is assigned the honour of having composed the largest number of pipe tunes. In the plaintive lament "Cumha na Cloinne" (Lament to the Children) he gives expression to his deep grief caused by the visitation of one of the most poignant afflictions known to man—the deaths of his children. According to Dr. MacLeod he was the father of eight stalwart sons. Proudly one Sabbath morning he and they marched to the church in their native glen. Before the close of that year he mourned the loss of all his sons who died in an epidemic of fever. Two other well-known laments, the composition of which is assigned to him, are, "The Lament to the only Son" and "The Lament to John Garbh MacGhille Chalum of Raasay," who was drowned in 1646 while crossing the Minch.

In 1651 Patrick Mór MacCrimmon was in all probability an old man, but not too old to accompany the clan in support of Charles II. At this time MacLeod of MacLeod was a minor, and the command of the clan devolved upon his uncles, Norman MacLeod of Bernera and Roderick MacLeod of Talisker. According to Angus Mackay's account, both these men were knighted by Charles II. before the battle of Worcester in 1651 and on that occasion, Patrick Mór having had the honour of playing before the King, and his performance having greatly pleased His Majesty, Patrick received the further honour of being allowed to kiss the King's hand. Mackay states that the well-known port, "Fhuaireas pog o spog an Righ," was composed by MacCrimmon in honour of the distinction then conferred upon him. Various accounts of this outstanding MacCrimmon honour have been published, no two of which entirely agree. Dr. William Mackay of Inverness has frequently rendered signal service in the department of Highland history, and I am indebted to his labours and scholarly research for what I regard as a complete elucidation of the circumstances surrounding the composition of this tune. Dr. Mackay edited *The Chronicles of the Frasers*, an old MS. of events embracing the period 1616-1674. There are many MS. histories bearing upon Highland matters, some of which have been fabricated, but no suggestion of falsification besmirches the reputation of this MS., which has been published under the auspices of The Scottish History Publication Society. Referring to the year 1651, the date of the battle of Worcester, the MS. states that at Stirling, in the month of May, "there was great competition betwixt the trumpets in the army; one Axell, the Earle of Hoome's trumpeter, carried it by the King's own decision. The next was anent the pipers; but the Earle of Sutherland's domestick carried it of all the camp, for non contended with him. All the pipers in the army gave John Macgurmen (MacCrimmon) the van, and acknowledged him for their patron in chief. It was pretty in a morning (the King) in parad viewing the regiments and bragads. He saw no less than eighty pipers in a crould, bare-headed, and John Macgurmen in the middle covered. He asked what society that was? It was told his Majesty—'Sir, yow are our King, and yonder old man in the middle is the Prince of Pipers.' He cald him by name and comeing to the king, kneeling, His Majesty reacht him his hand to kiss; and instantly played an extemporanean port, 'Fuoris Pooge i spoge i Rhi'—I got a kiss of the King's hand—of which he and they were all vain." The writer of the manuscript has made an attempt to render the Gaelic phonetically, and Mr. Mackay in a footnote gives the correct Gaelic spelling "Fhuaireas pog o spog an Righ."

DONALD BAN MACCRIMMON

MacLeod of Dunvegan, when Prince Charles Edward made his romantic if impossible attempt to seize the crown of his forefathers, declined to lend his services to the Prince, and consequently incurred the deep displeasure of many of his clansmen. Had he remained simply neutral, the resentment which his refusal to follow the Prince aroused would have been less bitter, but he openly supported the reigning house. Opinions differ as to which of two men, Malcolm MacCrimmon and Donald Ban MacCrimmon, held the office of hereditary piper, but most authorities agree that Donald Ban performed the duties of the office when MacLeod led out his men against the Prince. Many of the MacLeod men refused to follow their chief, and preferred to follow the standard of the Prince, under the leadership of the heads of cadet families sprung from the Dunvegan line. MacLeod's position was a difficult one. Had the Prince landed in Moidart with sufficient money, equipment and arms, MacLeod would probably have given him all the support within his power. It is persistently stated that his was one of the signatures to the document inviting the Prince to raise his standard in Scotland. In these circumstances it was necessary for MacLeod, by some overt act, to give practical evidence to the Government of his non-adherence to the Stuart cause. He was in close correspondence with, and being actively advised by, President Forbes, who realised the importance of securing the services of MacLeod, thereby lessening the likelihood of the Macdonalds of Skye joining the Prince's forces. MacLeod gathered around him a substantial body of men who held the lands in the vicinity of the castle, and led them from the castle to the shore, where boats waited to convey them to the mainland, and thence to the east of Scotland.

We are constantly reminded of the romance of the Forty-Five. We too often forget the dark tragedies of those days. The spectre of looming disaster entered the home of the MacCrimmons. Donald Ban MacCrimmon had heard the note of the Banshee presaging a journey from which for him there would be no returning. He was told to inspirit the men by the rousing strains of " MacLeod's March," but true to his hereditary instincts he could

THE PIBROCH

From the Painting by Lockhart Bogle

only play a port in harmony with the mood of the moment. In place of the " March " his pipes attuned themselves to that most touching of all laments, " Cumha Mhic Cruimein." The pages of the *Brahan Seer* do not contain any instance of second sight more circumstantially fulfilled than that concerning Donald Ban MacCrimmon. Contemporary history supplies us with the information. The scene is changed from Dunvegan Castle to Moy Hall, the residence of The Mackintosh, a few miles east of Inverness. In the absence of her husband, the wife of The Mackintosh, better known as " Lady Anne," kept a watchful eye, in the interests of the Prince, on the movements of his enemies. The Prince had accepted the hospitality of Moy Hall for the night. News reached " Lady Anne " that a body of men, under Lord Loudon, including MacLeod and his men, were to attempt to capture the Prince under the cover of night. " Donald Fraser, a blacksmith, and other four with loaded muskets in their hands were keeping watch upon a muir out some distance from Moy towards Inverness. As they were walking up and down they happened to spy a body of men marching towards them, upon which the blacksmith fired his piece and the other four followed his example. The laird of MacLeod's piper (reputed the best at his business in all Scotland) was shot dead on the spot. Then the blacksmith (Fraser) and his trusty companions raised a cry (calling some particular regiments by their names) to the Prince's army to advance, as if they had been at hand, which so far imposed upon Lord Loudon and his command (a pretty considerable one) and struck them with such a panic, that instantly they beat a retreat and made their way back to Inverness in great disorder, imagining the Prince's whole army to be at their heels."

Tradition states that Donald Ban's body was buried not far from the spot where he received his fatal wound, and I am informed that a large stone on the moor marks the place of interment.

THE HOMELAND OF THE MACCRIMMONS

Pipers throughout the world will probably welcome a short description of that part of Skye which will for all time be associated with the MacCrimmon family. We may safely assume that the lands of Galtrigal and Boreraig have undergone little physical change during the last 300 years. Standing on a lofty plateau, the MacCrimmon practice ground, we find ourselves in the centre of a district possessing great natural charm and an unparalled sea view. Dunvegan's ancient towers are a prominent landmark reminiscent of bloody feuds, when Macdonald and MacLeod, though connected by marriage, were continually at one anothers throats. Johnson, Boswell, Pennant and Sir Walter Scott all testify to the hospitality they received within its walls. Dun Boreraig, to the east, one of many interesting brochs on the island—silent witnesses to the strength and ingenuity of a past race—still keeps its sentinel watch. To the west stand out in strong relief the rocky cliffs of Dunvegan Head, and in the south are the marvellous Coolins with their ever-changing aspects. At the time when Angus Mackay's publication appeared in 1838, the ruins of the "college" remained *in situ*, disclosing thick walls, massive cabers or rafters, and other characteristics of old Highland habitations. Mackay says that the building was divided into two parts, one forming the class-room and the other the sleeping apartments.

It was the practice of the MacCrimmons to enter into formal indentures of apprenticeship with their pupils, one of which has been published in the Inverness Gaelic Society's Transactions. So many years of study were prescribed, regular lessons were given out, and certain periods for receiving the instructions of the master were fixed. The Rev. Archibald Clerk, son-in-law of Dr. Norman MacLeod (Caraid nan Gaidheal), writing in 1845 states, that the whole tuition "was carried on systematically as in any of our modern academies; and the names of some of the caves and knolls in the vicinity still point out the spots where the scholars used to practice respectively the Piob Mhor or large bagpipe, before exhibiting in presence of the master. MacLeod endowed this school by granting the farm of Borreraig to it, and it is no longer than seventy years since the endowment was withdrawn. The farm had originally been given only during the pleasure of the proprietor. For many ages the grant was undisturbed, but when the value of land had risen to six or seven times what it was when the school was founded, MacLeod very reasonably proposed to resume one half of the farm, offering at the same time to MacCrimmon a free lease of the other half *in perpetuam*: but MacCrimmon, indignant that his emoluments should be curtailed, resigned the whole farm and broke up his establishment, which has never been restored."

Any description of the home of the MacCrimmons would be incomplete without referring to Clach MacCrimmon, a stone which is almost as well-known as the MacCrimmons themselves. Although the account of this matter savours of exaggeration, there can be little doubt that the incident is believed in firmly by the people of the district. The incident as narrated to me was as follows: One of the MacCrimmons was in the habit of tethering his horse, in accordance with the custom of the country, by a rope attached to a cipean driven into the ground. Some maliciously disposed persons removed the cipean from its place on more than one occasion, thus causing MacCrimmon's horse to roam and to do damage to the surrounding crops. In exasperation, MacCrimmon vowed that he would so fix the cipean that no mortal man would ever remove it again. He thereupon looked about for a stone sufficiently large to suit his purpose, and, observing one about 200 yards distant, he immediately proceeded, unaided, to lift it, carried it that distance and placed it upon the top of the cipean. The spot from which MacCrimmon removed the stone, and the spot upon which he placed it, were both pointed out to me. The stone is about 3 feet long by 2½ feet broad, and 2 feet high. I endeavoured to lift the stone an inch or two from the ground and failed to do so. To satisfy certain south-country sceptics, not very long ago, several men, including Murdoch MacLeod (who accompanied me upon the occasion to which I have been referring), succeeded in removing the stone from the bed in which it had lain so long, and by using a wall as a lever, rolled it down a gradient of several yards to the spot where it at present lies. A most remarkable sequel followed.

It was stated to me, in all seriousness, that underneath the stone when it was removed, was found an ancient rusty cipean much worn away. Murdoch Macleod stated to me that he not only saw it, but handled it.

MACCRIMMON PUPILS

If the genius of a master can be measured by the success of his pupils, then, apart from other considerations, the MacCrimmons of Boreraig must truly be regarded as kings among pipers. The fame of their college, long recognised throughout the Isles, spread to the mainland, and pupils from all parts of Scotland eagerly travelled long distances to avail themselves of the tuition the college afforded. No piper's education was regarded as complete until he had passed through the hands of the masters at Boreraig. Rival chiefs buried for a time their jealousies, and sent their pipers to the college on MacLeod's lands. The method usually adopted was to apprentice the young pipers to the MacCrimmons for a period of years, and, in the case of those men who had already otherwise been trained, to send them to Skye for a short period. In a series of articles upon the History of the Parish of Kiltarlity, written by the Rev. Archibald Macdonald, I find the following: "There is an indenture drawn up at Beaufort on 9th March, 1743, in which William Fraser, tacksman, Beauly, is described as his Lordship's (Simon Fraser, Lord Lovat) musician. The brother of this William—David Fraser—had been educated by David Macgregor, his Lordship's piper. His Lordship, however, was now to send David to the Isle of Skye to have him perfected as a Highland piper by the famous Malcolm MacCrimmon, whom his Lordship was to reward for educating the said David for a year."

It in no sense belittles the importance of the MacArthurs, who, as a family of pipers, were second only in excellence to the MacCrimmons of Boreraig, to state that the musical education of a member of this family, Charles, was perfected by Patrick Og MacCrimmon. The MacArthurs were hereditary pipers to the MacDonalds of the Isles and, like the MacCrimmons, had a school for instruction in pipe music. Pennant, who visited the Hebrides in 1774, was hospitably entertained in this building and listened to the playing of many pibrochs. He describes the building as consisting of four apartments, one of which formed the hall set apart for students. Of Charles MacArthur the following interesting incident is told. Sir Alexander Macdonald, being at Dunvegan on a visit to the laird of MacLeod, heard the performance of Patrick Og MacCrimmon with great delight, and desirous if possible to have a piper of equal merit, he said to MacCrimmon one day that there was a young man whom he was anxious to place under his tuition, on condition that he should not be allowed to return until such time as he could play equal to his master. "When this is the case," said MacDonald, "you will bring him home and I will give you ample satisfaction for your trouble." "Sir Alexander," said Patrick, "if you will be pleased to send him to me I will do all that I am able to do for him." Charles was accordingly sent to Boreraig where he remained for eleven years, when MacCrimmon, considering him as perfect as he could be made, proceeded to Mugstad to deliver his charge to Sir Alexander, who was then residing there, and, where Iain Dall Mackay, Gairloch's blind piper, happened also to be. Macdonald hearing of their arrival, thought it a good opportunity to determine the merit of his own piper by the judgment of the blind man, whose knowledge of pipe music was unexceptionable. He therefore enjoined Patrick Og and MacArthur not to speak a word to betray who they were, and, addressing Mackay, he told him he had a young man learning the pipes for some years and was glad that he was present to say whether he thought him worth the money which his instruction had cost. Mackay said if he heard him play he would give his opinion freely, and he requested to be informed previously with whom the piper had been studying. Sir Alexander told him he had been with Patrick Og MacCrimmon. Then Mackay exclaimed, "He could never have been with a better master!" The young man was ordered to play, and when he was finished Sir Alexander asked the other for his opinion. "I think a great deal of him," replied Iain. "He is a good piper; he gives the notes correctly, and if he takes care he will excel in his profession." Sir Alexander was pleased with so flattering an opinion, and observed that he had been at the trouble of sending two persons to the college that he might retain the best, and that now the second man would play, so that an opinion on his merits might also be given. Mackay observed that he must be a very excellent performer to surpass the first, or even to compare with him. When Patrick Og (who acted as the second pupil) had finished playing, Sir Alexander asked the umpire what he thought of his performance. "Indeed, Sir, no one need try me in that manner," returned the blind man. "Although I have lost the eyes of my human body, I have not lost the eyes of my understanding; and if all the pipers in Scotland were present I would not find it a difficult task to distinguish the last player from them all." "You surprise me, Mackay, who is he?" "Who but Patrick Og MacCrimmon," promptly rejoined Mackay, and, turning to where Patrick was sitting, he observed, "It was quite needless, my good sir, to think you would deceive me in that way, for you could not but know that I should have recognised your performance among a thousand." Sir Alexander then asked Mackay himself to play, and afterwards he called for a bottle of whisky, drank to their healths, and remarked that he had that night under his roof the three best pipers in Britain. So much admired was Charles MacArthur for his musical taste, that a gentleman in MacLeod's country prevailed on Malcolm MacCrimmon to send his son Donald for six months to reside with MacArthur, not with the idea of adding to his musical knowledge, but in order that he might be improved by studying MacArthur's particular graces.

About the same time one of the MacCrimmons, better known as Padruig Caogach (obviously not the Patrick Caogach No. 3 on Mr. Ross' list, if Mr. Ross' order is correct), because of his habit of frequently winking, was endeavouring to compose a tune. Two years had passed since the first two measures of it had become known, and still the tune remained half finished. Poor Patrick utterly failed in his frequent attempts to finish what he had begun so well. Mackay succeeded where Patrick failed, finished the tune and called it "Lasan Phadruig Chaogaich."[1] Annoyed because of Mackay's success, or perhaps because of the perpetuation of his physical weakness, Patrick bribed the other apprentices to hurl the blind Iain from a height of twenty-four feet. Iain, however, landed on his feet without injury. The place in

[1] "The anger of winking Patrick."

question was thereafter known as "Leum an Doill."[1] It is said that the completion by Iain Dall of Patrick's unfinished tune resulted in great praise being bestowed upon the former, and gave rise to the saying, "Chaidh an fhoghluim osceann Mhic Cruimein," *i.e.*, "the apprentice outstrips the master."

MACCRIMMON LEGENDS

The legends associated with the MacCrimmons are numerous and interesting, but I can only refer to one or two of them. The "Cave" legend is well-known, and I make no further reference to it except to say that variations of it are to be met with wherever piping has been practised.

Neil Munro, whose stories of the Hebrides are redolent of peat reek and quaint Gaelic idioms, has used the following Breadalbane legend to excellent purpose in his story of the Red Hand: Ross, an old Breadalbane piper, in a fit of jealous rage, forced the right hand of his brother into the fire until it became a charred lump, to prevent him becoming a better piper than himself. Somewhat akin to this old tale is one concerning the MacCrimmons. Although proud of the state of perfection to which they had brought the art of piping, and while encouraging the dissemination of their art by returning young men to their homes from the college at Boreraig trained to a high degree of efficiency, they nevertheless retained among the members of their own family certain movements known only to themselves. They were rightly proud of the position they occupied, and were jealous lest they lost it, even though the honour were to descend upon a pupil of their own training. The story goes that a girl, friendly with the MacCrimmons, acquired the knowledge of how a certain hitherto secret combination of notes was accomplished and imparted the information to her sweetheart, who was not of the MacCrimmon family. Upon this fact reaching the ears of her family the drastic step was adopted of instantly cutting off her fingers so as to prevent possible leakage of information in the future.

In the beautiful Gaelic song, said to have been composed by Donald

[1] "The blind man's leap."

Ban MacCrimmon's sweetheart at Dunvegan, one of the lines refers to the wailing of the fairies when they heard that their friend was leaving to return no more. These little people play no small part in Highland legends generally, and we are therefore not surprised to learn of the existence of the following MacCrimmon fairy legend. On one occasion, when Dunvegan's chief was entertaining within his hospitable walls a goodly company, including many representatives of the leading clans, accompanied by their pipers, it was agreed that the pipers should compete for the post of honour. MacLeod, as a good host, naturally left his piper to come last. The competition went on, piper succeeding piper, until there remained two, including MacLeod's piper, MacCrimmon, to compete. MacLeod glanced in the direction where he expected to see MacCrimmon preparing to acquit himself bravely, but to his annoyance there was no sign of him. Calling a boy, a young MacCrimmon, to him, he bade him search for and bring back MacCrimmon. In a short time the boy returned with the tidings that MacCrimmon was hopelessly drunk. The chief was plunged into the depths of despair with the certainty staring him in the face of being disgraced in front of his guests in his own castle. Seizing the boy by the hand, he whispered in his ear as the eleventh piper stepped forward, " You are the twelfth piper from your chief." Realizing the impossibility of the task imposed upon him the poor lad fled from the hall and threw himself down upon the hillside bitterly bewailing the helplessness of his condition. Suddenly there arose out of an adjacent hillock a beautiful little fairy, who, doubtless realizing the importance of time, handed to the lad a silver chanter and bade him play upon it. He did so, and through the silent glen there floated music the like of which had never before been heard by human ears. With a radiant countenance the lad immediately returned to the hall and, as he entered, the last notes of the eleventh piper were dying away. Proudly the little fellow lifted his master's pipes, and to the surprise and merriment of the great gathering, took the place just vacated by the previous piper. The virtues of the silver chanter stood him in good stead and the looks of amusement quickly turned into admiration, as there came from the pipes the notes of a master player.

In my own youthful days I heard the following MacCrimmon story. On the occasion of a great competition among the pipers held at Dunvegan Castle, the leading MacCrimmon of the day and his nephew, to whom MacCrimmon had imparted his whole store of knowledge, save one particular tune, resolved to compete. The old master had specially refrained from communicating this particular composition to his pupil in order that, while priding himself upon the accomplishments of his own pupil, he might yet retain one item, the knowledge and playing of which would secure for him the coveted honour at the coming competition. On the night before the great event master and pupil slept together at a certain inn. Believing his companion to be sleeping, the old man conned over to himself the air by which he hoped to distinguish himself on the morrow. The arm of the apparently sleeping lad was lying stretched across the bed, and the old piper's hands, mechanically searching for something upon which to " finger " the tune, seized upon his pupil's arm. Time and again the old man practised the notes, at the same time quietly humming the notes, ignorant of the fact that his pupil, though feigning sleep, was very wide awake, and gradually becoming the possessor of the coveted port. On the morrow the pupil entered the lists before his master, and to the mortification of the latter, carried off the leading honour by reason of his manner of playing the tune of which MacCrimmon believed himself at that time to be the sole possessor.

* * * * * * *

Once again, I find myself in " Eilean a' cheó." Six weeks of almost constant rain, disappointing to others who are not accustomed to the vagaries of the weather, have not chilled the affectionate ardour which contact with the island and its people invariably inspires in me. The mists have ever hung heavy on the hills in times of deep, heart-breaking sorrow, and the present tempestuous weather is but in keeping with the sad aftermath of War.

To-day, there came from a distant part of the Island one who served his country well in the late war and who was sorely wounded in that service. To the home of Pibroch he brought his pipes, and in the seclusion of the Pipers Cave in Galtrigal he played two well-known MacCrimmon ports ;

" Cumha Ruari Mhor," and " Tog orm mo phiob." An ardent student of MacCrimmon Pibroch, and a cultured exponent of their art, he came to do honour at their shrine. It was fitting that one of those who heard the haunting notes as they welled forth across the loch was Sir Rory's lineal descendant Macleod of Macleod.

There are many pipers who look hopefully for the day when the memory of the MacCrimmons and of their immortal genius shall be enshrined in a College of Piping, where pupils from far and near may receive instruction in all that is noblest and best in the art of bag-pipe playing.

A GOSSIP ABOUT THE GORDON HIGHLANDERS

By J. M. Bulloch

If the Great War has reversed some preconceptions and ruthlessly rationalised many traditions, it has confirmed, and actually enhanced, the fine fighting reputation of the ten Regiments of the Line—half of them kilted—which Scotland contributes to the British Army. We now know of a certainty that this reputation is well founded as we did not know it before. True, there has long been a legend to that effect, but of recent years there has been a disposition to question its validity. Scotland, or rather the articulate part of it, has borrowed the deadly doctrine of self-depreciation, from which the dominant partner has suffered severely, and the suggestion has not been wanting that the praise of Scots troops, which received such an impetus from the enthusiastic pen of the author of *The Romance of War*, was somewhat overdone. We were reminded that our Army had not had to face troops on the Continent of Europe since the days of the Crimea; one Scots Regiment had not done so since 1799, while the Gordons had nothing to show for it since Waterloo.

If that was true of the old "Contemptibles" generally, it was still truer of the auxiliary forces, which had seen no fighting at all, except in South Africa; but to-day all of them have stood the acid test of the greatest war in history. The old "Contemptibles" were never finer, and we have lived to see one of the best Divisions in the Army composed entirely of kilted Territorials. Indeed, a cloud of witnesses has arisen to prove that all the 126 Battalions, into which the 69 composing the Scots Regiments expanded themselves for the purposes of war, have rendered magnificent service. If we relied merely on the word of the Commander-in-Chief we might suspect bias, for Earl Haig and more than one of his Generals are Scots by birth ; but we have the appreciation of the special newspaper war-correspondents, and not one of them hailed from north of the Border.

We have, moreover, the testimony of the enemy, who very quickly recognised the valour and skill of all the Scots Regiments, particularly those of the 51st Division. Indeed, the Scots soldier, although he represented only eleven per cent. of the British Army against eighty-one per cent. of England itself, took hold of the imagination of the Germans to such an extent that their caricaturists turned John Bull into a Highlander, converting his traditional tall hat into a diced " cockit " bonnet, his white riding breeches into a kilt or tartan trews, and his top-boots into gaiters. The pages of *Simplicissmus, Kladderadatsch,* and *Jugend,* to name only a few, have throughout the war pictured a long procession of the " wife-men " as representing the British Army, at first in a spirit of incredulous burlesque, and latterly with something of the wholesome fear, which was popularly supposed to have overtaken George the Second when he started in his sleep in terror as he dreamed that the " Great Glenbogged " (Glenbucket) was swooping down upon him.

It was to the advent of the father of that monarch that we owe the raising of the kilted Scots—nearly all the trewsed Regiments arose in the previous century—though the connection was indirect, not to say inverted, and was touched with an irony (especially in the light of the greatest of wars), which has been largely lost on a certain type of popularly accepted English history. According to this reasoning, the Highlanders, on seeing the country in danger owing to the expansion adventures of the dominant partner at the expense of France, flocked to the colours at the call of the English Government, and thus not only helped to save the Empire, but gratified their own passion for arms, which had been severely suppressed after the Forty-Five.

The facts, however, are very different from this facile theory. To begin with, if the country as a whole had little consciousness of expansion, as Seeley argued, the Highlander had infinitely less, for one of the main troubles of dealing with him, even in our own day, has been his homing instinct, his intense love of his native soil, no matter how poor it may be. In the second place, the ambitions of the House of Hanover touched no responsive chord in the Highlander's heart, for the Clans had felt the full scourge of Teutonism in the ruthless work of Cumberland at Culloden.

Again, if France was the hereditary arch-enemy of the dominant partner, Scotland in general and the Highlands in particular, had no such quarrel with her. On the contrary, France and Scotland, linked together by racial, psychological, and historical similarities and identities of interest, had long been the best of friends, and it must have puzzled the average Highlander why he should be asked to fight against her. So strong is this community of spirit that it might very well be argued that the Highland Regiments have never fought better in their long history than they have done in the Great War, because they were fighting for France, as well as for their native country.

No doubt the Union had placed Scotland in the same category as England so far as France was concerned, but the kilted regiments arose, not so much out of a political necessity as from a revival of the spirit which had made the Scot in the sixteenth and seventeenth centuries a soldier of fortune wherever he was wanted, fighting now for Rome, and now in the ranks of Gustavus Adolphus against her; fighting to a large extent without passion, but as an artist in arms; and it was this absence of bias as much as anything else that made these venturers clean fighters, and raised their reputation as masters of their art wherever they took service.

From first to last the spirit which animated the soldier of fortune—out to gratify his instinct for adventure, his desire to make a living, and his passion for individuality—has always inspired the Highland regiments to a remarkable extent. It is true that the war with France involved the most momentous issues for the State, but the methods adopted for warding off the danger were far more personal and local than national. It might be argued that the real cause of the war with France was due to the imperialistic ambitions of individual adventurers, and therefore raised little national animus, but precisely the same methods of meeting a crisis coloured the early stages of Armageddon, when every one felt involved, the influence of one man, Lord Kitchener, being far more potent in rousing resistance than any abstract doctrine of State necessity.

The raising of troops to fight France was at no time the complete State undertaking that conscription has involved in our own day. At first the duty was taken up by individual landowners, who raised in turn Regiments of the Line and Fencible Corps; and when their pockets were exhausted, the task was assigned to local authorities like the Lords Lieutenant, who were commissioned to raise in turn Militia, Volunteers (1794-1808), and the very curious force known as Local Militia (1808-1816).

Scotland afforded a splendid ground for the exercise of personal influence because, although the Clan system with its chieftainship had broken down, the influence of the great landowners was still powerful enough to attract attention, although the devotion of the people had to be reinforced by bounties on a scale unknown in our day, and by all sorts of practical recognition, such as the adjustment of rents and the enlargement of holdings; for, although the armies thus raised had strong affinities with the levies organised under the feudal system, the Clan system was infinitely more democratic, and gave scope for greater individuality. This is so true that it often happened that the men raised in one glen declined to march to the rendezvous with the men of another glen who happened to be their hereditary enemies, and trouble arose over the demands of particular groups to be led by their local officers, some of them even believing that they should go forth to battle by Clans, as in the old days.

Of all the personal potentates interested in recruiting in Scotland, none was more powerful than the fourth Duke of Gordon who, although long in possession of vast tracts of Higland territory, was in no sense a Highlander, his family having migrated from Berwickshire to the north, and the trouble which existed for centuries between him and his Highland tenants, like the Macphersons, was due to the inability of his ancestors, or their representatives, to understand the true nature of the Celt. More motives than one urged His Grace forward as recruiter. In the first place, his immediate ancestors had played a very dubious part in the Jacobite risings, and the fourth Duke was anxious to remove the last doubts as to the loyalty of his house. Later on he married an extremely clever and ambitious woman, the famous Jane Maxwell, who had a great desire to play a big part in the State, and do something for her sons.

Whatever the motives, the recruiting achievements of His Grace were splendid, for from first to last he raised no fewer than four complete regiments, besides contributing two companies to corps raised by others. and he also played a very active part as Lord Lieutenant of his county, The forces organised by the Duke were as follows :

1759-65 - - -	89th Regiment.
1775-83 - - -	Company for the Fraser Highlanders.
1778-83 - - -	Northern Fencibles.
1790-1 - - -	Company for the Black Watch.
1793-9 - - -	Northern Fencibles.
1794 - - -	Gordon Highlanders.

The sole remnant of this mighty effort, which must have cost the Duke a fortune, is the regiment of Gordon Highlanders, which we have seen blossom out into eleven battalions, to say nothing of certain reserves; and although the regiment has not continued to be recruited on the ducal estates, its connection with the House of Gordon has all along been maintained, and has actually been strengthened in recent times. That connection of course has always been symbolised by the wearing of the clan tartan, but the links with the north were strengthened by the rearrangement of 1872, when infantry regiments were allotted to definite Territorial areas for the purpose of recruiting. About the same time the Gordon family motto, "Bydand," and the familiar crest were placed upon the bonnet in lieu of the hard-won Sphinx.

What is of much more importance is the fact that the genius of the family, admirably described in the alliterative phrase the "Gay Gordons," which inspired the original regiment, has passed into all its subsequent accretions, so that the 75th Regiment added to it in 1881, although actually of earlier origin, has been completely absorbed. The same can be said of the old Aberdeenshire Militia, which became the 3rd Battalion, and also of the various Volunteer Corps which were gradually absorbed, while the Service Battalions raised by Lord Kitchener displayed exactly the same spirit as the cradle corps. This continuity and identity of tradition are also emphasised, not only in the Gordons, but in all the Scots regiments, and especially in the kilted units, by the fact that they alone maintained during the War at least, part of their Peace equipment in the shape of the kilt—even if it was camouflaged with khaki aprons—and the trewsed regiments had their glengarries replaced by Kilmarnock and other braid bonnets.

Who can doubt that such a continuity of outward traditions is but the symbol of a spiritual identity which links up the Scots regiments of the present day with the Corps who did such splendid work of old from Fontenoy to Waterloo, from the Crimea to South Africa. True, when you come to define it, it is difficult to say what it precisely consists in. Nearly every Regiment of the Line has its own peculiarities, but the Scots regiments have them in even greater abundance, for with them they are reinforced by marked racial characteristics. It is perfectly true that the Highland regiments are no longer confined to Highlanders, or even to Scotsmen, although the idea industriously propagated some years ago that they were originally composed largely of Irishmen, is a fallacy, completely disproved by War Office Records. Even if it were otherwise, the fact remains that the *esprit de corps* which all these idiosyncracies help to form has a remarkably proselytising influence, very subtle and difficult to define, but very potent in actual practice.

The early history of the Gordons is full of curious little incidents which sometimes run counter to popular notions. For example, it used to be commonly supposed, especially in support of the now exploded theory that we have become "degenerate," that the first recruits of the Highland regiments were gigantic men. This is far from being the case. From the Description Book of the Gordons, one of the very few regiments which possess such data in an early form, it is proved that the average height of 914 men composing the greater part (940) of the original regiment, was only 5′ 5½″, only six of them being 6′ or upwards—the tallest, a Morayshire man, scaling 6′ 4″. Similar facts can be cited about the heights of other groups of men at the same period.

There were only 16 men actually named Gordon, against 39 Macdonalds, 35 Macphersons, and 34 Camerons. As to the occupations of the men, it is interesting to note that 442 were described as "labourers," and as most of them came from the Highlands, they were presumably farm servants. Of skilled artisans, 186 were weavers. Inverness-shire, where the Duke had vast estates, supplied 240 men, Aberdeenshire 124, Banffshire 82, Lanark 62, Ireland 51, England 9, and Wales 2.

There was a solitary German in the regiment, a musician named C. Augustus Sochling, hailing from Hesse Cassel. There was another German in the regiment later on, also a musician, named Friederich Zeigher (or Zugner) who fell at Quatre Bras. The appearance of these Germans was in its way a sort of return for the fact that the House of Gordon had given many good soldiers of its name to what we now call Germany, although most of them really took post in Poland. The descendants of at least four of these soldiers still exist in Germany, and have risen to the dignity of a von, including the founder of the von Gordon-Coldwells, of Laskowitz, in West Prussia, the von Gordons of Frankfort, and the family of Dr. Adolf von Gordon, the well-known Berlin lawyer, whose motto is "Byid Dand." Although at the beginning of 1914 he told a Berlin newspaper that he knew nothing more about it than that it was an "altschottischer Spruch," it is, of course, nothing more or less than the historic word "Bydand."

With regard to the pipe history of the regiment not very much is known. I fancy this is due to the fact that so much that has to do with the art of piping generally rests on oral and not written tradition. In the second place it must be remembered that pipers were not originally recognised by the State. They were purely a regimental, and not an Army, institution, and had no separate rank as the drummers had. Indeed, it was not till about 1853 that they got the same rank and pay as drummers. Thus, in May 1805, a piper named Alexander Cameron was taken on the strength of the Grenadiers as drummer, probably to get him drummer's pay, to which, as a piper, he was not entitled.

The rivalry of the two is brought out in a story told in Carr's *Caledonian Sketches*, of a dispute as to precedence between a piper and a drummer of a Highland regiment. When the Captain decided in favour of the latter, the piper expostulated with the remark, "Oh, sir, shall a little rascal that beats a sheepskin take the right hand of me that am a musician?" The differentiation of the two is still reflected in the fact that a piper is always a piper, whereas a "musician" returns to the ranks in time of war.

The first direct mention of pipers in the Gordons occurs in a regimental order of October 27, 1796, when the regiment was at Gibraltar, and when it was ordained that pipers were to attend all fatigue parties. An interesting sidelight on the use of the pipes occurs in a regimental order of November 12, 1812, when the regiment was at Alba de Tormes in Spain:

"The pibroch will never sound except when it is for the whole regiment to get under arms; when any portion of the regiment is ordered for duty and a pipe to sound, the first pipe will be the warning, and the second pipe for them to fall in. The pibroch only will, and is to be considered, as invariably when sounded, for every persons off duty to turn out without a moment's delay."

A pathetic little story about this function of the pipers is told by James Hope in his forgotten little book, *Letters from Portugal, Spain and France*, printed in 1819:

"At ten o'clock (on the evening of the day of Quatre Bras) the piper of the 92nd took post under the garden hedge in front of the village, and, tuning his bagpipes, attempted to collect the sad remains of his regiment. Long and loud blew Cameron, and, although the hills and vallies (*sic*) re-echoed the hoarse murmurs of his favourite instrument, his utmost efforts could not produce more than half of those whom his music had cheered in the morning on their march to the field of battle."

At the battle of St. Pierre in the Peninsular, December 13, 1813, two out of the three pipers of the Gordons were killed while playing the pibroch "Cogadh na sith" (with which they were to charm the ears of the Czar of Russia in the great Review at Paris in July, 1815). As one fell, another took up the tune, and it was suggested to Sir John Sinclair, as President of the Highland Society, that this "should be made known all over the Highlands." It may be noted that the Colonel, the gallant, if martinet, Cameron of Fassiefern, who fell at Quatre Bras, gave great encouragement to his pipers, especially as regards the specially Highland airs and the high-class music (Ceol Mor). Colonel Greenhill Gardyne attributes to this the fact that "all pipers in the Gordons are still taught to play Piobaireachd," and that the ancient and characteristically Highland class of pipe music is still played every day under the windows of the officers quarters before dinner.

The Gordons have enjoyed the services of one particular family of hereditary ear-pipers, the Stewarts. They came from Perthshire, where one of them was a piper to the Duke of Atholl, while his brother, known as "Piper Jamie," crossed the hills into the Parish of Kirkmichael, Banffshire—the cradle of a remarkable military family, the Gordons of Croughly—where seven sons were born to him. All of these strapping fellows entered the Aberdeenshire Militia, now the 3rd Battalion of the Gordon Highlanders, six of them becoming pipers. The best known of these was the eldest, Donald (1849-1913), who migrated to New Deer, Aberdeenshire, and was known all over Scotland as a champion piper. The family has been supplying pipers to the Gordons for more than half a century.

No doubt modern battles are not won by deeds of individual daring such as these pipers have achieved, but they are won in terms of the spirit which makes such conduct possible, for it is just the little things, the train of tradition, the idiosyncracies of uniform, and the rest of it, which go to form that *esprit de corps* which has made the kilted regiments famous the world over.

TO THE LION RAMPANT

By Alice C. Macdonell of Keppoch

Did ye hear the light feet marching,
  Marching down the birchclad glen ?
Did ye see the pipers' streamers,
  Floating free behind the men ?
Did ye hear the brave tunes ringing,
  As they swung the drones on high ?
Did ye watch the rythm of the kilt,
  Did ye hear the war march die ?
Behind the sharp bend of the road,
  Beyond the wild Ben Nevis range :
The strains of Donald Dubh again,
  Bore out the clans to battles strange.
But, it's O ! our tears ran sorely,
  As they left the Scottish shore ;
For who'd come back, and who would see
  Lochaber's wooded braes no more ?
Only the Lord of Hosts could tell,
  And the wae heart's own prophetic knell.

Did ye see the brave lads smiling,
  As they drew their bonnets' down,
With the shortened breath indrawn and tight,
  The flashing eyes, the steadfast frown ?
Did ye hear the whistling shot and shell,
  That swept the kilted foremost ranks

Like the snow wind's call before its fall,
  As clouds lie piled in fleecy banks ?
Ah ! no, t'was not the keen gust bite,
  That reddens cheeks with healthful glow,
Nor the hissing as the shapnel fell
  The sound of melting driving snow.
Did ye hear the war pipes calling,
  Like the mavis, in the van,
'Mid the thunder of the battle storm,
  To the valour of each Scottish man ?
The blood call of the march they knew,
  With bayonet charge was answered true.

O ! Piper lads ! O ! Piper lads !
  What magic woven spell
Amergin breathed within your reeds,
  Is not for mortal voice to tell.
The wizard winds thro' reed and drone,
  The soul draws on to follow after
To splendid heights of hero fame,
  Or, spellbound, led to grim disaster.
Great Fingal heard beyond the hills
  Your quivering grace notes heavenward soar ;
Old Ossian followed in a dream
  The "Broom of Peril"[1] *Oscar bore.*
Blow softly, then, O ! Piobaireachd's wail,
  Or loud and bold, to stir the heart ;
No music stirs as yours can stir,
  Wild glamour of the fairies Art.

Did ye hear the war pipes shrilling,
  Out beyond the German lines,

[1] "The Broom of Peril," the banner borne by Oscar in battle.

Where the gallant soldiers pressing on,
  Drove home their charge, despite the mines ?
Did ye see yon brave lad casting
  His broken pipes aside,
As he plunged among the German lines
  To do his part what'er betide ?
Did ye watch the tartans pouring down
  From hill, and trench, and sweep
The cruel Teuton from the field,
  Like herds of driven sheep ?
Did ye hear the shot that echoed,
  Till it reached a woodland lone ?
Did ye see the mother's auld grey plaid,
  Wrapped round her mourning head ?—Ochone !
Did ye see the tears that dropped like rain.
  For the lads we ne'er may see again ?

O ! Piper lads ! O ! Piper lads !
  What magic woven spell
Amergin breathed within your reeds,
  Is not for mortal voice to tell.
The wizard winds thro' reed and drone,
  The soul draws on to follow after,
To splendid heights of hero fame,
  Or, spellbound, led to grim disaster.
Great Fingal heard beyond the hills,
  Your quivering grace notes heavenward soar ;
Old Ossian followed in a dream
  The "Broom of Peril" Oscar bore.
Blow softly, then, O ! Piobaireachd's wail,
  Or loud and bold, to stir the heart ;
No music stirs as yours can stir,
  Wild glamour of the fairies Art.

True hearts, as ever ready, to guard their native land,
O! Scotland's sons are bonnie, and Scotland's sons are grand.
True hearts that never failed her yet, to-day as yester year,
O! Scotia rouse thine echoes, with one resounding cheer.
Let the Lion Rampant proudly raise his head on cloth of gold,
For the deeds of valour done to-day, in pages yet untold.
Gay Gordon lads, brave Seaforths, Black Watch and Camerons tell,
What steeled your dauntless hearts to face that living screen of hell!
The pipes of Loos, of Mons, of far and distant Dardanelles,
That spake in Gaelic tones to each who dared those deadly shells.
The old time slogan of the race, the spell that cannot fail,
"*À chlanna nan gaidheal! À chlanna nan, Gaidheal!*
Guillain ri Guillain a chèile!"[1]

[1] "Sons of the Gael shoulder to shoulder."

THE MUSIC OF BATTLE

By Philip Gibbs

THROUGH all the days and the years in which I served as a war-correspondent on the Western Front, it was seldom that I did not hear, from near by or from afar, the music of the pipes. It was a sound which belonged to the great orchestra of life in the war zone, rising above the deep rumble of distant guns, travelling ahead of marching columns up the long roads to Arras or Bapaume, wailing across the shell craters of that desert which stretched for miles over the battlefields of Flanders, and coming to one's ears like elfin music through the dead woods above the Somme. Before every big battle the skirl of the pipes went with the traffic of war and guns surging forward to the fighting-lines. For in every big battle there were Scottish troops and their pipers played them on to the fields of honour, and played them out again when their ranks had been thinned by heroic sacrifice. This music had an inspiring influence not only on the Scottish troops themselves, whose spirits rose to the sound of it when, after long marching, their feet were leaden on the hard roads and their shoulders ached to the burden of their packs, but also on English troops who were in their neighbourhood, and on their way to the same battlegrounds. For though an Englishman cannot, as a rule, distinguish one tune from another—does not indeed believe that the pipes play any tune—there is something in the rhythm, in the long drawn notes, in the soul singing out of those "wind-bags," so he calls them, which in some queer magic way, stirs the blood of a man, whoever he may be, and stiffens the slackening fibre of his heart, and takes him out of the rut of his earth to some higher plane of thought, and gives him courage. It is an Englishman who writes this, but I am sure of it, for many times in dark days of war I have been taken up by the sadness and the gladness of the pipes, borne by the breeze across the fields of war.

The 15th (Scottish) Division were special friends of mine, and I remember, years ago now, how I saw them marching through Bethune on their way to the battle of Loos, where they fought their first big fight in September of '15. Through the Grand-Place of Bethune, not yet wrecked by shell-fire, they came marching with their guns. Snow was falling on the steel helmets of the men and clinging to the long hair of their goat-skin coats. It was a grim scene, and away beyond the city of Bethune there was the ceaseless thunder of bombardment over the enemy lines. But above this noise, like a heavy sea breaking against rocks, rose the music of the Scottish pipers playing their men forward. One pipe band stood in the Square, and its waves of stirring sound clashed against the gabled houses, and I remember how all our English gunners, riding with their heads bent against the storm, turned in their saddles to look at the pipers as they passed and seemed warmed a little by the spirit of that Scottish march.

The 15th Division went into battle with their pipers, while the Londoners of the 47th had to be content with mouth-organs and sing "Who's your lady friend?" on the way to Loos through storms of shell-fire. The 10th Gordons were the first into the village of Loos, and some of them went away to the Cité St. Auguste—and never came back. It was an unlucky battle and cost us dearly, but it proved the immense valour of our men, who were wonderful. The pipers played under fire and some of them were badly wounded, but there were enough left to play again when the Scots were relieved and came out, all muddy and bloody, with bandaged heads and arms, to small villages like Mazingarbe and Heuchin, where I saw Sir John French, then Commander-in-Chief, riding about on a white horse, and bending over his saddle to speak to small groups of Jocks, thanking them for their gallant deeds.

In the early battles of the Somme there were many Scottish battalions of the 3rd and 9th and 15th Divisions, fighting up by Longueval and Bazentin and Delville Wood, where they suffered heavy losses under the frightful fire of German guns. The South African Scottish were but a thin heroic remnant when they staggered out of the infernal fire of "Devil's Wood," and the men of the 15th Division who captured Longueval left many of their comrades behind. That was one of the finest exploits of the war, and they were led forward by their pipers, who went with them into the thick of the battle. It was to the tune of "The Campbells are Coming" that the Argyll and Sutherlands went forward, and that music which I had once heard up the slopes of Stirling Castle when the King was there, was heard now with terror by the German soldiers. The pipers screamed out the Charge, the most awful music to be heard by men who have the Highlanders against them, and with fixed bayonets and hand grenades they stormed the German trenches, where there were many machine-gun emplacements, and dug-outs so strong that no shell could smash them. There was long and bloody fighting, and in Longueval village, across which the Highlanders dug a trench, the enemy put down a barrage, yard by yard, so that it was churned up by heavy shells. On that day of July 20, 1916, I met the Scots marching out of that place. They came across broken fields where old wire lay tangled and old trenches cut up the ground, and there was the roar of gun-fire about us. Some of our batteries were firing with terrific shocks of sound which made mule teams plunge and tremble, and struck sharply across the thunder of masses of guns firing along the whole line of battle. At the time there was a thick summer haze about, and on the ridges were the black vapours of shell bursts, and all the air was heavy with smoke. It was out of this that the Highlanders came marching. They brought their music with them, and the pipes of war were playing a Scottish love-song:

I lo'e nae laddie but ane,
An' he lo'es nae lassie but me.

Their kilts were caked with mud, and stained with mud and filth, but the men were splendid, marching briskly with a fine pride in their eyes. Officers and men of other regiments watched them pass, as men who had fought grandly, so that the dirtiest of them there and the humblest of these Jocks was a fine gentlemen and worthy of Knighthood.

Many of them wore German helmets and grinned beneath them. One brawny young Scot had the cap of a German staff officer cocked over his ear. One machine-gun section brought down two German machine-guns besides their own. They were dog-tired, but they held their heads up, and the pipers who had been with them blew out their bags bravely, though hard-up for wind, and the Scottish love-song rang out across the fields—whatever its words, it was, I think, a love-song for the dear dead they had left behind them.

During the battle of Arras in April of 1917 there was always a wonderful pageant of men in that old city which had been under fire since October in the first year of war and was badly wounded, with many of its ancient houses utterly destroyed, but still a city with streets through which men could march, and buildings in which they could find comfortable, but unsafe billets. It was the headquarters of the battle which lasted in the fields outside by Monchy Hill and by Fampoux and Roeux, Wancourt and Havinel until the end of May. Arras is a city built above deep tunnels and vaults made in the Middle Ages when the stone was quarried out of them to build the houses, and lengthened and strengthened by our own engineers and tunnellers, so that our men could live in them under the heaviest shell-fire, and march through them to the German lines. Above, in the old squares and streets, in houses still standing between gulfs of ruin, several of our Divisional generals and some of our battalion commanders established their headquarters, and when the first fierce shelling eased off—though it never ceased until the last German retreat in the autumn of 1918—the streets were always filled with a surging traffic of men and mules and guns and motor lorries. Many Scottish battalions of the 15th and 51st Divisions among others were quartered here, and on one historic day there were assembled no less than five pipe bands in full strength, who played up and down one of the Squares amidst crowds of fighting men of English and Scottish regiments. I remember one such day when the pipers of the 8/10th Gordons, commanded then by Colonel Thom, were playing in the square. The Colonel had a proud light in his eyes as the tune, "Highland Laddie," swelled up to the gables and filled the open frontages of the gutted houses.

Snowflakes fell lightly on the steel hats of the Scots standing in a hollow square, and mud was splashed to the khaki aprons over their kilts as they smiled at the fine swagger of the pipe-major and the thump of the drumsticks; an old woman danced a jig to the pipes, holding her skirt above her skinny legs. She tripped up to a group of Scottish officers and spoke quick shrill words to them. "What does the old witch say?" asked a laughing Gordon. She had something particular to say. In 1870 she had heard the pipes in Arras. They were played by prisoners from South Germany, and as a young girl she had danced to them. It seemed to me a link between two strange chapters of history in the city of Arras which had been crowded with the ghosts of history since those days when Julius Caesar had his camp outside its walls on the very ground—at Etrun—where our Scottish troops had their huts.

The pipes of Scotland sounded in many villages of France and Flanders, where for all time the wail of them will come down the wind to the ears of men who hear with the spirit. They were played not only in the roads and fields, but often at night in farmhouses where Highland officers had their messes, or in cottages where some battalion headquarters were established or in old houses within city walls where there was a feast or a guest night. It was my privilege to spend some of those evenings, when down the long table in a narrow room the pipers marched, solemnly standing behind the guest's chair and playing old dances and marches of Bonnie Scotland. Then the colonel would offer the pipe-major a glass of whisky, which he would raise high, toasting the health of the officers in Gaelic. After that, on many a good evening in a bad war, the tables would be cleared, and the young officers would dance an eightsome reel, with laughter and simulated passion, and shrill cries of challenge and triumph which stirred a stranger's soul. Or the pipers themselves would be asked to give a dance, and in stocking feet on bare boards, dance as lightly as gossamer and as nimbly as Nifinsky the Russian, though big, brawny men. In small rooms the music of the pipes was loud—too loud for any but Scottish ears—and it was hard on a French "padre" who was trying to sleep upstairs in one small cottage, with thin walls and cracks between old timbers of the ceiling, while downstairs late into the night the pipers played merrily for those who would fight in the next battle, near at hand. The effect of such pipe-music within four walls was prodigious on a French officer whom I took one night to the mess of the 8/10th Gordons. The full pipe-band marched in as usual, and I saw my friend open his eyes wide and stare with amazement at this apparition. When they stood behind his chair playing lustily, so that the very glasses quaked on the table, he became very pale, and after the second " strathspey " I saw him collapse in his chair in a dead swoon. The Gordons thought this a fine tribute to their pipers. They enjoyed the incident justly though full of consideration for the French officer. He explained to me after the symptoms that overcame him. " I felt," he said, " enormous waves rolling up to me and passing over me ; my heart beat wildly, and vivid colours rushed past my eyes. Then I knew no more ! " Nothing would induce him to suffer such musical agony again.

I shall always remember one piper I saw in the ruins of the Château of Caulaincourt. How he came there, or why he stayed there, I do not know, because few of our troops were in the neighbourhood, and the place was a desert. The château had been a vast place, with high walls and terraces and out-houses, but the whole place had been hurled into ruin by the Germans on their first retreat in the spring of 1917. They had opened the family vaults and pillaged the coffins, and I remember being struck by the pathos of a little marble tablet I saw on a refuse heap, to which it had been flung. On it were the words in French, " The heart of Madame la Marquise de Caulaincourt." Poor dead heart of Madame la Marquise ! In life it would have broken at the sight of all this ruin. But there, quite alone, on the central avalanche of stones, stood a Scottish piper playing a lament. . . . I heard from other officers that he was seen there later, still alone, and still playing his pipes, but why we could not tell.

The last time I heard the pipes was at the end of the war. They were playing Scottish troops over a bridge across the Rhine, at Cologne, and at the journeys' end of all that long and tragic way through which our men had fought with heroism, through frightful fire, with dreadful losses, until victory was theirs, final and complete. Along those roads the pipes of war went playing, month after month, year after year, from one battle to another, and in their music for ever, as long as remembrance of this war lasts, there will be the tears and the tragedy and the triumph, reminding the world of all that gallant youth of Scotland which fought in France.

THE PIPES IN THE EVERYDAY LIFE OF THE WAR

By Arthur Fetterless

I do not think any one can write with greater pleasure than I for the Pipers' Record. My only regret is that, personally, I never chanced to see the pipes go into direct action. I know that, in the earlier stages of the war, and in a few celebrated cases later, the pipes went into the charge, but I had not the good fortune to be present on one of these occasions. Others, however, will have written of these things, and I do not think I can do better than speak of events actually known to myself relating to the pipes and the pipers in the general life of the war.

The pipes! Ah! No memories of the great war will ever be complete to any member of a Highland regiment without the recollection of the pipes, for they are unquestionably the finest battle instrument ever created. They mourned with us in hours of sorrow. They cheered us in hours of weariness. They played gaily in hours of rest and merriment.

Back in billets, in ruined villages, half the battalion would turn out to hear "Retreat" played by the pipe-band. It was one of the events of the day, in the summer in the sweltering heat of the dust-laden huts behind the front-line, in the winter in the dank cold mid the seas of mud, in the midst of which the pipers played upon an island that was sometimes almost a floating raft.

At these times the rumble of the guns was overwhelmed, and the horrors of war and the atmosphere were for a little time forgotten. And the fact that the pipes were the pride of the battalion was evident from the remarks of the men, if several Highland battalions were billeted together.

"Your pipes are no' a patch on ours!"

" Aw, away wi' ye, look at yer big drum ; he canna twirl his sticks above his heid."

" Umph ! We've got a pipe-major, onyhoo."

" Aye." A grudging admission.

Such remarks were of the everyday talk of the men who heard the pipes.

Again, at the periodical meetings and games of Highland brigades, the massed bands of the battalions were always there playing a mighty skirl. There were, of course, piping competitions in conjunction with competitions in Highland dancing and sport.

All these occasions did much to rob modern war of its dismal character, and bring back something of the glamour of arms, and the glory of strong men.

But enough of general remarks. I wish to write of five typical scenes from the life of the war relating to pipes and the pipers.

* * * * * * * *

In the first I am standing at the entrance to one of the low dug-outs, covered over with turf, which used to lie, and perhaps still exist, a few hundred yards from the Café Belge up the road to Ypres. Most people who fought in that sector found a billet in them at some time, or knew them—filthy they were.

Overhead a couple of aeroplanes are hovering, very high up. An occasional shell can be heard, coming from a long distance away, with a rolling noise. The shells are probably 9-inch or perhaps larger, and they are bursting with crash and splash in the fields around or near the road.

From the direction of the Café Belge I see a company of men in kilts advancing, men heavily laden with all the usual impedimenta of packs, rifles, etc. They look, in the distance, tired and grim, and in formation they are straggling, owing to the appallingly muddy state of the road.

A shell bursts in the field to the left of the road along which they are coming. There is a heavy cloud of smoke, and streams of mud and slime are spued upwards and around. For a moment the leader seems to hesitate, and the party halts. Then they move on again.

Suddenly there is a sound as of tuning up, and two pipers commence to play. The advancing men steady in formation and come slogging through the mud, with step almost rhythmic to the music.

"Crash!" Another shell bursts nearer them, splashing some of the platoon with mud. The pipes play on.

"Crash!" A third shell bursts short of them.

The pipes play on, and the men march steadily past to the music of the pipes. They cover another hundred yards, and a shell bursts in the road where the platoon were marching a few seconds before. I say to myself, "Thank God, they got through in time."

As I look back it seems to me that that was not too bad an example of steadiness of pipers and men under dangerous fire. But of course it was all just an everyday sort of thing—a few men relieving trenches with a couple of pipers to cheer them on the way up—part of the everyday life of war.

The pipes only began to play after the shelling broke out.

* * * * * * * *

My second scene is an incident taken from life in France. I think the pipes did their share in fostering the *entente*, and the arrival of Highland battalions with their pipe-bands marching in front did much to engrave in the hearts of the French people memories which will be carried on from generation to generation.

In this second scene I stood at the entrance to a French town when a very famous battalion entered the main street marching to attention, with pipe-band playing. It was the first Scottish battalion to enter that town.

Near me stood a little girl in a white dress. Her face, on seeing the band, first expressed astonishment. The expression changed to pleased interest, and finally she burst into gleeful smiles.

As the band came near her she danced along beside the pipers, a beautiful golden-haired child, supremely happy.

The people standing around cheered and waved with French enthusiasm. To them undoubtedly, in one of the darkest hours of the war—those magnificent men and the music of the pipes bore a message of hope and determination, with the promise of ultimate victory.

To any people who are inclined to be supercilious about pipe-music, the recollection of the unfeigned pleasure of a beautiful child on hearing the pipes for the first time has often seemed to me to supply an answer. Those who cannot understand pipe-music might be able to do so if they were ready to receive it in the same simple spirit.

* * * * * * * *

About the end of October 1915 the trenches on Hill 60 in front of Ypres, were in a particularly sodden state. The rotting sandbags which formed the parapets were a mass of oozing earth, continually being scattered by shell-fire and rebuilt again by the toilsome labours of mud-covered " Jocks."

The Hun sniper, too, was exceptionally vigilant in these parts, and, as he had the advantage of ground and of enfilade fire from several points, to put a head above the parapet in daylight meant almost certain death. Men also were being continually wounded and killed while passing along the trenches at points where the parapet had become too low, and it had not been possible to build it up quickly enough.

As the combined result of shell-fire, sniping, and the bad state of the trenches, the amount of work which could be done in daylight was small. Repairs were done at night. There were also, on account of these difficulties and others, very few loop-holes available, so that, excepting through periscopes, the average man saw very little of the enemy. He scarcely ever got a shot at him by day. I suppose it was the result of all these things put together which created the scene.

On a very dull morning a party of Seaforths were gathered in a bay of one of the trenches. I was round the traverse in the next bay. One of the party of men was on sentry duty with a periscope ; the rest were cleaning rifles.

Owing to the dullness of the day, mud and filth, the *ensemble* was dismal. Suddenly there sounded from the direction of Sanctuary Wood the music of pipes playing. Why they were playing then, or where exactly they were playing, I have never known, but there certainly floated across to the dismal trenches the music of " Horo, My Nut Brown Maiden."

To us in the trenches the distant music sounded perfectly glorious, and the burdens of the hour were for a time lifted away. That the men found it so was evident from their action.

Everybody knows the soldier's version which runs to the same air, and it apparently struck the fancy of the men as applicable to the occasion, for there burst forth from the adjoining bay a cheerful chorus :

" Aa canna see the tairget,
Aa canna see the tairget,
Oh, aa canna see the tairget,
It's owre far awa."

The last line was converted by one of the chorus party into the line :

" For Jerry he's owre fly."

On looking round the corner of the traverse I saw the concert-party incredibly cheerful, and entirely oblivious of war, mud or danger, for the pipes had asserted their sway.

* * * * * * * *

There are many marches which the pipers made, including marches to battle, of which I might write, but I think my second last reminiscence had best be taken from the journey of the conquering Second Army which tramped from Ypres to the Rhine on the last great triumphal march.

Of the 250 miles odd which the Army covered, I am certain that the pipers of my battalion piped at least a good half, perhaps more.

What could we have done without them on that march ? As we tramped through village after village and town after town, neath welcome banners and cheering crowds, men wearied with marching, not always too amply rationed, yet swung forward with assured tread to the lilt of the pipes through every village and town.

Welcoming bands played the Marseillaise, the Brabançonne, and the British Anthem, and the crowds shouted their " Vive les Alliês," etc. The pipes played their regimental and national marches in return, and if inter-communication through language was not perfect, yet there was complete accord through music.

Undoubtedly, on that never-to-be-forgotten march, the pipes were indispensable.

* * * * * * * *

The last scene is taken from Germany. Perhaps I should speak of massed bands parading in the main squares and streets of the great towns of the Rhine, bringing home to the Hun as forcibly as in any way the destruction of his ill-judged schemes; or perhaps I should speak of the pipers on some of the great occasions—presentations of medals, presentations of colours, etc.

I prefer to write of a very simple event. Happening where it did, it seemed so homely.

I was riding through a forest not far from Cologne when I heard the music of pipes. I turned off the road and proceeded along a pathway which led to a green sward in the forest.

There I saw a solitary piper marching slowly up and down playing a lament. His loneliness seemed to me to symbolise two things—the completeness of victory, and the detachment of the conquerors. The music sounded very beautiful among the trees.

I did not interrupt the piper, but if I know anything at all of piping, I am sure that that piper in the forest felt for a little while almost as if he were treading his native heath again, and dreamt of the Highland hills and forests from which he had come.

After all, in Germany, we were strangers in a strange land and not wishing to stay there. Having done our work, we said in our hearts, "let us away!" for the Huns will always be Hunnish. But we are Highland, and the pipes are calling us home.

* * * * * * * *

Beat on drums; let the pipes play and the banners be unfurled for every triumphal march that shall be. But when the marches are played let us never forget that every march has grown more glorious by the war and the blood of the men who fell; that every march has woven around it a thousand memories of life and death, of hardship, of danger, and of victory.

In days to come we will remember—to battle we went by *that* march;

to Longueval we went by *that* march ; and from Loos we came by *that* one. And for every battle march that the pipers play, we know that a million feet and more have marched to its song.

That record of great work—that, with death and other things they did not count—*that* is the Pipers' Record.

THE OLDEST AIR IN THE WORLD

By Neil Munro

Col Maclean, on two sticks, and with tartan trousers on, came down between the whins to the poles where the nets were drying, and joined the Trosdale folk in the nets' shade. 'Twas the Saturday afternoon ; they were frankly idling, the township people—except that the women knitted, which is a way of being indolent in the Islands—and had been listening for an hour to an heroic tale of the old sea-robber days from Patrick Macneill, the most gifted liar in the parish. A little fire of green wood burned to keep the midges off, and it was hissing like a gander.

" Take your share of the smoke and let down your weariness, darling," said one of the elder women, pushing towards the piper a herring firken. Nobody looked at his sticks nor his dragging limb—not even the children ; had he not been a Gael himself Maclean might have fancied his lameness was unperceived. He bitterly knew better, but pushed his sticks behind the nets as he seated himself, and seated, with his crutches absent, he was a fellow to charm the eye of maid or sergeant-major.

" Your pipes might be a widow, she's so seldom seen or heard since you came home," said one of the fishermen.

" And that's the true word," answered Col Maclean. " A widow indeed, without her man ! Never in all my life played I *piob mhor* but on my feet and they jaunty ! I'll never put a breath again in sheep-skin. If they had only blinded me ! "

There was in the company, Margaret, daughter of the bailie ; she had been a toddling white-haired child when Col went to France, and had to be lifted to his knees ; now she got up on them herself at a jump, and put her arms round his neck, tickling him with her fingers till he laughed.

"Oh bold one! Let Col be!" her mother commanded; "thou wilt spoil his beautiful tartan trews."

"It is Col must tell a story now," said the little one, thinking of the many he used to tell her before he became a soldier.

"It is not the time for wee folks stories," said the mother; "but maybe he will tell us something not too bloody for Sunday's eve about the Wars."

Col Maclean, for the first time, there and then, gave his tale of The Oldest Air in the World.

* * * * * * * *

"I was thinking to myself," said he, "as I was coming through the whins there, that even now, in creeks of the sea like this, beside their nets adrying, there must be crofter folk in France, and they at *ceilidh* like yourselves, telling of tales and putting to each other riddles."

"*Ubh! ubh!* It is certain there are no crofters in France, whatever," said William-the-Elder. "It is wine they drink in France, as I heard tell from the time I was the height of a Lorne shoe, and who ever heard of crofters drinking wine?"

"Wherever are country people and the sea beside them to snatch a meal from, you will find the croft," insisted Col the piper. "They have the croft in France, though they have a different name for it from ours, and I'll wager the bulk of the land they labour is as bare as a bore's snout, for that is what sheep and deer have left in Europe for the small spade-farmer."

"Did'st see the crofting lands out yonder?" asked Margaret's mother.

"No," said the piper; "but plenty I saw of the men they breed there; I ate with them, and marched with them, and battled at their side, for we were not always playing the pipes, we music-fellows.

"And that puts me in mind of a thing—there is a people yonder, over in France, that play the bagpipe—they call them Brettanach—the Bretons. They are the same folk as ourselves though kind of Frenchmen too, wine-drinking, dark and Papist. Race, as the old-word says, goes down to the rock, and you could tell at the first glance of a Brettanach that he was kin to us though a kilt was never on his loins, and not one word in his head of the Gaelic language. 'Tis history! Someway—some time—far back—they were sundered from us, the Brettanach, and now have their habitation far enough from Albyn of the mountains, glens and heroes. Followers of the sea, fishermen or farmers; God-fearing, good hard drinkers, in their fashion—many a time I looked at one and said to myself, 'There goes a man of Skye or Lewis!' "

"And the girls of them?" said Ranald Gorm, with a twinkle of the eyes.

"You have me there!" said Col. "I never saw woman-kind of the Brettanach; the war never went into their country, and the Bretons I saw were in regiments of the army, far enough from home like myself, in the champagne shires where they make the wine.

"We came on them first in a town called Corbie, with a church so grand and spacious a priest might bellow his head off and never be heard by the poor in the seats behind. 'Twas on a week-day, a Mass was making; that was the first and last time ever I played pipes in the House of God, and faith! that not by my own desiring. 'Twas some fancy of the priests, connived between them and the Cornal. Fifteen of us marched the flag-stones of yon kirk of Corbie playing 'Fingal's Weeping.' "

"A good brave tune!" remarked the bailie.

"A brave tune, and a bonny! I'll warrant yon one made the rafters shiver! The kirk was filled with a corps of the tribe I mention—the Bretannach—and they at their Papist worshipping; like ourselves, just country folk that would sooner be at the fishing or the croft than making warfare.

"My eye fell, in particular, on a fellow that was a sergeant, most desperate like my uncle Sandy—so like I could have cried across the kirk to him 'Oh uncle! what do ye do so far from Salen?' The French, for ordinary, are black as sloes, but he was red, red, a noble head on him like a bullock, an eagle nose, and a beard cut square and gallant.

"When the kirk spilled out its folk, they hung awhile about the burial-yard as we do ourselves in Trosdale, spelling the names on the head-stones, gossiping, and by-and-bye slipped out, I doubt not, to a change-house for a dram, and all the pipers with them except myself."

DUNIQUAICH, LOCH FYNE

From the Water-colour Drawing by George Houston, A.R.S.A.

" God bless me ! " cried Ronald Gorm.

" Believe it or not, but I hung back and sought my friend the red one. He was sitting all his lone on a slab in the strangers' portion of the graveyard, under yews, eating bread and onion and sipping wine from his flask of war. Now the droll thing is that though I knew he had not one word of Christian Gaelic in his cheek, 'twas the Gaelic I must speak to him.

" ' Just man,' says I to him. ' Health to you and a hunter's hunger ! I was looking at you yonder in the kirk, and a gentleman more like my clansman Sandy Ruadh of Salen is surely not within the four brown borders of the world nor on the deeps of ocean. Your father must have come from the Western Isles, or the mother of you been wandering.'

" Of all I said to him he knew but the one word that means the same thing, as they tell me, in all Celtdom—*eaglais.* To his feet got the Frenchman, stretched out to me his bread and wine, with a half-laugh on him most desperate like Uncle Sandy, and said *eaglais* too, with a flourish of the heel of his loaf at the kirk behind him to show he understood that, anyway. We sat on the slab, the pair of us, my pipes stretched out between us, and there I assure, folk, was the hour of conversation ! "

" But if you could not speak each other's tongue ? " said a girl.

" *Tach!* two men of the breed with a set of pipes between them can always follow one another. 'Tis my belief if I stood his words on end and could follow them backwards they would be good Gaelic of Erin. The better half of our speech was with our hands ; he had not even got the English ; and most of the time we talked pipe-music, as any man can do that's fit to pucker his lips and whistle. The Breton people *canntarach* tunes too, like ourselves—soft-warbling them to fix them in the memory, and blyth that morning was our warbling ; he could charm, my man, the very thrush from trees ! But Herself—the *piob mhor*—was an instrument beyond his fingering ; the pipes he used at home he called *biornieu,* fashioned differently from ours. Yet the same wind blows through reeds in France or Scotland, and everywhere they sing of old and simple things ; you are deaf indeed if you cannot understand.

"He was from the seashore—John his name—a mariner to his trade—with a wife and seven children; himself the son of a cooper.

"I am a good hand at the talking myself, as little Margaret here will tell you, but his talk was like a stream in spate, and the arms of him went flourishing like drum-sticks. Keep mind of this—that the two of us, by now, were all alone in the kirk-yard, on a little hillock with the great big cliff of a kirk above us, and the town below all humming with the soldiers, like a byke of bees.

"He bade me play on the pipes at last and I put them in my oxter and gave him 'Lochiel's awa' to France.' A fine tune! but someway I felt I never reached him. I tried him then with bits of 'The Bugle Horn,' 'Take your gun to the Hill,' 'Bonnie Ann' and 'The Persevering Lover;' he beat time with a foot to them, and clapped my shoulder, but for all that they said to him I might as well be playing on a fiddle.

"It was only when I tried an old *port-mor*—"The Spoil of the Lowlands now graze in the Glen" that his whiskers bristled, and at that said I to myself 'I have you Uncle Sandy!'

"Before the light that flickered was gone from him I blew it up to a height again with 'Come to me Kinsman!'

"He was like a fellow that would be under spells!

"'The Good Being be about me!' cried he, and his eyes like flambeaux, 'what tune is that?'

"You never, never, never saw a man so much uplifted!

"'They call it,' said I, 'Come to me Kinsman,' (*Thigibh a so a charaid!*), and it has the name, in the small Isles of the West, of the Oldest Air of the World. The very ravens know it; what is it but the cry of men in trouble? It's older than the cairns of Icolmkill, and cried the clans from out of the Isles to Harlaw. Listen you well!' and I played it to him again—not all the MacCrimmons that ever came from Skye could play it better! For grand was the day and white with sun, and to-morrow we were marching. And many a lad of ours was dead behind us.

"When I was done, he did a droll thing then, the red fellow—put his arms about my shoulders and kissed me on the face! And the beard of him like a flaming whin!

"What must he do but learn it? Over and over again I had to whistle it to him till he had it to the very finish, and all the time the guns were going in the east.

"'If ever you were in trouble,' I said to him—though of course he could not understand me, 'and you whistled but one blast of that air, it is Col Maclean would be at your side though the world were staving in below your feet like one of your father's barrels!'"

II

The day was done in Trosdale. Beyond the rim of the sea the sun had slid to make a Sabbath morning further round the world, and all the sky in the west was streaming fire. Over the flats of Heisker the light began to wink on the Monach islets. Ebbed tide left bare sand round Kirkibost, and the sea-birds settled on them, rising at times in flocks and eddying in the air as if they were leaves and a wind had blow them. Curlews were piping bitterly.

Behind the creek where the folk were gathered on the sea-pinks, talking, Trosdale clachan sent up the reek of evening fires, and the bairns were being cried in from the fields.

The Catechist, sombre fellow, already into his Sabbath, though 'twas only Saturday nine o' the clock, came through the whins and cast about him a glance for bagpipes. He had seen Maclean's arrival with misgiving. A worthy man, and a face on him like the underside of a two-year skate-fish.

Col Maclean turned on him a visage tanned as if it had been in the cauldron with the catechu of the barking nets.

"Take you a firken too, and rest you, Catechist," said he. "You see I have not my pipes to-night, but I'm at *sgeulachd.*"

But the Catechist sat not; and leaning against a net-pole sighed.

"'Twas two years after that," said Col, again into the rapture of his story, " when my regiment went to the land of wine, where we battled beside the French. I assure you we did nobly! nobly! Nor, on the soul of me! were the Frenchmen slack!"

"The French," ventured Patrick Macneill, "are renowned in story for all manly parts. Oh King! 'tis they have suffered!"

"'Tis myself, just man, that is not denying it! We were yonder in a land like Keppoch desolate after the red cock's crowing. The stars themselves, that are acquaint with grief, and have seen great tribulation in the dark of Time would sicken at the sight of it! Nothing left of the towns but *larochs*—heaps of lime and rubble where the rat made habitation, and not one chimney reeking in a hundred miles. Little we ken of trees here in the Islands, but they were yonder planted thick as bracken and cut down to the stump the way you would be cutting winter kail. And the fields that the country folk had laboured!—were the Minch drained dry, the floor of it would seem no likelier place for cropping barley or for pasturing goats.

"There was a day of days, out yonder, that we mixed up with the French and cleared the breadth of a parish of *am boche*, who was ill to shift. But the mouth of the night brought him back on us most desperate altogether, and half we had gained by noon was lost by gloaming.

"Five score and ten of our men were missing at the roll-call.

"The Cornal grunted. 'Every man of them out of Lewis!' says he; 'they're either dead or wandered. Go you out Col Maclean with your beautiful, lovely, splendid pipes, and gather at least the living.'

"Not one morsel of meat had I eaten for twenty hours, and the inside of me just one hole full of hunger, but out went Col and his pipes to herding!

"Oh King of the Elements! but that was the night most foul, with the kingdom of France a rag for wetness, and mire to the hose-tops. Rain lashed; a scourging wind whipped over the country, and it was stinking like a brock from tatters that had been men. The German guns were pelting it, the sound of them a bellow no more broken than the roar on skerries at Martinmas, the flash of them in the sky like Merry Dancers.

"I got in a while to the length of a steading with a gable standing; tuned up *piob mhor* and played the gathering. They heard me, the lads—the living of them; two-over-twenty of them came up to me by the gable, with no more kenning of what airt they were in than if a fog had found them midway on the Long Ford of Uist. I led them back to King George's furrows where our folk were, and then, *mo chreach!* when we counted them, one was missing!

"'It is not a good herd you are, Maclean,' said the Cornal, 'you will just go back and find Duncan Ban; he's the only man in the regiment I can trust to clean my boots.'

"So back went Col in search of Duncan."

"Oh lad! weren't you the gallant fellow!" cried Margaret's mother, adoring.

"I was that, I assure you! If it were not the pipes were in my arm-pit like a girl, my feet would not keep up on me the way I would be pelting any other road than the way I had to go. But my grief! I never got my man, nor no man after ever found him. I went to the very ditches where *am boche* was lying, and 't was there that a light went up that made the country round about as white-bright as the day, and I in the midst of it with my pipes in hand. They threw at me grey lead as if it had been gravel, and I fell."

"*Och, a mheudail bhochd!*—Oh treasure!" said the women of Trosdale all together.

"I got to my knees in a bit and crawled, as it might be for a lifetime, one ache from head to heel, till I came to a hole as deep's a quarry where had been the crossing of roads, and there my soul went out of me. When I came to myself I was playing pipes and the day was on the land. The Good Being knows what I played, but who should come out across the plain to me but a Frenchman!

"He moved as spindrift from spindrift,
As a furious winter wind—
So swiftly, sprucely, cheerily,
Oh! proudly,

Through glens and high-tops,
And no stop made he
Until he came
To the city and court of Maclean,
Maclean of the torments,
Playing his pipes."

The Catechist writhed; the people of Trosdale shivered; Patrick Macneill wept softly, for Col Maclean, the cunning one, by the rhyming trick of the ancient sennachies, had flung them, unexpected, into the giddiness of his own swound, and all of them, wounded, dazed, saw the Frenchman come like a shadow into the world of shades.

"He flung himself in the hole beside me, did the Frenchman, gave me a sup of spirits and put soft linen to my sores, and all the time grey lead was snarling over us.

"'Make use of thy good hale feet, lad,' said I to him, 'and get out of this dirty weather! Heed not the remnants of Col Maclean. What fetched thee hither?'

"He put his hand on my pipes and whistled a stave of the old tune.

"'How learned ye that?' I asked him.

"Although he was Brettanach he had a little of the English. 'Red John our sergeant, peace be with him! heard you playing it all last night,' said he, 'took a craze at the tune of you and went out to find you, but never came back. Then another man, peace be with him! a cousin of John, heard your playing and went seeking you, but he came back not either. I heard you first, myself, no more than an hour ago, and had no sooner got your tune into my head than it quickened me like drink, and here am I, kinsman!'

"'Good lad!' I cried, 'all the waters in the world will not wash out kinship, nor the Gael be forsaken while there is love and song.'"

"Vain tales! Vain tales!" groaned the Catechist, and his face like a skate.

THE PIPES: ONSET

(Somme, September, 1916)

By JOSEPH LEE, Lieut.

Dedicated to Major Angus MacGillivray.

The cry is in my ear,
The sight is in my eye,
This is the dawning of the day
That shall see me die:

What is the piper playing
That battles in my blood ?—
Winds in it,
Waves in it,
Waters at the flood ;
Sadness in it,
Madness in it,
Weeping mists and rain—
What is the piper playing
That beats within my brain ?

Sobbing and throbbing
Like a soul's unrest ;
I drink his madd'ning music in
As milk at my mother's breast :
Flame in it,
Fame in it,
Love and all desire ;

The clean hills,
The clear rills,
The smouldering peat fire ;
Glances sweet,
Dancing feet,
Beating on the floor ;
Maidens fair,
Comrades rare
I shall meet no more.

The cry is in my ear,
The sight is in my eye,
This is the morning of the day
That shall see me die :

What is the piper playing
That surges in my blood ?
The soft breeze
In pine trees,
The hawthorn i' the bud ;
The lone tarn,
The golden barn,
Fields of waving grain—
What is the piper playing
That beats within my brain ?

Red war screams from his reeds
And in the thrumming drones
There lurks the lapping of men's blood,
And sobs, and dying groans :
Night in it,
Fight in it,
Wraiths of stricken men,
Ghosts of ancient clansmen

Sweeping down the glen ;
      Life in it,
      Strife in it,
Whisp'rings—it is well,
   If you bear a foeman down
Right to reddest hell !

*   *   *   *

What is the piper playing ?
   For now I may not hear . . .
The glamour comes across my soul,
   And the cry is in my ear.

FLESH TO THE EAGLES

By Boyd Cable

It was during the retreat of 1914 that a Highland regiment was quartered for a night in one of the French villages, and billetted in houses, barns, anywhere the hospitable villagers could give them room. The officers established their Mess and quarters in "The Chateau," a big house on the outskirts of the village. Many of the villagers had already cleared out, but in the Chateau the officers found the mistress of the house, her daughter, and her servants, standing staunchly to their place; the master of the house being, as they were told, in the French Army.

Madame spoke English fairly well, the daughter very well—when she did speak, which was seldom. She was a young and pretty girl of perhaps fifteen to sixteen years of age, fresh come from a convent school, reserved, timid and shy, in the presence of the officers almost to a point of shrinking when they spoke to her. Yet, although they could see her shiver and blanch at the sound of the distant grumble of the guns, she supported her mother bravely and asserted stoutly that she was not afraid to stay, when the C.O. and some of the other officers questioned the wisdom of the household waiting for the Germans to advance.

"Perhaps, monsieur," said Madame, "your soldiers will possible arrest the advance before the Allemands arrive at us here. And if it is not so, it is, after all, soldiers of the Allemands that will come, and they will not harm women and old men and boys who make no provocation or resistance."

Unfortunately the practices of German soldiers were not then sufficiently known to the officers to make them press their argument beyond reasonable limits, and they gave in reluctantly to Madame's reasoning. "We cannot the children and the very old to march away," she said, " and one could not go and leave them here. Me, I stay to speak with the enemy officers and see my people do nothing foolish. I cannot run away and leave them."

So they left it at that.

Madame gave them dinner that night in the dining-room, and it was after dinner that one of the regimental pipers was heard parading round and playing tune after tune. Madame and Mademoiselle were greatly interested and asked many questions.

" But there," cried Madame at one tune, " there is the music most fierce. It sound—"

" It is battle music, Madame," explained the C.O. " Music of a war song of the Highlands—of the Écossais. Ask Monsieur l'Adjutant for the words of the song."

So the Adjutant recited " The Macgregors' Gathering," with all the fire and ardour of a fiery Scot, and a Macgregor at that. Madame sat with brows knit, plainly struggling to follow the English words ; her daughter, as plainly understanding them clearly, held her breath and listened spell-bound and wondering to the words. Her head lifted and her eye lit to some of the lines :

While there's leaves in the forest and foam on the river,
Macgregor, despite them, shall flourish for ever.

But at others, delivered with fierce emphasis and dramatic fervour, she shrank back with quivering lip and pain on her face :

If they rob us of name and pursue us with beagles,
Give their roofs to the flames, their flesh to the eagles.

When the Adjutant had finished and had sat down, looking a little shame-faced at having allowed his feelings to so carry him away, Madame and the girl spoke rapidly in French for a minute.

Then Madame shook her head. " But no," she said, " I do not like it, this song. It is cru-el, cru-el. How says it—' The roof to the burning, and the bodies, the dead, the flesh, to the birds of prey. But no, that is the war of savage."

The C.O tried to explain to her, while the Adjutant did so even more eagerly to the girl, that it was war of the most savage and relentless kind that ran in those far back days in the Highlands of Scotland; but again Madame protested. " It is too cru-el. I do not like it that you make such song and such music now. War, it is no more so. What is it your song says of the burning of *la maison?*" She made the Adjutant repeat the lines and repeated after him, " Ah, m'sieu, ' Give their roof to the flames, their flesh to the eagles.' That is, burn the shelter of the women and children, and leave the dead unbury. You would not do that; even the Boche that we despise would not do this thing. It is cru-el, cru-el."

Mademoiselle said nothing, but they could all see the shrinking in her eyes as she looked at them, the wonder if, even now, the Écossais could be so savage as to make such war. The Adjutant set himself to remove such an idea of their barbarity from her mind, and with some success apparently, since there was little shrinking and no more than a faint blush of timid friendship when they said good-night and retired.

Next morning the orders came, sharp, urgent and imperative, to move at once, and there was little time for farewells. But Madame and the girl were both out to see them off and watch the battalion tramp by. The pipes at their head were screaming their vengeful music, " Give their roof to the flames, their flesh to the eagles," until the Adjutant, seeing the protesting motion of Madame's hands to her ears, hurried to the pipers and asked them to change the tune.

. . . .

After the ebb of our retreat and the period of the Marne, came the full flood-tide of our advance, and the sweeping forward of the French and British over the ground the Germans had taken and held a space. As the luck had it, the same Highland battalion came back through the same village where they had billetted that night—or rather to the shell, the wreckage, the remains of the same village. The men by now were coming to know what sort of treatment had been served out to the conquered country by the Germans, and were angry enough at some of the sights they had seen, the tales they had heard. But the anger had been cold and impersonal until now, when they came swinging in to this friendly spot, through the shattered houses and streets littered with broken bottles and household goods, saw the gaping windows to the houses, the smoke-blackened shells here and there, the signs of pillage and wanton destruction everywhere. The cavalry and an advance guard regiment had been through before them, but it was plain that no fighting had taken place here, that no shell-fire had wrought this damage, that cold-blooded " frightfulness " alone had to answer for it. They were roused to fresh wrath by what they saw, but to a still greater pitch of fury by the tales they heard from the quaking villagers who were left, or who came creeping in from the fields and ditches to which they had fled on word of approaching soldiers. The sights were no more than the men had been seeing in any of a dozen villages passed, the tales no more than they had heard a score of times in the past few days ; but in this village they had been made welcome, had been treated to the best, had made quick but happy friendships ; and they felt a personal injury and pity for the brutally treated villagers.

The battalion halted there for an hour or so and ate their midday meal—or rather gave it to the hungry women and children and watched them eat—and heard fresh and more horrible tales and half-tales that were too bestial to be told in full.

The moment the battalion had fallen out and he was free, the Adjutant had asked the Colonel if he might go to the Chateau and make enquiries. . . .

But when he and another officer came there they found none to make enquiries of. The house still stood, intact so far as the building itself went, but otherwise no more than a litter of rubbish and wreckage. Every stick of furniture that would break was broken, every crock and dish and bottle was scattered in splinters over the floors, every curtain, blanket and sheet, every item of bed and table linen, every piece of clothing was torn, dirtied, and defiled as completely as men and beasts could do it ; every shelf and door and balustrade and fitting was hacked and broken and wrenched out of place ; every room on the ground floor had been used as horses' stables and left as foul as a stable could be ; every upper room was so befouled that, by comparison, the places of the animals below was the cleaner.

The two officers hunted through the house, outside and round the out-buildings, and found no one ; and, nauseated by what they had seen and heart-sick at thought of the women who had been there, returned to the village. As they entered it again they heard pipe music softly played, and seeing down a bye-street a cluster of their men, and hearing the sound of a woman's voice raised loud above the pipe music, they turned off and pushed in to see what was afoot.

They found a woman in the centre of a close-pressing ring of their men, a woman wild-eyed, with grey hair in disorder, with black and blue bruises on her face, with her clothing torn and grimed with dirt.

" Good God ! " exclaimed the Adjutant. " Madame ! "

He thrust a way through the men to her, but when he spoke to her and asked her to come with him, she clutched and held his wrist, and stood there and made him—short of using force to her—stand and listen with the men. A dozen times he tried to interrupt, but she would not be interrupted, so at last he left her to go on with her tale and asked the other officer to go and bring the C.O.

But before the C.O. came, he, like the men, was under the spell of the woman and of her tale, was listening, like them, with his heart turning cold and a deadly bitter anger rising in his heart. She spoke to them in English, breaking off at times into voluble torrents of French, checking herself and going back and repeating as best she could in English again. But although French words and phrases and sentences were mixed through her English, the tale was horribly plain and clear, the stories detailed and circumstantial enough to make it evident they were desperately true.

She told of women, girls, girl-children, outraged, and afterwards, in some cases, mutilated and bayoneted ; she told of old men and boys haled out and stood against a wall and shot while their women were made to stand and look on ; of one woman who refused to make coffee for the Germans until they dipped the head of her infant in a pan of boiling water ; of another woman who was crucified, pinned to the door with bayonets while the arm of her child was broken and its body was flung down on the ground before her and left there writhing . . . all this and more she told, and helped her story out with rapid gesticulations and imitative motions and sounds of the child squirming and whining and the helpless mother wrenching at the pinning bayonets, while the men pressed in, glowering and cursing under breath, and behind them the pipe music skirled and wailed " roofs to the flames, and their flesh to the eagles."

And then, lastly, she told them of herself and her daughter, the girl of fifteen, fresh from a convent school, timid as a child and shrinking from the look, much less the touch of a man . . . and of what they had done to her, while they held her daughter and made her watch; and then had done to the daughter, while she in turn was held to see and not allowed to look away or even close her ears to the cries. She told it all, sparing herself and her child no word and no item of their shame; and then—this was just before the Colonel arrived—she paused and looked round at the ring of savage faces about her, and lifted her two hands and shook them above her head.

" I am French, and you are Anglais," she cried, " but I am woman and you are men. I have told you, so that you may know the animals you fight. I have asked your music-man will he play this song you have, that with the music I say it to you 'Give their roofs to the flames, their flesh to the eagles.' And if ever you have Germans soldat at your mercy, and they cry for pity, remember this village, and its women and my daughter, and me. Give us revanche . . . their flesh to the eagles. . . ."

The Colonel broke in here, and, finding she was not to be stopped, turned and ordered the men away, and when they had gone, handed Madame over to some of the village women who watched timidly from their doors. Madame had told nothing but truth they assured him. Mademoiselle? Ah, ma'm-'zelle could not be seen; she hid in a cellar and screamed like one mad if any entered or spoke—like mad did one say, but truly she was mad; and Madame scarcely less mad.[1]

They had one more glimpse of Madame as they marched out, a glimpse of her standing in a door and waving and calling something to the pipers

[1] All the atrocities mentioned above are not fiction but fact. Day and date, names and places can be given for all of them.

as they came past. They knew or guessed what she wanted and the tune they were playing swung abruptly into " The Gathering," and the battalion tramped past the woman to the vengeful skirl of ". . . flesh to the eagles."

. . . .

Affairs had not gone well with the battalion, or what was left of it, through the battle. They had been ordered to advance and take a certain position in what was supposed to be the flank, had forced their way forward over the open under a scourging shell-fire, had suffered heavy losses, and at last gained the point from which they were to make the final attacking rush. But now that they were here it seemed impossible for men to go further and live. A stretch of open still lay before them, and this was swept with a tornado of rifle and machine-gun fire. What was supposed to be a flank of the enemy had become a frontal position, strongly held and evidently meant to be bitterly defended. It was vital to the success of the day that it should be taken, for various tactical reasons we need not touch here. The Colonel had passed the word through his officers and N.C.O.'s of what they were needed to do, and, briefly, why and how much depended on them.

The moment came.

A battalion on their left surged out and went plunging across the open, the high-explosive shells bursting and flinging fountains of spouting black earth and smoke amongst them, the ground puffing and dust-spurting under the hailing bullets. The Highlanders were supposed to wait until this other battalion had gained a certain line before they, the Highlanders, attacked ; so they lay in their ditch, watching the line struggle forward and the men falling in swathes under the pouring fire, watched it stop at last and drop flat and then begin to break back to cover. It was no time to wait longer, and the Colonel, making up his mind swiftly, launched his attack. It was met by a devastating storm of fire, even heavier and more deadly than the one they had watched. The battalion, barely clear of their cover, wilted under the storm, hesitated, stopped, and began to fire back at the enemy they could not see. Those of the men who stood firing were cut down quickly, the others dropped prone or jumped into shell-holes or such cover as they could find. The officers did their best, jumping up and running forward and calling on their men to follow. But few of them ran more than a score of paces before bullet or shell fragment found them, and they fell; such men as rose and tried to follow only followed them into the next world. The air was alive and trembling to the whistle and whine and hiss of bullets, their snap and smack and crack, and to the quick following crash on crash of the earth shaking shell-bursts.

Again some of the officers tried to rally and start the line forward; but, by now, so great was the noise, so dense the air with smoke and dust, so chaotic and confused the whole business, that the officers' attempts resulted in no more than spasmodic and isolated movements of little groups, movements that were worse than useless, because each could be dealt with in detail, and, one after another, the sweeping machine-guns sluicing bullets on each and cutting them to pieces in turn. Those that made these separate attempts were mostly cut down; those that watched their failure were more convinced than ever that the whole was useless.

The Colonel, too, saw that it was useless and vain slaughter unless by some desperate chance the line should move together . . . and even now it was perhaps too late, because the battalion on the left, lying in the open and scourged with fire, was giving way solidly and struggling back to cover.

It was a crisis in the battle, and where in the crisis many brave men had failed, one brave man tried and won. From somewhere down the line high over the roar of the battle there rose a wailing skirl of the pipes. There was no note of the music that was not familiar to every man there, that they did not know each word to fit to it. The pipes might have been crying the very words aloud to them instead of the music:

> "*Thro' the depths of Loch Katrine the steed shall career,*
> *O'er the peaks o' Ben Lomond the galley shall steer,*
> *And the rocks of Craig Royston like icicles melt*
> *Ere our wrongs be forgot, ere our vengeance unfelt.*"

It was the voice of their own Highlands, their own clansmen, their own regiment, that was calling to those crouching men in the ditch. They stirred, lifting their heads and looking for the piper. They could not see him, but the pipes shrilled on :

"*Then gather, gather, gather . . .*"

The men knew what was coming. "*Gather*" sang the pipes, and, when they were ready gathered, the word or the sign would surely come. The music was rousing them to other memories beyond their Scotland and their name and fame in the Highlands. "*Landless, landless, landless,*" cried the pipes, and the men remembered those women back in the village, houseless and homeless, tortured and shamed past telling, remembered too a woman's final word, "But we are women and you are men."

Along the line the wild and useless fire was steadying and dying away ; they could see now that this was no time for shooting, but for the cold steel. The Colonel saw and felt that the moment had come, rose crouching to his knees, made ready to leap out and forward. He, too, had been looking for the piper without seeing sign of him. But now, just as he rose,—"*Hulloo, Hulloo . . . Gregorlach!*" skirled the pipes, and down the line a figure leaped from cover into full view, halted, marked time for a few steps to the beat of the music, moved steadily forward, the kilt swaying, shoulders and pipe drones swinging, streamers fluttering, and the pipes screaming their hardest.

All along the line men were scrambling to their feet and into the open. "*. . . Gregorlach!*"

The Colonel was out and running forward, the line was up and away—"*Hulloo, Gregorlach!*" and the pipe streamers still fluttering and dancing ahead of the solid rushing wave of kilt and khaki and glinting steel. "*Give their roofs to the flames. . . .*"

In that rush many fell and died ; but at the end of it so did many Germans. For this time no bullet storm could stay the charge, the position was reached and taken, and the cold steel came to its own again—came to its own and drove home the meaning of the music that alone had brought it there—"*Their flesh . . . to the eagles.*"

THE BLACK CHANTER

By Charles Laing Warr

It was April above Lucerne, in the year of grace nineteen hundred and fourteen, and everything was young. A witchery of sunlight and scent and blossom etherealised the earth and the heavens; and fields, green as the green diamond at the heart of the world, rioted wantonly to kiss the white dazzling peaks that glittered in the sapphire sky.

On a fallen tree, its bark all frosted with lichen, two young people sat at the edge of a pine copse. They were both in the springtide of life, and they sat in enchanted silence inhaling the perfume of the trees and listening to the birth song of an awakening universe. She was not much over twenty, perhaps, and she was enhaloed with the soul of France. It lurked in the dark glistening coils of her hair, in the gestures of her shoulders and white, nervous hands, her lips. Her eyes, half mystic, half tigerish, wells of lightly slumbering passion, told the eternal story of that indomitable race whose destiny it seems to have been to demonstrate to the world that the life of a nation's soul may be unquenchable, though drowned in every century with blood.

He was obviously from across the Channel; clean built, healthy and handsome. One versed in the characteristic physiognomy of the denizens of our islands would have told you after a moment's observation that he was a Celt. And indeed, the Honourable Gordon Niall, son and heir of the fifteenth Baron Niall of the Western Isles, could play the *piob mor* and speak the Gaelic as his mother tongue. Twelve years of public school and university life had left him still dreaming foolish dreams and seeing great visions. Which is a proof that he was born into this world a trifle late.

They were happy, these two, in their nest in the hills. They looked out on the world as the good God made it. Among the flower-smothered fields stretched at their feet a placid-minded peasantry lived and moved and had their being. Content with their tree-bowered, log-built chalets and their daily bread, they follow the slow-footed oxen and their wooden ploughs, just as their fathers did a thousand years ago. From day to day their stainless, uneventful life unfolds to them the secret of the untroubled heart, and they believe in the beauty of the world they see and the goodness of the Creator they one day hope to see. They are simple folk, of course.

Helene von Behr loved it as she looked. It made her remember so vividly an old-age worn chateau in the peace of southern France. She felt again in her inmost soul those scents of childhood which outlive all human forgetfulness. She sat and dreamed of it all, and as she dreamed her thoughts became words, and she told them to her companion, who listened with his blue eyes full of a boyish unconcealed adoration for the lovely girl beside him. Her eyes sometimes puzzled him ; they puzzled him now. A sad, lambent light was in them ; like sunset glints on the shadowing hills of vanished years.

She talked on : about the moat round the grey creeper-covered house, the moat into which she had fallen one day when only six years old. And the forest—so deep and dark and wonderful—with the great oak, into whose branches Napoleon III. had climbed to smoke his everlasting cigarette in peace when he had been the unwelcome guest of her great-uncle, a *grand seigneur* who had despised the new régime. Old Jean Barbé, the coachman, was remembered too—old Jean, who was always cross but didn't mean to be ; and what a funny scar it was over his left eye where her white cat had scratched him !

Then there was the village curé. She said, with simple innocence, that her nurse had told her as a secret that it was whispered he was her uncle, and would have reigned in the chateau had he only travelled into this life down the broad road which leadeth from the altar. But, what a dear he was ! She remembered when she made her first confession to him, and how she had wondered if he was smiling, or angry, behind the grating when she told that she had stolen a cigarette from the big silver box on the writing-table of M. le Vicomte de Fontaigne, her father, and had smoked it surreptitiously in the stable beside her pet horse. He used to dine with them every Wednesday evening; and in the calm summer night the table was laid beneath the pear tree at the end of the terrace near the river, which glowed so red in the light of the westering sun. How shabby his soutane always was, and all brown with the stains of snuff!

So she rambled on and spoke of her father, that proud aristocrat, bearing a name to be found in the most abbreviated histories. She laughed when she said that he lived there in magnificent isolation, too proud to serve the Republic!

Then she sighed, and did not tell that nevertheless he had married her against her will to that dull old German diplomatist sitting down there in the Schweizerhof immersed in the voluminous correspondence which was the breath of his life: that correspondence which she secretly blessed in her heart for the free, careless hours it had given her these last ten days with this fresh-faced boy, the only occupant of the scantily filled hotel with whom her lord and master would allow her to associate.

She sat silent, and gazed dreamily at the undulating countryside, radiant in bloom and light and colour, with old Pilatus in the distance, sentinel of ages. The shimmering sunshine quivered all over it, and the scattered chalets, and orchards pink and white with foam, seemed lulled to sleep in the security of God. Once a priest passed, trudging down the white dusty road beneath; once a peasant, the smoke of his long black cigar hanging in a blue filmy wreath about his round felt hat. Far down in the valley tinkled the music of cow bells. A little stream, crystal clear, trickled at her feet . . . flies danced in clouds above the edging rushes. The warm smell of the earth was intoxicating like incense. . . .

She was dimly conscious that her companion was whistling softly. He had a habit of doing this when deep in thought, and she recognised the odd little refrain. She had heard him whistle it a dozen times—queer, uncanny, elusive as the mountain mist, with the mystery of the hills in it, and sorrow, and the spirit of brave men. She glanced at him. She knew that this boy had begun to exercise a strange fascination over her, stronger and more dangerous than she dared to confess even to herself. It was not unnatural, for her life these last three years in that grim, dull old schloss in Hanover had been very lonely. The bud will not mate with the yellow leaf, but spring must call to spring; albeit the mongers of the matrimonial market prattle as they please.

"What is it you whistle, my Gordon?" she asked suddenly. "There are strange things in the air. Has it a story from your Scottish hills?"

He sat back and laughed his gay laugh.

"Yes, it has," he answered. "I'll tell it you, if it won't bore you."

"But no: tell me," she said, and prepared to listen, her chin in her hand.

It was a tune they played on the pipes, he said: and it was a wild, barbaric story of war and the fierce passion of men and the tottering fortunes of his race. Six hundred years ago Castle Niall had been besieged by a neighbouring clan, for the Niall of the day had carried off the daughter of its chief, and held her within his walls. The beleaguered garrison was on the verge of starvation, when to Niall came a dream which told him that deliverance would come from a black chanter which would drop from heaven upon the castle roof. Three times, and three times only, would it play a mysterious tune, which none but the head of the house would be able to awaken from the reed; and in the hour of peril or distress the playing of the chanter would bring salvation. When the morning dawned grey over the castle ramparts, they found, lying on the roof, a black chanter as had been foretold. The chief blew on it with trembling lips, and lo! it played of its own accord. Immediately Niall and his men sallied from the fortress and drove their enemies into the sea.

In the intervening centuries the chanter had again been used and brought deliverance. Its virtue would be efficacious only once more. The strange, haunting air had become the battle charge of his race. It was that which he had been whistling. The last time it had been played, in the sixteenth century, the family piper had caught the air and fixed it indelibly on the scroll of memory. He laughed nervously when he had finished. He was afraid she would treat it lightly. But he had told his tale with an old-world seriousness, and although she had felt inclined to smile when he had ended his recital of it, something in his face restrained her. Instead, she patted his brown curly head.

"Come," she said, "it is late. We must go home."

. . . .

It was their last evening together, for Helene and her husband were leaving the following day. As they walked along under the chestnut trees on the Schweizerhof Quai, Niall was dull and silent. She had stirred the very depths of his young, impressionable heart, this girl. He didn't attempt to deceive himself: he knew he was passionately in love with her. He felt that he hated old von Behr. But—it was all so hopeless.

That night he dined with them. The dinner was not a great success. They were all pre-occupied—Helene and Gordon with crowding thoughts that were very much akin, the Count with a disquieting dispatch from the Wilhelmstrasse and a severe attack of indigestion. At ten o'clock he excused himself: he had writing to do. He pointedly suggested that his wife should go to bed; and he made his adieux to Niall, remarking that they were leaving early in the morning and would not likely see him. Furious with stifled anger, the boy said a conventional good-bye to the woman he loved. She moved away. Count von Behr lingered for a moment, and then betook himself with shambling gait to his accustomed corner of the writing-room, which, for some reason, he preferred to his own private apartment.

The moment he was out of sight Niall hurriedly left the lounge and hastened upstairs. On the first floor he saw her, obviously lingering, a little way down the corridor. She came back as she saw him approach. The boy blushed deeply as he took her hand, and stammered something about not being able to say good-bye in such a beastly cold fashion. His head seemed to be swimming. He had some confused impressions about the white of her evening gown and a great crimson rose at her breast.

"My Gordon," she said softly, with that fascinating inability to control her r's that thrilled him; "Whistle me your tune once again—quickly, for I must go. I shall remember you by it, boy. Perhaps, some day if we meet again, I may be able to whistle it to you!"

She smiled, but her eyes were moist. And Niall drew his parched lips together and managed to whistle the strange, mysterious air. He finished and stood awkwardly facing her, tall and distinguished in his evening clothes. No word of love had ever passed between them, but as they looked into each others eyes, each read the secret that nothing could hide.

"Adieu, my Gordon," she whispered hastily. "You have been good to me. I won't forget you . . . and you'll help me often . . . but be sensible, boy—and forget me!"

A moment later she was running down the corridor and vanished at the end. The boy stood for a minute or two rigid where he was, staring blankly at a red rose in his hands, his head reeling with the delicious joy of the knowledge that for one never-to-be-forgotten moment her arms had been thrown round his neck, and on his mouth her warm lips had pressed a swift, burning kiss.

II

Captain Gordon Niall of the Uist Highlanders lay flat on his face beside a loophole in the wall. With a subaltern, two men, and a stray sergeant of the Yorkshire Rifles, he occupied the remains of a former farmstead, now a jumbled heap of bricks and mortar. The only portion of this mass of refuse that looked like a house was a right angle formed by the ends of two walls which rose like a skeleton from the shattered piles of rafters, rubbish, stones, lime, and dead bodies of mangled men.

It was one of the supreme moments resultant upon the German break through near Armentières, that grim, bloody month of April, 1918. The British line existed only in the imagination of an exhausted and bewildered Staff, their faculties half paralysed with fatigue and over work. No one knew with anything even approaching certainty what the situation was. Only one thing was certain because it was obvious, and that was that the very existence of our Armies was hanging in the balance. The British front was hopelessly, irretrievably broken; and a disorganised rabble of tattered regiments, half crazy with weariness and strain and hunger, were retreating in mixed, irregular bands back from the river Lys, through a withering hail of bullets and a raging tornado of shrapnel and high explosive; valiantly and uncomplainingly to take up new positions and renew the desperate struggle against overwhelming odds.

Gordon Niall had arrived at the stage when all emotion had been frozen to its depths. He looked phlegmatically out upon a dreary, muddy countryside literally alive with the grey advancing hordes of the enemy. The little group huddled in the shelter of the tottering walls manipulated a Lewis gun with the dull ceaseless energy of men in a dream. Dirty, ragged, verminous, with a week's growth on their smoke-grimed emaciated faces, they were unquestioningly carrying out to the last their final act in the mighty drama of that last awful month which clouded their minds like a nightmare from Hell.

They had been all through the sickening horror of the struggle on the Somme, and after three weeks hard fighting had arrived a week ago at Armentières for a rest, to find themselves swirled into the vortex of the new German offensive. Gordon Niall as he stoically waited for death, knew very little about the facts of it all. He had been told that the Portuguese who held the line on the left had broken; and that out of the welter of shattered, scurrying, disordered units, he had been ordered to take up an advanced position, to stem the rush with a handful of men he had managed to gather round him out of the retreating forces. And there he was, with four others—all that were left—with the German masses two hundred yards ahead, and behind him the river Lys, its muddy waters splashing under the bursting barrage, ironically emphasising the fact that for him there was no retreat.

It was only a matter of minutes, and at last the end came. A confused babel of sounds; a smothering avalanche of men, stamping, yelling, pushing; the collapse of the whole universe about him; a deadly pain in his head; a strange, swift, kaleidoscopic vision of home . . . his mother's face . . . then darkness.

He didn't know how long afterwards it was that he felt himself jerked roughly to his feet. As his senses slowly returned he realised that a German officer was searching him. He watched the man stupidly as he went through the papers in his pocket-book: then something fell from a letter to the ground, something brown like a dead leaf, and Niall lurched forward with a snarl.

"Give it me!" he said hoarsely.

The officer looked up, surprised, and then down at his feet. He stooped and picked the little fragment from the ground, glanced at it casually, and handed it to Niall with a look of half amused wonder in his eyes. Then he went on reading. Niall thrust the recovered treasure into his tunic pocket—only a faded rose given to him four years ago by a girl at Lucerne, whose memory the passion of war had not succeeded in effacing.

The officer soon finished, and Niall was marched off with a small escort. It all seemed like a bad dream, that scurry over the fire-swept zone, the arrival at the battered hamlet where more prisoners were waiting. Then the long weary march, hour after hour, their numbers constantly swelling, on through the fading twilight and a dark drizzling night. Like drunken men the straggling column reeled along, half delirious with hunger and fatigue, past stores and camps and dumps and villages, while ever past them the reserve masses of horse, foot and artillery incessantly pressed on the heels of the advancing German forces. At last, long after midnight, they reached a smallish town; and, packed into an empty building, they fell on the cold concrete floor and slept the sleep of utter exhaustion.

Early in the morning they were marched to the station, and Niall found himself in a third class compartment with eleven other officers. Some time before the train started a bowl of some sticky, soupy substance was handed in, with a loaf of bread; and on this they subsisted during the twenty-six hours which elapsed before they were detrained at their destination, a dreary, drab little town; and, cramped and weak as children, they marched two miles out into the country to the wire-encircled encampment which awaited their coming.

III

Those unfortunates who endured the lonely monotonous horror of prison life in Germany will tell you what " barbed-wire madness " was. They will tell you of men who got the disease ; and of that furtive, piteous look that haunted the tragic sunken eyes of weary creatures who became frenzied with the longing for freedom. It is perhaps difficult to appreciate from the depths of an arm-chair the terrible gnawing pain of this consuming passion to which some natures were so very susceptible. But strong men who have lived, if only just lived, for three long ghastly months, without letters or parcels, on a diet of turnip-soup and small lumps of black bread, till the skin was stretched tight over their protruding cheek-bones like yellow parchment, their filthy, ragged clothes hanging like mildewed sacks on their emaciated bodies, and their hollow eyes gleaming like the eyes of famished beasts—they understand how easy it was to fall a prey to " barbed-wire madness."

Gordon Niall got it, and got it badly. It was inevitable. The restless Celtic spirit was the first to fall a victim to the mania for escape. Five times he eluded his watchful guard, and five times was recaptured, sullen and still determined, taking his punishment of solitary confinement as a matter of course, with a purpose dogged and unbroken. For solitary confinement in cells was no cure for the disease : it was like malaria, once in the system it was ineradicable. The weeks dragged on. Parcels and letters arrived from home and conditions gradually improved, but Niall remained obsessed with his yearning for liberty. Other men who had escaped and been recaptured began to realise the futility of it, and the news which filtered through the German newspapers of the turn of the tide and the progress of the Allied forces tended to encourage them to settle down to await developments. And one night the camp was electrified with the announcement of the defection of Bulgaria. It was the beginning of the end, and the star of hope shone clear in the firmament. Yet it had no effect on Gordon Niall, for the following night he made yet another attempt to escape.

He had thought it out carefully; and at midnight, three friends, strenuously protesting at his foolishness, hoisted him up to the little window of their hut which overlooked the prison yard. It was not more than twelve yards from the wire enclosure, and within four feet of it rose a telegraph pole. The window had been very carefully prepared, and it did not take Niall many minutes to remove the glass, drop the panes into the keeping of his friends below, and wriggle on to the narrow ledge. He listened carefully, and looked up and down the yard, white in the searching glare of the great electric lamps which turned night into day. A high wind and a driving sleet favoured him, for the sentry who passed shortly afterwards on his beat by the barbed wire was walking quickly with his chin sunk in the collar of his coat. Niall waited till he had gone, then, crouching for a moment on the window ledge, he sprang forward, clutched at the telegraph pole, clung to it for a few seconds, then laboriously hauled himself up to the cross-bars. Here he rested for a while and allowed the sentry once more to pass. Then, judging that he would just have time to reach the further pole, which was a few feet on the far side of the wire, before the man returned, he commenced his perilous journey. Painfully and cautiously he straddled across the wires and began to work himself along. The swirling blasts of the strong wind more than once almost swept him from his precarious hold, and the icy rain numbed his cut and bleeding hands. Beneath his weight the wires swayed and sagged . . . yet he struggled on his desperate way. It was more difficult than he had supposed, and sick, with nervous strain and physical exhaustion, he determined to risk discovery and hang where he was, halfway across, until the sentry passed again. The minutes dragged, and then round the corner of the next hut the man appeared, his shoulders hunched in the driving rain, his eyes on the ground. Above him, clinging frantically to the wire, Niall waited, his heart in his mouth. The man walked almost beneath him, seeing nothing; and in a few seconds the prisoner again began to toil along the wires. At length, almost fainting with fatigue and strain, he clutched his goal and drew himself across the cross-bars, and waited, panting, his heart throbbing as if it would burst, until the sentry should repass him. He soon approached. Nearer and nearer he came. He tramped beneath the crouching figure on the top of the telegraph pole. Niall muttered a prayer of thankfulness for the fierce wind and the torrential rain.

The blood suddenly roared in his ears with excitement . . . the man had stopped . . . was he going to look up? . . . he stamped his feet for a minute or two, then resumed his monotonous beat.

Niall quickly clutched the pole with his arms and knees and slithered to the ground. Bending low he ran swiftly across the area illumined by the glare from the prison yard, and found himself in the enveloping darkness of the night.

. . . .

The fugitive had a roughly accurate knowledge of the immediate countryside, gained by constant observation during the occasional walks which had been permitted the prisoners, under escort. He purposed making for a thick wood which lay about two miles to the westward, and there concealing himself during the following day when the hue and cry would be in full swing. When night again came round he would push ahead; if possible, keeping a general course to the north-west, which, he anticipated, would in time bring him to some point on the Dutch frontier. He had saved up a quantity of food, which, with strict economy, he hoped might last him at a pinch for a fortnight. If, by that time, he had not reached the frontier, things might become awkward; but this was an eventuality too distant to be considered at the moment.

He found himself at the outskirts of the forest an hour later, and forged ahead through the crowding trees and thick undergrowth until dawn broke, when he searched about for a secure hiding-place. He resolved not to climb a tree as he felt that sleep was a necessity. Fortune favoured him by the discovery of a large fox-hole in a dense thicket; and down this he forced his way feet first, carefully wound up his wrist watch, and in five minutes was fast asleep.

It was one o'clock in the afternoon when he awoke. Scarcely a sound broke the tense silence of the wood. The rain had passed and the sun shone clear above the trees. He ate some biscuits and a meagre slice of tinned meat, washed his face and hands in a neighbouring stream, made some rough calculations on a sheet of paper as to direction, and settled down to wait for nightfall. With the advent of dusk he again set off through the forest.

For twelve long weary days and nights he successfully eluded capture and kept up the same monotonous round—hiding by day and pushing ahead by night. He had been forced on many occasions to retrace his steps or make circuitous rounds owing to coming suddenly on villages or towns, and he had not made the progress he had resolved to make. His food, too, he had miscalculated ; and at the close of the twelfth day he found himself with his rations at an end, and hopelessly befogged as to his whereabouts. For another day and night he held out bravely, and then narrowly avoided detection in a fruitless attempt to steal a chicken from a farmyard. At the expiry of a fortnight he was starving and in the throes of a fever.

He came to a final decision. He would start again at dusk and press on. If by daylight there was no sign of the frontier he would give himself up. There was nothing else for it. He was in desperate straits : his clothes were torn to rags and he was almost overcome by the fierce grip of the fever that was rapidly consuming his little remaining strength. He had given up all hope of winning to the haven of neutral territory ; it might not be far away, perhaps, but his power of endurance was at an end. However, he would forge ahead that night, whatever happened.

As soon as darkness rendered it safe he emerged from his concealment and struck westward along the edge of a rough country road. For hours he toiled along meeting with nobody, but making poor progress. He was becoming light-headed, and he lurched heavily as he walked. At intervals he burned and shivered and sweated fiercely. Time and again he fell on his face, but on each occasion he staggered to his feet and struggled ahead.

The night wore on, and through the clouds on the eastern skyline a palish light began to filter. The skies grew dull grey and then softer like the wing of a dove. Over the fields and hedgerows the luminous glow grew clearer as the wheels of the Dawn rolled on, touching the bare branches of the trees and silvering the green stagnant water in the ditch, by whose edge reeled and pitched an exhausted atom of humanity.

Niall raised his bloodshot eyes to the heavens.

"Well, this is the end of it," he muttered, "and probably the end of me too. I don't mind . . . it's been a good effort, and I'm so tired . . . my God, how tired I am!"

A hundred yards ahead a high wall began, evidently the bound of some large country residence, and not much further on was a small iron gate. Inside, a footpath led winding among the trees of a wide parkland. With shaking hands Niall unlatched the gate and followed the path. He could not see now where he was going: a red mist hung like a veil before his eyes. Once he ran against a tree, striking his head violently against the trunk. Dazedly he raised his hand to his forehead and felt it wet. . . . Shortly afterwards he reached the end of the parkland. Things grew clearer again, and he saw before him, not three hundred yards away, the grey battlemented towers of a stately castle. For a few moments he stared at it in a fuddled manner, then he collapsed into a ditch full of rotting leaves.

. . . .

When he regained consciousness it was night. He must have lain there all day. Slowly past events came back to him, and he raised himself with difficulty on his elbow and looked at the winking lights in the castle windows. The fever did not trouble him now: all he was conscious of was a fierce, overpowering craving for food and warmth and rest. The twinkle of the lights called to him. It was a German house, certainly, but he would get something to eat there, and they would let him rest—how he wanted rest! His thoughts flew back to his home in the distant western isles. Would they be thinking of him? he wondered. Thank God, they couldn't see him now. His mother, and Eileen his sister . . . they would be in the old library where they always sat at night, that vast stone-walled room above the cliff where the moaning of the sea rose eternally. And his father would be asleep in the red leather chair by the gun-room fire. He smiled as the vision rose before him. Would he ever see it again? Great God, why did men want to kill one another? . . .

His rambling thoughts switched off in another direction . . . if they could see him now, perhaps his old father would go to the glass case on the library wall, take from its resting place the black chanter, and blow on it for the last time! He laughed hoarsely—a good joke that! Delirious and cracked, his voice suddenly croaked forth the weird notes of the black chanter's tune. Horrible and broken it rose on the still night air.

In a few moments the delirium passed, and with a mighty effort he got on his hands and knees. Painfully and slowly he began to crawl across the damp grass of the park towards the shadowy mass of the silent castle.

"They'll give me food," he gasped . . . "and let me rest."

IV

The Countess von Behr sat in a deep chair by the open fireplace of her boudoir in the Schloss Bersenburg. On the white marble mantelshelf a painted china clock pointed to a quarter past eleven. The luxuriously furnished room was in deep shadow, the only light coming from two massive silver candelabra upon the grand piano in a recess by the window. The flickering glow from the red embers lit up fitfully the face of the woman who gazed abstractedly into the fire.

Four years of mental strain and suffering had left their mark on Helene von Behr, for there were lines about her eyes and her mouth had grown harder. These years had fallen with tragic weight upon the shoulders of the exiled girl, doomed by the exigencies of the times to live alone in this vast gloomy house, her heart in bleeding France, her body in a country which by hereditary instinct she had always disliked, but now hated with all the intensity of her passionate southern heart. So she had dragged out her solitary days in the seclusion of the Schloss, one of that vast multitude, young in years but old in suffering, whose souls have been ruthlessly crushed beneath the iron wheels of the chariots of war.

The Count had been keenly alive to the delicacy of his domestic situation, and from the outbreak of hostilities, though he had been almost constantly resident in Berlin owing to his important connection with the Foreign Office, he had deemed it the prudent course to leave his French wife in the solitariness of his country home; a policy which saved both himself and her from inevitable embarrassments which might at once prove detrimental to the interests of the one, and intolerable to the other.

The unutterable agony of the weary months in a position which was both false and horrible to her, conscious as she could not fail to be of the veiled contempt and cleverly concealed hostility of her servants, and the less disguised dislike of her few neighbours, had told heavily upon the lonely woman. Two months ago things had become almost insufferable when the news came that the Vicomte de Fontaigne had been laid in a soldier's grave. To fight for the Republic was one thing, but to fight for France was quite another: and so, at the hour of crisis, like the rest of his order, the haughty nobleman had put his politics in his pocket and offered his services to the Government. The grief of her father's death, borne alone, friendless and exiled, had almost crushed Helene. Yet it seemed as if her perplexities were never to end: for that very afternoon a telegram had come intimating in crude staring words, that the Count von Behr had been shot dead in the Wilhelmstrasse while endeavouring from a window to appease a revolutionary mob.

She had tried to analyse her feelings when the news was conveyed to her. She had never loved him, but in his own blunt way he had been kind and considerate to her; and the sudden tears which she shed were from the heart, for she sincerely regretted his death. Yet despite this fact she could not stifle the insistent thought that she was free—free to go back to France and to the Chateau Fontaigne, that pearl of her soul, when this holocaust of death was past and over; a thought rendered doubly moving by the knowledge that the dawn was already breaking! She had often wondered what it would be like in the future for a child of France to be wedded for ever to a German.

As she sat before the fire she felt restless and ill at ease. Her jumbled thoughts refused to be focussed on any one aspect of her affairs. She felt something strange in the atmosphere, something that oppressed her. It seemed in the air, it was all around, real yet indefinable. Time and again she looked round half nervously as if expecting to find someone in the room with her. . . .

She settled deeper into her chair and listlessly watched a morsel that fell red from the fire . . . it grew pink and then grey. It still smoked a little, then died. As the lonely woman stared into the embers there suddenly rose before her a boyish face, so clear and vivid that she was startled by it. There was pain in the eyes that looked at her, pain and dull weariness, and the dumb suffering of a yearning spirit. Helene shivered. . . . How often during these last years had that face risen before her, and the sunlight and happiness of ten brief days in a deserted Lucerne had fallen on her tired heart like the dew of heaven. She had never forgotten him—how could she? She had wondered so often where he was. She knew he was not dead: for he was first in that list of names which she had given to a friend in Berne, desiring him to keep her acquainted with their fortunes. She often thought, had she done wrong that night when she kissed his young mouth? But it didn't really matter, after all: she had done him no harm, and long ago he would have forgotten her. Men forgot so quickly. For his own sake she hoped he had: yet—in spite of herself she prayed that he hadn't. And as she looked ahead, to-night, to her coming liberty, she wondered. . . . But the face in the fire made her uneasy. A queer tune throbbed in her head—his tune! She had heard it in her thoughts all night; wild, unrythmical, it seemed to have vibrated in the stillness of the shadowy room—mysterious, passionate, compelling. Once it had been so realistic that she had been convinced that she actually heard it—out in the night; and she had pulled aside the curtains and peered out into the darkness.

She stretched her arms above her head. She felt stifled: surely the room was very hot. Rising, she moved restlessly to the window and looked out. It was a clear, starry night; with a silver moon peeping from behind some scudding clouds. She lingered, gazing up at the beauty of the heavens. Then, just as she was about to let the thick curtain drop, suddenly, muffled yet distinct, she heard a man's voice rise on the night air. It cried one English word—"Help!"

For a minute she stood startled and irresolute, then she flung open the window. Below, on the white of the wide gravel sweep, she could dimly see a dark form lying stretched before the massive steps of the doorway.

She leaned over the edge and called. No answer came. She drew back into the room and touched the electric bell. A few seconds later, an old sleepy-eyed footman appeared, their last remaining man-servant.

"Quick," she cried, "there is a man lying outside on the gravel. I think he is dead. Get some help and bring him into the hall. I'll come down myself immediately."

The man bowed solemnly and withdrew; and when five minutes later she descended the broad oak staircase, Helene saw an excited knot of servants depositing a human burden on the great fur rug before the cavernous hall fireplace. She approached and looked down upon the form of a man, little more than a skeleton, his clothes ragged and smeared with filth, his thin sunken face bearded and dirty. The cluster of servants stared at him open-mouthed.

The sick man moved an arm. He drowsily muttered a few words; feebly, but Helene and the domestics heard them:

"Must be near the frontier now. . . . Thank God!"

"English," said the old footman resentfully, but a quick look from his mistress silenced any further remark. She despatched the man for the local doctor and sent the women for blankets, hot water, brandy, pillows; and she herself knelt by the miserable creature and gently loosened his ragged collar. The emaciated face recalled nothing to her as she looked—but, a few seconds later, Gordon Niall opened his eyes, and, trembling like an aspen leaf, and white to the lips, Helene von Behr recognised him.

"Mother of God!" she gasped.

The floodgates of memory opened and the great waters poured over her soul. She felt the walls and the floor of the vast gloomy hall reeling about her; but, with an almost superhuman effort of will, she regained her composure, and met the eyes that looked into her ashen face with a look of wonder and amazement. The fever seemed to have left him, and for the moment Niall was perfectly conscious. She bent down and pillowed his head on her arm.

"Helene," he whispered, "is it you? . . . where am I?"

"It's all right, dear," she said soothingly. "You're quite safe. Don't speak—you must rest."

The servants returned and Niall was made as comfortable as possible. Helene thought rapidly. At all costs she must be alone with him for a time. She dismissed the whispering women upon various errands. Yes, she said to their enquiries, she would stay with him till they returned.

When they were alone Niall looked up.

"I escaped, you know," he said weakly. "I've had an awful time—but I'm safe now, Helene, am I not? . . . across the frontier, eh?"

"Yes, yes, my Gordon," she answered, smoothing back his matted hair, "you're across the frontier, and you'll soon be well." She almost choked as she remembered that the frontier was only five miles away.

He sighed contentedly and closed his eyes. For a while he lay very still; then he spoke, with difficulty.

"My left tunic pocket," he gasped, "feel in it, Helene . . . that's right . . . now, open that flap."

From the tattered leather pocket-book she pulled out a dried withered flower. His eyes gleamed as he saw it. He turned his face to her.

"Your rose," he whispered—"at Lucerne, you know."

A severe fit of shivering seized him. His eyes closed. From the corners of his mouth two thin rivulets of blood began to trickle . . . he opened his eyes.

"Helene," he muttered spasmodically, "Helene—the frontier . . . I must get across the frontier . . . before the morning."

The end was near and she knew it. With her left hand she extracted from her bosom a little gold crucifix and held it before the dying eyes. In a voice, choked with emotion, she said in his ear,

"Say after me, my Gordon . . . 'Jesu, have mercy!'"

"*Jesu—have—mercy!*"

"Now, and in the hour of death"—

"*Now, and—in—the hour of—death*"—

"Have mercy on me, a sinner!"

"*Have mercy—on—me—a sinner!*"—

He shivered as in a blast of icy wind, then smiled like a tired child and nestled his head against her breast. And very quietly he crossed the silent frontier of that shadowy country, whence no traveller returns.

. . . .

The servants were clustered about her, and the stout village doctor was bending over the thin body stretched on the fur rug ; but Helene, her head bowed, neither looked up nor spoke. . . .

THE PIPES

BY EDMUND CANDLER

ON Christmas night the pipers came into the mess. They had piped the regiment across many a hot place in France and escorted bombing parties down many a German trench. In one action four out of the eight were hit and two killed. They touch a chord deep down somewhere which no doubt has its proper scientific name. The eye of the piper which conceals his gladness, denying all rapture, is a key to the undemonstrative temper of the men who would rather die than throw up their bonnets and shout.

A subaltern of nineteen years put the case for the pipes to me in his own eloquent slang.

" Of course I get cold feet sometimes " he said, " like everyone else. But the pipes soon warm one. MacFarlane, the Company Piper, piped us across on the 25th, the regimental slogan, you know. By Jove, it was top-hole."

We called him the Chicken. Being bigger in the beam than in the shoulders and having a slightly forward stoop he looked in his kilt like a preternaturally large nestling just emerged from the egg. To see him walking reminded one of a determined young chicken. He had an assurance unnatural in the new-born which set off his callowness and puzzled one. It was not side. To hear him talk made one smile, You would think he had plumbed experience and was already convinced about the main issues of life, celibacy or marriage, the rights and wrongs of Demos, peace and war, and the like. One smiled in sympathy, not in derision, accepting the indisputable explanation that the Chicken had had special privileges in the egg. And one thanked the war for an ingenuousness of speech, the bloom of which would have been rubbed off in a week of peace-time conditions in a mess.

"MacFarlane was killed with a bombing party," the subaltern went on. "They let hell loose,—all their machine guns, rifle grenades, trench mortars, and every rifle thirty rounds at least. Our fellows came in half an hour afterwards, having been snug in a shell-hope through the whole show. Only two of our men were hit—by a trench mortar. One was MacFarlane. It was a horrid sight—made me feel a bit green. Nothing was left of them, and you couldn't tell who they were save by their identity discs. I put a sentry by the traverse on both sides and gave orders that no one was to pass. It wouldn't have done for these young recruits to see the mess," this pink-faced subaltern of nineteen explained with paternal solicitude.

His tenderness for the recruits amused me, for the absence of down on his chin made the Chicken look younger than his years. But I marvelled more at the complacency with which he found himself in command. He spoke of his blooded veterans—Perthshires, if you please, the salt of the British Army, as if he were a huntsman holding them in the leash; yet it was only in spirit that he had attained to man's estate. One phrase struck me. He was describing the capture of Hun murderers, or if not actual murderers the comrades and accomplices of murderers, men whom his Highlanders wanted to kill.

"They were all holding up their hands," the boy told me, "and trembling with funk and holding out pictures of their Fraus and kids, and calling out 'Don't shoot, Kamarade! Don't shoot!' and my men wanted to shoot them. The Perthshires had been out for blood since the 9th of May when the Huns had burnt their wounded comrades, shooting them with petrol bullets so that their clothes burst into flame and they died in agony, and men who couldn't stick the sight of it any longer crept out of their trenches, in spite of orders, to drag them in and were burnt alive too. That day my company swore that they would take no more Prussian prisoners, and now word had been passed round by the Brigade, 'The 15th Prussians are in front of you, who burnt the men of your regiment. You will know how to behave.' My men wanted to shoot them all down, make the place a shambles;

but, of course, I wouldn't have it. I told them they had to take the men prisoners."

"Did they obey you?" I asked.

The Nestling looked at me in surprise as if I were a very ignorant person.

"Obey! They knew very well that the first man who fired I'd blow out his brains with my revolver."

After all, the Chicken's assurance was a compliment to the regiment, where discipline is an elemental fact. And it spoke well for the boy too, that he realized what admission into that Kingdom, or corporation, meant, —all self and chickenhood being merged in the subaltern of the Perthshires, whose powers were as natural and inalienable as the properties of carbon or oxygen.

Yet this callow youth on whom authority sat so lightly spurned his profession. It appeared that he had ambitions. He scoffed at the idea of sticking in the army after the war. He wanted "to do something," he said. I could not understand how he could resist the glamour of it all. His Colonel thought well of him and he knew it. The O.C., a reserved man, and sparing of praise, had been talking to me about the Chicken before dinner; he told me that the boy had the right spirit and no fear in him. "I sent him on a patrol," he said, "a day or two after he arrived at the front, to a building between the lines which was supposed to be occupied by Germans. My orders were, 'Find out if the house is held. Find out for yourself, remember, and don't take your men's word for it. They'll always see Germans, especially on a wet night when they want to be snug in the trenches.'"

The Subaltern had the sight of an owl, but he was determined not to come back until he had seen Germans. So far he had seen none, having arrived at the trenches straight from Winchester, where he held a commission in the O.T.C. and had just won a scholarship for New College. He swore he would see Germans that night or promenade the empty house between the lines.

A slip of a moon showed above the clouds and the rain ceased when they were within fifty yards of the building. The Corporal touched the Subaltern's sleeve and said, "They're there, Sir. I can see about a dozen of them."

"Where? I don't see."

"Straight ahead, Sir, by the wall."

The Chicken approached nearer. Within forty—thirty yards. The Corporal warned him again in a throaty whisper :—"There's 'arf a company, Sir, lining the side of the house. We're almost agin them."

Still the Chicken could not see. He gave the order to move forward.

At fifteen yards the Germans opened fire. A quick volley. The patrol threw themselves flat. Luckily they were concealed in a slight depression, and in a few seconds the moon went under a dark cloud.

The Subaltern whispered the order to return the enemy's fire, and his four men blazed away into the shadow under the house. The Germans replied vigorously; by a miracle none of the little party were hit. Then the Huns turned the machine gun on to them from somewhere farther back. The Subaltern heard the spray of bullets coming nearer, spattering the earth, searching every inch of soil, passing with a thirsty sucking noise overhead. He was the most exposed of his party, but he felt for the body of the dead man he had stumbled against, and drew it into a close embrace. The current of lead passed an inch over them where they lay interlaced, the live man clinging for life to the dead. The fire dropped. The body received a bullet and shook as if it were wrestling with him. It's head butted his own. A faint smell of cigar fume clung to its moustache. The boy had let the situation go for a moment, and was wondering, with a detachment at which he was surprised, whether all Germans smoked Havanas in the trenches, when a new kind of explosion added to the din. It was "A" Company's patrol bombing the house. The little scouting party received their first casualty from them. The man behind the Chicken uttered a cry of pain. A splinter from a bomb had taken away part of his right ear.

This extended attack was too much for the Huns, who thought the whole line was advancing and decamped. The moon peeped out again as they were going off, and the Subaltern, Corporal and the two men accounted for at least half a dozen of them. These dark figures which rolled up like rabbits were the first Germans the Chicken had seen.

The Subaltern entered the house with the two privates and sent the

Corporal back to tell the Colonel that we were in possession. He had taken a rather important Observation Post marked 2.22 on the map.

I had some of the story from the boy and some from the Colonel, but I will let the boy finish it.

" The next day we had some burying," he said. " From the new post we could send out patrols to bring in our fellows who had been knocked out on the 12th. You won't mind me talking about things which make you feel a bit squeamish, will you, Sir ? "—the boy called everybody above the age of forty " Sir "—" Tell me to shut up if it is too beastly ; but, you see, most of these bodies had been out for six weeks and were more or less decomposed. We dug a shallow trench towards them, threw out a hook on a bit of rope and drew them in. We had to find their identification discs. It was not a pleasant business taking off a man's shirt and not always easy, and my Corporal being sick every minute didn't help things either. I generally went for their pockets for letters ; that was easier, but . . ." I omit here some details which are too unpleasant to print. " The Corporal with his weak stomach was a bit of a nuisance, especially at night, for if the Germans heard him they would send up a flare."

Then he told me about a frontal attack at Loos. The Chicken had seen and suffered more and lived more in six months in France, and done more for England than I had in two score odd years. He was clearly a born soldier. He was happy in the regiment and quite one of them—one of the new incarnation at least who approximate in some ways to the old. I could not see what more he desired.

" You really think of throwing up the army after the war ? " I asked. The Chicken turned on me the wistful smile that talk of " after the war " evoked among the sanguine at the time. " In war time of course everybody has got to be a soldier," he said, " but in peace time—no thank you ! "

" But what are you going to do ? "

" Anything, but inspect meat and tunic buttons. Something that counts. I suppose I shall go into the Bar or Parliament."

I would have asked him if he really thought these talking shops counted more than the Perthshires ; but the pipes were coming in again and they were playing the regimental slogan. It gave one the most extraordinary feeling in the pit of one's stomach and all down one's back.

" I'm not sure, though," the boy said ingenuously when they had gone out, " I may stick to the regiment on the chance of another show."

I understood, I had passed through the two moods myself in a long route march when the pipes took over charge from the brass band.

www.ingramcontent.com/pod-product-compliance
Lightning Source LLC
Chambersburg PA
CBHW060838100426
42814CB00016B/417/J

9781847340894